PRAISE FOR SAVING FAITH

"*A lively and engaging memoir that documents Elizabeth Osta's call to service and years as a nun, Saving Faith meditates on strength, womanhood, friendship, and redemption. The "chores," "errands," and "decisions" of daily life "flood" with deeper meaning as the voice of this luminous prose intertwines the tangible and the ethereal, the visible and the not-yet-revealed, the quotidian and the philosophical – all while remaining intensely personal, wildly imaginative, and refreshingly direct. This is a book that shows us all how strength, femininity, spirituality are intricately connected, offering an inspiring and intensely moving glimpse into that "inner harmony" that "starts with the sound of a bell."*

-Kristina Marie Darling, author of *Dark Horse* and *The Disappointment Acts*

"*What good Catholic girl in the 1960s didn't think about joining the ranks of dedicated nuns who taught her? In Saving Faith: A Memoir of Courage, Conviction and a Calling, Elizabeth Osta bravely bares her soul to reveal her journey as a young religious sister, struggling to find her place in both the turbulent inner world of the Catholic Church and the magnetic outside world of community activism. Deeply personal, mesmerizing and even humorous, this memoir enthralled me.*"

-Jane Sutter, author of *Sutter's Sodas Satisfy: A Memoir of 90 Years of Sutter Drug Co.*

SAVING FAITH

A Memoir of Courage, Conviction, and a Calling

ALSO BY ELIZABETH OSTA

JEREMIAH'S HUNGER

SAVING FAITH

A Memoir of Courage, Conviction, and a Calling

Elizabeth Osta

Rochester, New York

DISCLAIMER: Memories can be like gauze, translucent and
beyond clear definition. Some names have been altered where it
seemed best.

*For permission to reprint portions of this book,
or to order a review copy, contact:
ElizabethOsta.com*

ISBN-10: 0-692-95379-5
ISBN-13: 978-0-692-95379-2

THE FLEUR-DE-LIS IS SAID
TO SIGNIFY PERFECTION,
LIGHT, AND LIFE.

I don't know Who—or what—
put the question.
I don't know when it was put.
I don't even remember answering.
But at some moment I did answer Yes
to Someone—or Something—and from
that hour I was certain that existence is
meaningful and that, therefore, my life,
in self-surrender had a goal.

—Dag Hammerskjöld, *Markings*

Dedicated
to the
Sisters of Saint Joseph,
past and present,
who inspire me to continue
to say Yes.

And to my husband, Dave VanArsdale,
whose love continues to be proof
of the presence of God.

CONTENTS

PART ONE

For we are so preciously
loved by God
that we cannot even
comprehend it.

-Julian of Norwich

PROLOGUE

I LAY ON MY BACK, outstretched, my breathing deep and steady. The light envelops me. I get lost in the elegant crisscross pattern of the ceiling's dark wooden beams, their function of support exquisitely accomplished. My eyes roam from beam to beam, the symmetry breathtaking, intricate carved fleur-de-lis designs identical and precise, reminiscent of the French influence on the congregation.

I breathe in and out, listening to the soothing voice of the instructor as she tells us to let go of distractions. In and out, in and out. As I slowly exhale, pushing breath through my diaphragm, despite my efforts to release distracting thoughts, images from more than forty years ago come swirling in, a kaleidoscope of memories.

I breathe in and smell the incense that once filled the chapel sanctuary where I now lie. I breathe out and see the center aisle of black and white tiles, gleaming with polish, leading up to the altar. I hear organ chords accompanying the voices of over one hundred Sisters singing the High Mass antiphons and hymns written by choir director Sister Flora. I hear the squeak of rubber-soled shoes worn by the older Sisters as they come down the tiled main aisle, pausing to genuflect before entering the pew, some with a more steady deep knee bend than others; cloth swishing, rosary beads clicking. Images of long ago, still so real.

*"Now gently roll over to your right side. Slowly sit up."
The words break my reverie. The lights come back up and
the space that had once been my place of worship and worry,
contemplation and concern, music and mystery comes back
into today's focus. The raised floor that once held the altar
and served as the place where young women were admitted
to the congregation, kneeling in bridal gowns, symbols of their
status as brides of Christ, is gone, leaving only the polished
wood floor. The cutting of hair and donning of black habits
that cover anything bride-like, completing their ceremony of
commitment to Christ and his Church, took place right here,
where I lie on my back in yoga tights, my hair spread on the
bare floor. The entire altar and all its accouterments are gone,
the space filled by a gleaming grand piano, which tonight is
positioned off to one side to allow room for downward dog
and other yoga poses. The confessionals on either side, where
I once knelt and shared my failings of faith, are now stacked
high with metal chairs. The sacristy where I once arranged
the altar flowers is stripped; the shelves empty of candlesticks,
wine cruets, chalices and vases.*

*I sit up, bearing awareness of this historic transformation.
The entire Motherhouse, chapel and all, has been changed to
a college education center, no longer home to the Sisters of
Saint Joseph. I am no longer a twenty-three-year-old postulant
asking admission to an order of Sisters who practice vows of
poverty, chastity, and obedience.*

*A retired teacher, wife, and stepmother, a breast cancer
survivor and a writer, here I am, living in the present, practicing
a Hindu discipline aimed at training the consciousness for a
state of perfect spiritual insight and tranquility through the
three paths of actions, knowledge, and devotion.*

*I revel in the wisdom of both paths to enlightenment, the
first learned here forty years ago.*

1

THE MISTRESS OF POSTULANTS

THE MASSIVE OAK DOOR OPENS with a tug and I climb the black and white tiled stairs, colors of things to come. My white Chevrolet convertible with its black top and red interior is parked just outside.

This four-story building is where I will begin postulant year, the first step on my journey to becoming a nun.

Am I really doing this?

The door closes behind me. I climb the steps to the cell I've been assigned, an area curtained off within a space on the third floor of this massive building. The long, wide room I step into looks like a hospital ward from the World War II movie Sahara starring Humphrey Bogart. White bedsheets hang from metal rods and create small areas for each postulant. My space, closest to the door, has a small single iron bed, a nightstand, and a small chest of drawers. Outside the curtains, locker-sized oak cupboards line the wall, providing room to hang our clothes.

Thankfully no one else is here to watch as I open the small footlocker my father carried up on the elevator an hour ago. I relish the time alone to settle in, sort my things and my thoughts.

My friends and family wonder why I am doing this. I wonder too.

My parents hadn't stayed long. Time for lingering was not

built in to the afternoon schedule. Goodbye hugs were warm, and brief. Mom and Dad seemed as overwhelmed as I was, none of us knowing exactly what the future held. How soon would I be able to see them, call them, or visit? How often could they visit me? Would they?

My family's response to the news that I am entering the convent has been varied. My younger sister, Kathleen, asked, "Don't you have to be a virgin to become a nun?" My four brothers for once keep their comments to themselves. My older sister, Mary Jean, has already decided which of my clothes she'll take.

My father had piped up that until this point, he didn't know any nuns who smoked, drank, or told dirty jokes. "You, my dear," he said, brown eyes smiling, "might just change that."

I fill the dresser drawers with pajamas, underwear, and socks, all tagged with sewn-in BETTY OSTA labels left over from my college days. I smile as I pull the bathing suit from the trunk; I had been surprised and delighted to find it on the list of recommended items. Swimming is one of my favorite activities—and had not been one I had pictured continuing as a nun.

I'm so glad for this time to settle in and take a deep breath. I take things out slowly. I tuck new blue slippers under the bed. I hang three brand-new white blouses and three dark skirts in my assigned cupboard, ready to wear to my job at the neighboring Foreman Center, where I'll continue teaching children with special needs.

As I unpack my toothbrush and deodorant, I breathe into the fact that today, in this year of our Lord, 1968, a new era exists in convents across America. Vatican II has opened the doors wide to what is being called relevance: expanding the horizons of work and service. The concept of *aggiornamento*, literally translated as "bringing up to date," is now allowing the church to address itself to the world instead of away from it.

As I tuck my green missal, a confirmation gift from my parents, into my nightstand drawer, I realize I am daring now to live out—within a religious community—my evolving belief that the sacred is to be found in the secular. I hope the beliefs and values I embraced at the adjacent Catholic college, run by this congregation, will be mirrored here.

I decide not to change out of my green plaid cotton skirt, matching jacket, and white short-sleeved blouse. Remembering my mother's maxim that first impressions are lasting, I hope this smart-looking suit gives a good one. I climb yet another flight of stairs to find the meeting room on the fourth floor. Sister Maureen, the Mistress of Postulants, will be welcoming us shortly.

My stomach churns as I traverse the highly polished brown terrazzo floors to a room on the left that overlooks the front of the building. A few other newcomers have already gathered, chairs arranged in a semicircle. I drift toward the windows to gain my bearings. Amidst the rolling lawns and tall pines, I search for Smyth Hall where so many of my college classes were held. I see traces of the stone wall that runs along the tree line, the one we guessed nuns could jump over back to freedom. At this sight, a sense of finality overwhelms me. This is it. I am on the other side of the infamous wall.

I gulp and look back to the circle of chairs, more of them filling up. With a deep breath, I find a chair, noting fidgeting hands and staccato laughter. I'm not the only one who's nervous.

Sister Maureen, petite with pale skin and tawny hair protruding across her forehead from under her simple, contemporary black-and-white headdress, takes her seat. As the last few are seated, I count thirteen. Sister Maureen makes fourteen. She gives a weak smile and clears her throat. "Beginning is in itself always so beautiful."

I recognize the quote from the German poet Rainer Maria Rilke. My mind flashes back five years to another beginning, where I found the same quote on a card left on my dorm room dresser when I was a freshman in the all-girls' college founded by these same Sisters of Saint Joseph.

I'd proudly worn the purple and gold beanie of the college student, pleased to have escaped the persistent inklings of a calling to religious life that had haunted my parochial school years. I felt safe surrounded by girls my age, preparing for a college degree, and was totally enchanted. I loved student assembly, academic gowns, alma mater singing, and our class songs. Our class of '67, we were told, was the largest freshman group ever enrolled, the cusp of the baby boomers.

So how did I end up here?

I remember the November sun, bright in the height of afternoon, streaming through the stained glass windows of the college gymnasium during Friday student assembly. "Make us worthy of thy lofty standards and thy noble teachings prove," we sang proudly, the strains echoing. Then Sister Josephine Louise, Dean of Students, had approached the microphone. We were quiet as she spoke, her voice unsteady.

"Girls, we have just received official word. President Kennedy has been shot and killed."

The same golden sun still streamed through the window,

but everything was changed. The air had been sucked out of the room; a terrible silence held us. And then came muffled sobs. Sister led us in prayer. It seemed a feeble response.

After the final "Amen," I ran from the building, my black academic gown flailing as tears fell to my cheeks.

How could this be happening? Our handsome young Irish-Catholic president? Killed!

In my room, I shut my door, tore off my gown, and threw it on the bed and pounded the pillow, howling at this injustice.

I could hear the President's voice: his vigor and his Boston accent underscoring his call, "Ask not what your country can do for you. Ask what you can do for your country." I could see his gray-green eyes staring out into the future, eyes inviting me to join him. It was more than the heart could hold. Numbness set in.

What indeed could we do for our country? We who would be the next generation of teachers, social workers, physicians, lawyers, nurses, engineers, accountants, theologians, mathematicians, and leaders. Who now would inspire us to become all we could be for our country? Our country's leader, our President, was gone.

Sister Maureen's inquiring tone draws me back to the present moment. I'm sitting in the community room gathered with other young postulants. She is asking us to introduce ourselves. I listen carefully to each of my new colleagues. One is a licensed practical nurse, another a businesswoman, one a college sophomore. I am the only college graduate. I wonder if that will make a difference. I hope not.

My mind slips back again to college days. In sophomore year

I had stopped going to Mass. Anger at injustice overwhelmed me. Old theology that spoke of sin and punishment, filled with complacent responses about "God's will," didn't speak to the needs of the time. Instead of looking to lessons of the past, I dug into philosophical readings trying to make sense of what made no sense. The existentialist philosophers Sartre, Kierkegaard, Nietzsche, and Camus became my mentors. I questioned with them, letting their questions fill me. I let myself be submersed in the intellectual and artistic environment of college life.

One night, watching the college's spring theatrical presentation of Jean Anouilh's Antigone, I felt myself become one with Antigone as she told her uncle Creon that she could not live a life with his idea of happiness, humdrum happiness she called it- of life that he said must go on come what may. She told him she wanted more of life, to be sure that everything would be as beautiful as when she was a little girl. If not, she told him, she wanted to die. The dilemma that was hers was so real for me.

I read, researched, and submitted papers for my classes in Greek Drama, Philosophy, and Theology, receiving accolades for my fashionably existentialist thinking, for the insights I shared, my outrage on behalf of my generation.

But President Kennedy's assassination was always in the back of my thoughts. I eventually realized the campus could no longer be my hiding place. No longer could I look the other way or think someone else should do it. I had to do something. I had to determine how I would make a difference.

I wondered at Sartre's lack of belief in God, knowing, as he says, that his whole being cries out for God. I was consoled by Kierkegaard who told me life was not a problem to be solved but a reality to be experienced. I was fascinated when I saw the stark cover of the April 8 issue of Time repeating Nietzsche's declaration: GOD IS DEAD. I laughed when I saw the reply posters appearing on campus: NIETZSCHE IS DEAD. -GOD.

I chuckle to myself, remembering, and come back to the present.

Sister Maureen is outlining the horarium, the daily schedule we'll be following, as well as what lies ahead. Formation— the time of being formed into a Sister through a postulant year (time of asking), two novitiate years (a time of being new), and a juniorate year (time to practice as a junior nun in preparation for final vows)—has been a long-established process with little variation over the years.

But this year the traditional entry date, September 8, the feast of the Holy Name of Mary, has been changed for the first time. The entrance of our band of thirteen, the smallest band ever to join this congregation, will enter on August 30, a date of no particular canonical significance.

Additionally, a second year has been added to the postulancy, perhaps an acknowledgement that it might take modern young women longer than a year to discern if this life is for them, the competing forces of the women's liberation movement and the sexual revolution muddying what may have been clearer choices in the past.

The program is new and in flux. Sisters across the country have been leaving congregations in droves, spurred by a compelling call to social justice issues and frustration that the church is not moving fast enough.

I'm entering to help speed things up. I hope I can.

2

THE DIRECTOR OF VOCATIONS

"STOP IN ANYTIME IF MY DOOR IS OPEN," Sister Mary Ann had offered.

I've only been a postulant for a month, but my concerns are still the same. I'm afraid entering the convent means I'll be "leaving" the world—the world I continue to believe is very much part of the sacred. I am reticent to share my beliefs openly just yet, not knowing whom to trust. But I find myself called to Sister Mary Ann's office anyway, wondering if she's a person I can confide in.

I peek around the open door to see her sitting at her desk, a book open in front of her. A small bronze desk lamp illuminates the room with a welcome glow. What is she reading? I hope I was right to take her at her word.

When she sees me, she waves me in and closes the book. I snatch a peek at the title: St. John of God. Never heard of him.

A framed quote from Rilke hangs by the doorway— the one I can't seem to get away from, this time a slightly different translation: "Beginnings in themselves are always so beautiful." An appropriate quote, I think, for the Director of Vocations.

On her bookshelf a small flag from Brazil is displayed, the site of one of the missions of the Sisters of Saint Joseph. Another shelf holds a photo of an African American child with several Sisters, probably from the congregation's mission in

Selma, Alabama. Sister Mary Ann gestures me to a chair as she comes out from behind the mahogany desk and sits opposite.

"I'm sorry if I'm disturbing you."

"Truthfully," she says, "I'm so glad you stopped by. I couldn't keep my eyes open. It's a good book, but this is my sleepy time of day, always has been. Do you know John of God?"

I shake my head, and she continues. "You might find him fascinating. Today they'd probably say he has an attention disability. He left home as an eight-year-old to follow God. His adventures are fascinating."

She offers me chocolate candy from a small dish. I decline. She takes one and smacks her lips as she finishes it. Her eyes are bright as she talks about her day, starting with a possible candidate for the novitiate. She chats casually with me, and I find myself relaxing.

"What charges do you have?" she asks, referring to the tasks assigned Sisters to see to the upkeep and maintenance of this huge building.

"I'm shining the stainless steel sinks and counters in the kitchen." I sigh. "I don't really see the point. They're stainless, after all."

"Oh, that's an easy one," she says as she waves her hand in dismissal. "Wait 'til they have you clean hallways that are already gleaming." She smiles. "But you'll soon discover there's some fun to be had amidst all the work."

I smile back in spite of myself. Her nonchalant manner is contagious. Her office is simply yet cheerfully decorated, and I note more of the details. Topping one shelf is the plaster statue of the Blessed Virgin Mary dressed in blue, with bare feet standing on a star-studded sky, the same as the one we had one at home. Next to it is a small vase of fresh wild flowers, probably picked from the back fields—acreage owned by the congregation, stretching up to the top of French Road.

On the opposite end, on the shelf below, stands a carved wooden statue of Saint Joseph holding carpentry tools. Alongside him, I'm delighted to spot a stack of books by authors I recognize and admire: Harvey Cox, Paul Tillich, and Hans Kung.

Except for once or twice in the refectory, I hadn't seen Sister Mary Ann since my first interview last March. Her dark hair shows the beginning signs of silver; her dark eyes still sparkle like I remember. It feels good to be back in her presence.

During that interview, Sister Mary Ann had assured me that rather than leaving the world, I would be dedicating myself to helping serve it. I found myself trusting her vibrant spirit and with-it attitude. Her shoulder-length veil, white blouse, black skirt, and matching jacket—the modified habit—were the newest phase in religious life. They replace yards of gabardine, starched headdresses, and bibs that cover the breasts.

As we chat, I note the small pewter cross on a silver chain she wears around her neck. I'm reminded of what one of the Junior Sisters—those who had finished their two years of novitiate and are now preparing for their final vows—had said about the letter designations used to determine the best length on the bosom crosses should be worn: A) up near the neckline and upper chest, B) suspended between the breasts, C) below the breast near the waistline. Sister Mary Ann is a definite B.

And she doesn't wear the traditional profession crucifix anymore. The profession cross, as I've heard it referred to, is the one presented once final vows are taken. It's the one many of the older Sisters still wear, and is actually a crucifix. I've held one, its weight not insignificant. They are bound by brass, the small corpus of Christ affixed on a black surface. The reverse side is solid brass and at the bottom there is place to pry the two pieces apart, revealing a small space for a relic.

Many also no longer wear the oversized rosary beads that the Sisters who taught me in grade school wore on a cincture around their waist, a distinct clicking sound familiar and prominent when my third-grade teacher, Sister Wilmett, was charging down the aisle on a rampage to straighten out some perceived misbehavior. I imagine that many of the rosary beads and brass profession crosses of the past are being relegated to memorabilia as the doors open wider for the modern nun. I wonder if Sister Mary Ann or any of the others miss them or their habits. I wonder if they've saved them. Someday I may ask.

Sister Mary Ann shares stories from her journey to the convent and I respond with some of my own. I realize that nuns have been in my life since age five when I first started kindergarten at Most Holy Rosary in Syracuse, New York. Then it hits me. "Actually, it was even before that! I'm named after my aunt, Sister Betty, a Sister of Saint Joseph who for many years taught at Saint Agnes High School. She now serves as librarian at the College."

Sister Mary Ann just nods, and I feel myself hoping she is not too familiar with my aunt.

As Sister Mary Ann and I continue to talk, I observe not only her office but also her demeanor. I find no hints of parochialism or narrowness, no scolding eyes or stiff tone in her speech. And yet I can't bring myself to share my doubts with her. As I stand to leave, I spot Jesuit Louis Monden's *Sin, Liberty and Law* on her shelf. I had read it in my Senior Theology college course.

It was senior year. I had started to go to Mass again, hoping for solace and support. I found the liturgy on campus had evolved in the time I had been away to be far more inclusive, informal, and inspiring. My Senior Theology professor, Father Shannon, had summarized the change: "We'd been teaching a theology of damnation and should have been teaching a theology of salvation." I'd never much believed in hell or fire and brimstone, and now I felt I could be more open about what I did and did not believe.

An inner harmony began to warm me. The more I read, the more I became convinced I might be able to answer John Kennedy's call to service—not only service of my country, but also of my Church. I was cautious and watched carefully what was happening around me and to me, waiting to be sure I had found a path. It felt like the path I had long felt called to, even though at one time I had been relieved to pass it by. Now it seemed like it might be the path out of existential conundrums and into action.

At the Christmas concert, Handel's Messiah resonated deep within me:

> *And the Government shall be upon His shoulder.*
> *And His name shall be called Wonderful, Counselor.*

I was ready to act. I joined classmates in this era of protests in a feeble and ultimately misguided attempt to block the building of the proposed Modern Arts Center, our mission to protect the large sloping green lawn. Our lack of success didn't dampen our spirits, our efforts a small badge of courage against the establishment—a point of pride as we neared graduation that would be held on the adjacent lawn. It was a genuine gesture yet it didn't satisfy what I hoped to do.

What to do next plagued me. I was lucky enough to have three job offers to consider, but I was confused and needed help. I sought out Sister Tee, a dorm advisor who wore the modified habit and had round brown eyes that were kind. She occasionally frequented "the smoker" that was in the lower part of Lourdes dorm—I imagine she visited to connect with students. Amidst pop machines, mailboxes, pianos, plastic couches, chairs, televisions, and smoke, Sister Tee listened as I shared my dilemma.

I had inhaled from my Lark cigarette, smoke escaping from my lips and nostrils, and finally said out loud my innermost secret: that I was wrestling with thoughts of entering the convent.

I felt my face redden.

While students came and went, picking up mail, buying Cokes, and scurrying about, Sister Tee listened, acknowledged my struggle, and never steered me to any single option, not even the convent.

I treasured her response. I knew I needed time.

The Church was in flux, and so was I.

In my final semester, Father Shannon introduced the book by Jesuit Father Louis Monden: *Sin, Liberty and Law*. Its cover design displayed an orderly pattern of small squares with one turned on its axis. The opening page of the book asked, "Was the square turned on its axis an example of sin, of liberty, or of law?"

From my window seat in the library, overlooking the budding trees that graced the nearby cloister walk, the frost of winter gone, I read my way into a new freedom of thought:

> *Mankind as well as the individual is facing a choice . . . In his personal decision each one commits the others and bears the responsibility of the decision of his time.*

Did he mean what I thought he meant: that what I did and what I chose affected others? That, in a sense, I was choosing for us all?

> *Each one throws the weight of his conscience, light or heavy, on the scales of history in an exceptional hour, which might be the hour of the daimon but is also that of the Spirit.*

I remember looking out over the courtyard, the potential of blossoms not far away. Would I be able to throw my weight of conscience on the scales of history in a way that would matter? Is this, I wondered, the calling I had worried and wondered about since childhood? I was still, at some level, fascinated by the mysterious life of nuns and prayer, yet not able to reconcile "leaving the world," the world that was full of the goodness of God.

When I had received my little nun doll from my aunt, Sister Betty, as a present, I had hoped she didn't think I should be a nun. She didn't inspire me, nor did her older sisters, my aunt Veronica or my mother, encourage me to look to her for guidance. They were more of the world than of the church.

Then there were the nuns at school. Many were stern. But a few—like Sister Lizbeth, my sixth-grade teacher who was kind and fair and in whose class I excelled— made me pause. I observed several of these women who carried a bit of truth with them, shining a light on the possibility of religious life—not a popular choice among my peers who were edging up to be a rebellious generation. We were teenagers then. Parties and boyfriends and plans to skip school were far more prevalent conversations than what we wanted to do after graduation.

Yet here I was, coming to realize that I'd run from these thoughts as long as I could.

Did the caring nuns who had surrounded me since my earliest school experiences know something I didn't? Did they understand something I had thus far missed? Could there be a way, through service, to make the world better, brighter, safer, stronger?

While older practices were being abandoned in favor of more contemporarily relevant ones, some older Sisters continued to wear the traditional habit even though the option to change was open to them. Self-flagellation was never spoken of, but a Sister much older in religion than I told me in confidence about the use of a discipline—a small handheld wooden stick with a spiked ball on a chain—used to strike one's legs to remind oneself of the sufferings of Christ. She knew of Sisters who drew blood. I heard no open talk of this, glad for new theology.

Women, the backbone of the educational systems many of the men in ruby robes at Vatican II have been educated in, would wait no longer. They were ready to take off their veils and come out from behind the walls to serve. Yet the changes offered by Vatican II primarily orchestrated by men didn't address women's issues or rights.

While the African American Civil Rights Movement continued to explode around the country during the 1962–65 Vatican Council, women's rights were not on the Church's mind. No single woman actually spoke during any of the four sessions of the Council in Rome. A female relative of Cardinal Giovanni Battista Montini (who would go on to become Pope Paul VI) was actually denied entry when she showed up for a Mass held for participants during the Council.

Just as participation in the anti-slavery movement fed the nineteenth-century women's movement, the advances being sought and made by black citizens were inspiring women to stretch their wings as well. The new energy was creating the future for all of us.

Seeing *Sin, Liberty and Law*, a book I had cherished for its liberating philosophy, sitting on Sister Mary Ann's shelf during our talk, coupled with strong, optimistic, forward-looking Sisters like her, helps me become more clear that this is what I want to be a part of.

3

PRAYER OF THE CHURCH

IT'S 6:38 A.M. I slip into the pew and hope I'm not noticed. Ahead of me are polished pews filled with postulants, novices, and junior Sisters kneeling in front of the side altar dedicated to Saint Joseph. No one looks up. I kneel behind three others from my band and look over to see if Sister Walter Anne noticed.

Mornings have never been my best time, yet here I am asking to live my life in a religious community that starts the day at 6:30 a.m. with Lauds, the morning prayer of the Divine Office. I reach down on the shelf under the pew and pull out my black leather-bound breviary and quickly join in the recitation:

> *Have mercy on me, O God, in your goodness;*
> *In the greatness of your compassion*
> *Wipe out my offense.*

The Divine Office, or Litany of the Hours, is the official set of prayers "marking the hours of each day and sanctifying the day with prayer." In my classes I am taught that these prayers are said by religious and laity around the world in order to provide one road to salvation for all. I read in the introduction of the Breviary that, recited daily, these prayers can lead to personal interior growth.

As I keep rhythm with the others, my mind races in its own direction, wondering if these prayers really can save the world. I laugh inwardly at the prayer I've just recited, wondering if I should ask that my offense of being late to morning prayer be wiped away.

From my earliest childhood days, I had my own personal indoctrination to prayer. At nine o'clock each Sunday night, my father called through the house, "Prayer time!" Television shows came to a halt, and once assembled, the seven of us, along with my mother, would kneel on the living room carpet, Dad facing us. We would follow as Dad led us in the Rosary, each decade following one of the three Mysteries: Joyful, Sorrowful, or Glorious.

The carpet scratching my knees seemed an intrinsic part of penance, something I'd learned about in religion class. My favorite part of the ritual was Dad's closing prayer that he taught us to recite in unison: "God Bless y and Daddy, Mary Jean, John, Jim, Tom, Betty Anne, Donald Mark, and Kathleen, all of our friends and relatives, especially . . ." Dad would insert a name of someone in need and we'd pray for a speedy recovery or a happy death.

My first-grade teacher, Sister Norman, reminded us to save room on our seats for our Guardian Angels and taught us to pray to them;

Angel of God, my guardian dear,
to whom His love entrusts me here,
ever this day be at my side
to light and guard, to rule and guide. Amen.

We also memorized all the answers to questions from The Baltimore Catechism, the blue paperback book that was the text for Catholic schools throughout the United States:

Q. Who made us?
A. God made us.

Q. Why did God make us?
A. God made us to show forth His goodness and to share with us His everlasting happiness in heaven.

The seven sacraments are church rituals, we were taught, that signified God's presence in our lives. Baptism was followed by Penance (Confession) and the Holy Eucharist (Communion). At age twelve, the sacrament of Confirmation was conferred by the Bishop and marked the coming of age as a young Christian, the song "Onward Christian Soldiers" accompanying the occasion. The three remaining sacraments, Marriage, Holy Orders (for priests), and Extreme Unction (Anointing of the Sick) were yet to come.

At age seven, I was told I had reached the age of reason, responsible for my actions. I went to Confession in preparation for Communion. The intrigue of going behind the big velvet curtain and into the darkened space was momentous. There I found the kneeler and heard a voice from somewhere beyond a dimly lit grate say, "Yes, my child."

I launched into my memorized verse: "Bless me Father, for I have sinned. This is my first Confession. I disobeyed my mother two times and fought with my brother once."

I waited in the dark for the priest to tell me my penance: three Our Fathers and three Hail Marys. My memorized act of contrition was my exiting prayer: "Oh my God, I am heartily sorry for having offended Thee."

My confessions frequently contained offenses against my mother. I strove for her approval as much as for God's. Her Catholicism was different from Dad's, who was a daily communicant. Hers was strong, yet laced with a streak of subversive humor and impatience with what she saw as stuffiness, and I came to share her view. She was a woman and a mother of the fifties who had managed an efficient and organized household of seven children all born within ten years of one another. I soon modeled household skills I'd learned from her when babysitting neighborhood children, and I was popular with the families of five and six children who kept me engaged often. Mom was proud to have me help them and to hear me praised.

But as she aged, and her work slowed, Chesterfields and Canadian Club became her more constant companions. I was being set free to fly, yet I still longed for a hug from her.

In sixth grade, I wrote an essay about her that got read over the public address system for Mother's Day.

She's My Mom

"Aw Mom" I argued "why can't I go?"
"The answer is no" she replied. I
left sadly walking toward my bedroom.
As I ascended the stairs, I heard her
say, "It's for your own good." She's
swell to care about me. I guess she's
great after all. She really does a
lot of things for me. I thought. She
irons my clothes, makes my lunch—Wait
a minute, she's not a walking work
machine, she's my Mom. I really should
appreciate her more. After all I'm
almost living with a saint. Think of
all the virtues she practices—clothe
the naked, feed the hungry, shelter
the homeless, comfort the sick, and
probably a lot more I don't even know
about. I never think how many things
she drops to do something for me.
Multiply that by six other children.
Wow! Quite some job. And to think I
argued with her to top off all her
other chores. I'd better get started
on that Mother's Day gift, even if it
does cost all the money I've saved,
cause after all,—she's my Mom.

I relished the praise and attention this essay earned me, and especially the way it let Mom know how much I thought of her. My Mom. Gorgeous and stylish, vivacious, smart as a whip. Kind and competent, nonjudgmental yet no-nonsense strict. Part of me idolized her. And part of me resented the Canadian Club and Chesterfields.

In years of confessing my every lapse, eventually I learn the difference between venial and mortal sins, and by my college years I'd come to challenge the concept of sin.

Now, as I kneel in prayer, watching the Motherhouse chaplain raise the host and the chalice, I remind myself of the new theology I've learned in Senior Theology, a theology of Salvation, not Damnation. Hell is losing its power.

I realize the power of past beliefs, not only for their meaning but also for the time and place they represent. I recall early morning weekday Masses I attended with my father, often the only one of the seven of us who arose at what I deemed an ungodly hour, dressing in the dark of the fall or winter morning and scurrying down the back stairs and out the side door to the waiting car. Even though I was not a morning person, the payoffs were too deep and wondrous to miss. As I climbed into the front seat of the Chevy wood-paneled station wagon, I smelled the Old Spice that Dad slathered on himself. We often rode in comfortable silence across town to the Church of the Assumption on the north side of Syracuse, where the Mass was held early enough to accommodate Dad's work schedule as one of Niagara Mohawk Corporation's vice presidents. Punctuality was his strong suit.

Though that was long ago, the soft lighting and pungent smell of incense in the little chapel still transport me back through time. The organ music and the cantor's sung responses became indelible imprints. *Ad introibo ad altari Dei.* "I will go unto the altar of God."

I realize I have grown in this religion—and with this family—to love the familiar rituals. Gregorian Chant, with its punctums and sacred melodies, lives deep inside me. Whenever I hum *Credo in unum deum, Patrem omnipotentem, factorem caeli et terrae*— one of my favorites—the smell of incense isn't far away.

Luckily Vatican II has introduced me to new music that I am also learning to love. This morning's consecration is one such song by a favorite composer, Father Lucien Deiss. It's a melody I'm not likely to forget called "Keep In Mind." I feel lucky to be tiptoeing inside the inner workings of a Church in flux, a congregation in flux, learning the existing rituals and routines, and the reasons that surround so much of the mystery. Questions are being answered and new ones are arising as I read and study. I hope for a time in the future when the rituals will bring their promised comfort and I can feel at home. For now, this is enough.

After morning Mass ends, I catch up with Katie, one of my "band," as the thirteen of us who have entered together are called. I've formed an easy friendship with her. She's blonde with the help of a bottle, and like me, a recent smoker. Before we entered, we had both just given up our Larks.

As we head down the backstairs to the refectory, I ask, "Do you think Sister Maureen saw me come in late?" Our postulant mistress sits ahead of us in chapel and to the right.

"She may not have, but I sure did," she says in her matter-of-fact way as she turns on the landing. "It's those late night hours you keep," she says in jest, our ten o'clock lights-out precluding any burning of the midnight oil.

Breakfast after Mass is held in the refectory—the large dining hall below the chapel—an experience that starts with the sound of a bell, followed by a recitation of a Maxim from a collection of one hundred sayings that reflect the spirit of the congregation, written out for the Sisters by the first priest to serve the order, Father Medaille. One of my favorites becomes:

Advance good works to near their completion and then if you can, without notice, let others perfect them and gain all the glory.

Once the bell is rung again, we can be seated. Second-year novices serve each table, bringing dishes of food that are shared family style—eggs, toast, hot cereal, and occasionally bacon.

Of my band of postulants, I've formed an early bond with both Katie and Ellen. Ellen is two years older than I. One of nine children, she has rapid-fire speech and a droll sense of humor, which she uses at just the right time to lighten a mood. She has come from the world of business, well-groomed brown hair and metal-rimmed glasses giving her an efficient look.

Marnie is another "older" one, not fresh out of high school, but rather a Spanish major at adjoining Nazareth College. She has an infectious giggle and ready smile, her noticeable limp the result of polio.

Amy, blonde and blue-eyed, is one of nine children and a graduate of the congregation's Nazareth Academy, a high school founded in 1871. She shares the experience of polio with Marnie, both of them granted special permission to use the elevator on a regular basis. The rest of us "hitchhike" when possible.

Other band members come from the Southern Tier: Diana and Celestine from Elmira and Carol from Horseheads. Diana's gorgeous dark hair and dark eyes go along with the fact that she is still writing to her boyfriend, trying to let him go. Cel's mischievous laughter after lights-out has more than once brought us a cautionary reprimand. I think Carol—blonde and blue-eyed, vivacious and energetic—must have been a high school cheerleader.

Terry hails from New York City and holds the distinction of being an accomplished cellist and the only African American in the congregation. Elaine, Karen, Rita, and Shirley are recent high school graduates and eager postulants. At our early recreation times together, we swap the stories of how we decided to enter. Sponsors, I learn, are key players as our stories unfold.

"My sponsor, Sister Joan," Amy shares, "met with me once a week after school. She really helped me want to join. She even got to know my whole family."

Katie, a nurse by training, is assigned to the infirmary, a modern brick building behind the Motherhouse. Before she entered, she worked at Saint Ann's Home, a state-of-the-art nursing facility on the north side of the city run by the congregation. It was there she was encouraged to enter by a Sister who became her sponsor.

Throughout my senior year in college, Sister Tee heroically listened to what must have seemed my endless ranting about all that I saw wrong with religious life. Yet I kept talking with her. During one memorable visit she looked at me, her eyes focused sharply on mine, and said, "Your questions are good ones. You have something important to bring to religious life."

I began to argue but she interrupted, something she rarely did. "You may be just the kind of person we need to attract. Think about it, won't you?" I had left in a quandary but found my thinking shifting.

I imagined others had similar stories and conversation with their sponsors, Sisters who recommended us to the congregation and remained mentors and friends. Though our band of thirteen is one of the smallest our congregation has ever had—previous bands had up to sixty—we do bring an element that is new and fresh.

I find the conversation at the tables enlightening, especially when I sit with canonicals (first-year novices) who offer tips to make life more livable. Kathleen becomes a favorite. She's the niece of Sister Christine Marie who teaches chemistry at the college and is a dorm mother for some of my friends. Kathleen has the same twinkle in her eye as her popular aunt.

"Don't ask for any special permissions," Kathleen says as she passes the breakfast platter. "They'll tag you as a trouble maker." Another tip she offers: "Keep your eyes down as you pass by the head table and fly under the radar."

The head table consists of the Reverend Mother Agnes Ceclia, a woman in her mid-sixties whose sister, Sister Joan, was my dorm mother freshman year. A passionate musician, Sister Joan had a temperament to match, the story of her throwing a desk out of the third-floor window of Smyth Hall having become legend.

Next to Reverend Mother is the second-in-charge, Sister Florencia, a well-groomed woman with regal carriage. She has two sisters in the order, one my freshman theology professor, Sister Mary Lourdes, whose passionate phrase, "God is good, girls, God is good," stays with me. Her younger sister, Sister

Margaret Marie, works as one of the kitchen cooks. The other councilors who run the congregation include Sister Agnes Ruth, a middle-aged, honest, no-nonsense woman, and Sister Rosalma, a physically fragile looking woman who I learn is a congregational giant, recently returned from the mission in Brazil she started.

I watch and listen. We scrape our plates into round, silver receptacles and stack them on a cart. We slosh the tableware in a bin of soapy water to ready it for the next meal. I'm a bit repulsed by the questionable hygiene of this, but I'm not sure about questioning procedures like this yet. I think of one of my favorite albums, *60 French Girls Can't Be Wrong!* Or can they?

When I report to do my charge, spraying the surface of the stainless counter, I think about this vocation I have been fighting for so long and about the Sisters of my childhood.

I remember Sister Virginae, my kindergarten teacher, as one of the kindest. No one and no activity was too small for her attention. She had the whole class come around in a circle to admire Jimmy McDonald's clay elephant, her praise genuine, her classroom safe.

I press the cloth against the surface, making circular swirls and strokes, and remember the twelve years of education with these Sister Servants of the Immaculate Heart of Mary, some of whom gave me ample examples of goodness and others examples of injustice—not the stuff that encourages vocations.

I move down the stainless steel counter and think of the young ones, like Sister Jacinta, who played baseball with the boys at recess, a direct counterpoint to others like Sister Wilmett, who shamed and bullied us as a disciplinary tactic.

A classroom of more than seventy students was not uncommon in 1950s parochial schools. And no doubt the nuns had to maintain discipline and order. But at what cost?

My place in the back of my third-grade classroom, seated alphabetically behind Mary Ann Neimeier, wasn't as safe as I thought. My skin crawled as the chalkboard liner hit high C as Sister drew lines for our practice of Gregorian chant. An uninhibited impulse came from my throat to my lips, an imitation of the chalkboard sound registering with classmates who giggled. Sister Wilmett spun around, her gray eyes fierce, her face unyielding as she threatened my classmates to identify the person who made the sound, evidently as irritating to her as the original sound had been to me. After a long duration with no traitors offering me up, my neighbor Joan pointed her finger at me. I was ordered up to the front of the classroom where Sister Wilmett demanded I make the sound again. I stared feebly at the chalkboard, wishing the small quarter note punctums were drawn and that we could go on and practice the Credo for Mass. Maybe that would calm her. I tried to make the sound but all I could produce was a squeak. Sister Wilmett bent down into my face, the sides of her headdress covering me, her nun's breath blasting up my nostrils and said, "Make it again, louder."

I did my best but by now I was no longer breathing regularly, terrified not of punishment but of this senseless woman. After several more "Louder!" commands and several more attempts to replicate the sound, she looked up to the class and demanded, "Who knows what class her sister is in?" Again, Joan volunteered and was sent off to the third floor to find my eighth-grade sister, Mary Jean. Then Sister Wilmett really lost it. She spun about and leaned once again into my face, her eyes level with mine.

"Get out of my classroom. Get your things and get out of here, now." Her voice trembled with anger.

At first I didn't believe my ears. I looked around to see eyes dart away from my gaze. I shivered as I went back to my desk and piled my speller, reader, arithmetic, and geography books, all neatly covered in brown paper bags, along with my black and white composition notebooks into my arms. No one looked as I carried my load out the door. The lesson on punctums went on.

Credo in Unum Deum, I heard my classmates sing. I put all the books down under the coat rack, pulled my yellow slicker from the hook, put it on, and picked up my books, balancing them carefully as I navigated down the stairway to freedom. I began to feel something surprising: delight. I knew my mother would understand.

Even though she defended the nuns when we complained, telling us to be respectful, Mom also intervened when necessary. The previous year she had successfully defended my older brother John when Sister Mercier challenged his paper route that caused him to miss daily Mass during Lent. After a talk with Sister Mercier, John's paper route continued. I knew with certainty Mom would understand this incident.

I peered out the window at the landing, soft showers continuing, and worried momentarily about my books. I could see Hubbell Avenue, my path to home and freedom. I continued down a few more steps and as I hit the next landing, standing above me, looking down on me, hands on her hips she appeared—Sister Wilmett.

"Just where do you think you're going, young lady?" she demanded, her dark eyebrows knitted in a scowl. She used the same contemptuous tone she used at the start of this tirade. I took a deep breath, shifted my pile of books, and looked her in the eye.

"Home, Sister," I said, my lips quivering, lost between anger and tears. "You told me to get my things and get out."

Sister Wilmett spat back at me, "Get back in here right now and don't try any smart stuff again, do you understand?"

"Yes, Sister," I said, the heaviness in my chest bringing me almost to tears. She returned to the classroom and I was so tempted to continue on home. But I didn't. I climbed back up the stairs, put my pile down, hung up my slicker, and slithered back down the aisle with my books, past staring eyes and several smirks of solidarity. Joan reported back with my sister, who was given a note for my mother. Behind her glasses, I detected a wink from Mary Jean as she left the room. I looked away quickly, afraid another tirade might erupt.

I was an A student and not a troublemaker, unless one considers talking trouble. I had already been awarded several molded plastic statues of the three children of Fatima, prized possessions marking the miraculous appearance of the Blessed Mother. During the following years I received more awards and accolades for achieving the most A's on one report card and for my Mother's Day writing assignment. I cruised through my studies and for the most part enjoyed what I am learning. My writing was singled out as worthy.

Still I remained wary of the way nuns dished out discipline. I had already seen Sister Norman, my first-grade teacher, tip my neighbor Eddie Dick upside down by the heels for talking too much. She just let him hang there, all the blood rushing into his head, and my head ached just watching him. The fifth-grade teacher, Sister Claudette, a young and inexperienced teacher, picked on Eddie as well. As he pulled down on the ancient window frame, as she had requested, the sixty-year-old oak separated from the glass. Sister Claudette verbally berated Eddie, telling him he would be in detention for the rest of the year. Our classroom of ten-year-olds knew it wasn't Eddie's fault, but the verbal barrage continued: "You should have known better. Don't you have any common sense?"

Finally another student, Steve, could take it no longer and stood up to her. "Sister, it's not his fault," he shouted. "It's the damn window." A collective gasp cleared the way for Sister Claudette as she ordered both boys to the office.

By sixth grade we had committed the Baltimore Catechism questions to memory, and I wish I could say that little by little, we bonded together as students and friends, aware that the women who were belittling us were not right to do so. We were innocents at the mercy of these women who showed little or no mercy. Unfortunately many of us internalized their messages of shame and our only hope was to go home to families that could undo some of the damage.

The final straw for me came in my senior year at graduation practice. Artistically tempered Sister Mario, our dark-eyed, olive-skinned music teacher whose love for order and outcome overshadowed her concern for students, was quick to shame and humiliate.

Graduation was the next day. All sixty-four of us stood on stage, excitement brimming as we practiced singing "America,

Our Heritage."

"Who's that talking?" a demon-like voice asked. With no warning, Gus Revuik was pulled from the stage down to the floor, then slapped, shoved, and shamed for talking out of turn. He was small and never raised a hand in self-defense. He was told not to report to graduation.

It was June 1963. In April the nation had been outraged as police dogs and fire hoses in Birmingham, Alabama, were used on non-violent protesters. Sixty-three speechless teenagers witnessed Gus's humiliation and not one of us said a word.

As we sang the rehearsed song on graduation day, the words ringing out into the darkness of the audience, I felt my eyes fill with tears.

Stout hearts and true hold fast what is ours.
God give us courage, through darkest hours.
God give us strength, and guide with thy hand.
America, our heritage, our homeland.

A cork finally popped inside me. As soon as I could, I ran from the auditorium, vowing never to return.

4

THE NEW NUN

DURING MY FOUR YEARS at Nazareth College, founded by the Sisters of Saint Joseph, I had discovered a new breed of nun, whose life commitment seemed to be to service and truth, not to shame and humiliation.

As a college freshman, I learned from Sister Mary Lourdes in Freshman Theology to see the good in God and the God in good; Sister Mary Clare, head of the Speech Correction Department, shared the basics of effective clinical practice and encouraged my to attend the American Speech and Hearing Conference in Chicago. National speakers came to her class, including Dr. Burton Blatt, whose work changed the face of special education. Sister Marie Martin brought tales from her years of work in the field that made our Human Growth and Development class come alive.

When I am not at work, at charges, or in communal activities, I have homework. As preparation to enter the novitiate, I'm assigned readings from a small paper-covered blue book simply titled: *Sisters of Saint Joseph of Rochester*. It was written in 1950 by "A Sister of Saint Joseph"—no specific author is acknowledged. Humility. I think back on the praise I've received for my writing and wonder about the Sister who toiled in obscurity on this well-researched and well-written piece. Was she pleased to be anonymous? Could I be?

A picture of Mother M. Agnes Hines, General Superior of

the Sisters of Saint Joseph of Rochester, 1882–1921 faces the title page. She is dressed in the traditional floor-length black habit. Under her long black veil, a white wimple surrounds her face and neck, leaving only the front of the face and a bit of the forehead uncovered. She is also wearing the profession cross, a replica of the very first cross as used by the founding Sisters in France.

As a college freshman I had lived in Medaille Hall, named after the founding priest of the congregation, Reverend Jean-Pierre Médaille; my sophomore dorm, Lourdes Hall, was another French connection. Le Puy, the valley town high up along Loire River where the Sisters of Saint Joseph first developed their mission, was also the name of the senior house during my time at Nazareth. A charming stone building that looked like it belonged along a French avenue, it stood apart from the dorms and academic buildings, off in its own pocket of trees. We all aspired to live there.

In Father Médaille's time, as now, Le Puy-en-Velay, France, clings on the edge of volcanic rock, its quaint winding streets leading to a grand cathedral standing high above the red terra cotta roofs of the homes clustered below. Dramatic outcroppings of rock punctuate the view. This beautiful and historic place, now a city of 20,000, is still noted for its unspoiled medieval atmosphere.

I discover in my readings that Father Médaille, a Jesuit, encountered a small group of unmarried women and widows anxious to devote themselves to works of charity: visiting the sick, instructing children, and aiding the poor. Under his direction, they began to work for the good of their neighbors and toward the sanctification of their own souls. In 1650, with the approval of Bishop de Maupas, the godson of Henry IV of

France, Father Médaille formalized the founding of the Sisters of Saint Joseph in Le Puy. The new congregation combined works of charity with contemplation, a winning combination it seems, as this innovative non-cloistered order of Sisters spread across France.

I imagine Jean-Pierre with gentle eyes and spirit, perhaps like Monsignor Schnacky, directing these women who scurry about the town in common garb of the day doing good works. Their habit comes later in their history, as it will come later for us as we enter the order.

In between charges, homework, and personal tasks, I curl up on the iron bed in my cell reading about the work of Daniel Berrigan, an American Jesuit priest whose prayer life is lived out loud on the streets. He gives me courage as I struggle with what I see as the "old ways." I seek out his writings and treasure each one I find, wanting desperately to be, as he is, part of the change that will make religious life viable in the coming years. I savor one quote in particular: "Unless we begin to think about the impossible, we cannot begin to understand the Resurrection." His autobiographical reflection on his experiences and beliefs, *No Bars to Manhood*, becomes a second bible for me.

I'm glad that the Sisters of Saint Joseph have redesigned the postulant year program to be two years instead of the traditional one, providing time for the thirteen of us to reflect on what we are getting into.

As the days unfold, I find that my "boundless" idealism—as Berrigan calls his own—and my hope that I can make a difference help me to tolerate prayers even though they don't seem relevant, like "for behold, your enemies shall perish." I'm not sure which enemies shall perish and if it's very loving to wish them that. Yet I learn to bite my tongue instead of arguing; I refrain from continued lashing out at the inane practice of polishing stainless steel that is already stainless or buffing already gleaming hallways. Instead, I learn to pray not to change my circumstance but rather my response to it. That feels holy.

In our postulant class, I have learned that all the convents of the Sisters of Saint Joseph of Rochester, including those in Brazil and Alabama, are bound together by communal prayer and at least one hour of "community" per day—time spent for the good of the group.

During these days, the community hour, which is in addition to meals and prayer times, is often spent in preparation for the upcoming General Chapter, the governance convocation of the congregation. It will meet over the summer and write Vatican II adjustments into official documents. One such adjustment will address the issue of dress. These adjustments will be submitted to and approved by Rome.

Approval for some experimentation has already begun. While many are already wearing the modified veils and black and white attire that we new postulants will likely receive when it is time, some have begun to wear "contemporary dress," ordinary street clothing of the day, in their everyday professions. I'm being swayed by some of the Sisters on the college faculty who seem to be at the forefront of this progressive thinking. Sister Mary Clare, my personal idol and college speech therapy instructor, is part of the program and dresses professionally and sharply, in a handsome gray suit with tasteful silver stud earrings and only a small pewter cross marking her identity. It's a new world. The fate of this "experiment" is to be determined at this summer's upcoming

Chapter.

Questions of identity and witness arise in the discussion. Religious dress has long been seen as a form of witness for Christ to the world. How important is the habit in this society and for this generation? This is the question on the floor.

I find a certain peace each morning in the gracious chapel, its wooden beams and stained glass calling for reflection and contemplation. I kneel, reflect, and observe, learning more about the congregation as I watch Sisters returning from Communion.

Only a very few older ones—gaits slow, some with somber expressions—still wear the traditional habit whose design dates from the middle of the 1900s. White starched linen surrounds their faces, holding hair out of sight. Flowing black veils cover the linens, tiny black-headed silver pins keeping them in place. Black serge material covers the bodice along with full sleeves and a full skirt. Large rosary beads that clink amidst excessive yards of serge are worn at the waist. The huge starched white guimpe (a French word pronounced "gamp"), a medieval high-necked blouse—in this case worn like a huge bib over the chest—covers any sign of curvaceous breasts.

A key feature that I note in the habit of these old ones is the profession cross, suspended by a black cord. They each received one upon profession of vows, usually in their early twenties. The crucifix with a molded brass body of the crucified Christ is large enough to cover a woman's palm. On its reverse side there is a small cavity that opens to house relic—if one is fortunate enough to possess these sought after saintly remains.

I count the number with this traditional garb and find

there are fewer than thirty in a chapel of one hundred. Many Sisters, even some older ones, have chosen the modified habit. New York's Bergdorf Goodman designed the headdress that replaces the starched facial linens: a soft, shaped white hat with a shoulder-length black veil, held in place by a narrow white band, it is worn in a fashion that leaves hair showing. A black skirt and jacket, white blouse, and a small pewter cross suspended by a silver chain generally complete the outfit. Flat, sensible shoes remain a standard.

As the parade of Sisters goes by, hands clasped, heads bowed in prayer, I observe the third type of dress, more infrequent here at the motherhouse. This is "contemporary dress" that blends with dress of the day: simple and straight unadorned skirts, blouses, or suits. There are certainly no miniskirts, and the colors are muted: grays, blues, and browns. This choice is still experimental, and those wearing it are scattered throughout the community, several of them at the College.

At breakfast, I wonder aloud about the dwindling number wearing the traditional habit. "I'll bet," I say to my postulant band, "one day we'll find the traditional habit on display in a museum, younger folks having no idea about it."

In our weekly meeting, Sister Maureen announces that the habit we will ultimately receive will include a small veil called a hat or headdress, some form of black and white dress, or a skirt, blouse, and jacket. As the date draws closer, she tells us, we will spend time learning to sew our own habit: a skirt, dress, or jumper.

I'm remembering my attempt in high school at shortening my loden-green stretch slacks. I measured and marked the new length carefully, and with great precision I cut the material at the marked length instead of leaving material for a cuff. I wonder how I'll do in this adventure.

After the meeting with Sister Maureen ends, Katie, Ellen, and I go to the kitchenette at the end of the long hallway. "You can sew a whole new nursing outfit, Katie," Ellen says to her.

"Right after I sew a button for your lip," Katie replies.

Their banter delights me.

I'm settled for now, this part of community familiar and fulfilling. And I'm excited to be a part of the change that is swirling about. Relevance. Sisters have their own allowances, and are often involved in decisions about where to live and how to dress. House superiors are now called coordinators; each Sister is now more responsible for her own decisions.

Despite my own excitement, I can see how these changes bring disruption and challenges for older nuns, and have sympathy for those whose lives are being turned upside down, perfectly summed up in the following joke:

> In one convent, each Sister received an allowance. An older Sister requested that Mother Superior put her allowance back in the common fund. The middle-aged Sister squirreled the money away for a trip she was planning. The youngest Sister took her money to the street. She found a man of dubious circumstance, greeted him, and pressed the money into his hand with the phrase, "Godspeed."
>
> Later that evening, after most had gone to bed, the convent doorbell rang. The middle-aged Sister answered. An unshaven man, reeking of tobacco and alcohol, wearing dirty and disheveled clothing,

asked if the young Sister he'd met earlier was available. Having difficulty hiding her disdain for the gentleman and his appearance at this late hour, the Sister backed up, covered her nose and mouth with her hand, and replied, "I'm sorry, sir, the Sisters have retired for the evening."

The undaunted visitor thrust forth an envelope and replied, "Well, please give her this envelope and tell her she can retire for the year. Godspeed was a long shot at the track today and came in first."

5

HOW MUCH DOES JOY COST?

ONE OF THE MANY CHANGES sweeping through religious congregations since Vatican II is the expansion of fields of study for professions that support personal interest and aptitude. I learn that a Sister who has been teaching for several years is in medical school; another has also left the classroom for cosmetology, providing her own brand of spiritual counseling while helping beautify her new clients. No longer just a teaching and nursing congregation, the Sisters of Saint Joseph are opening up their boundaries.

I find this heartening. I am relieved that religious women are no longer saddled with only teaching or nursing as choices, happy that they can find fulfilling work and happy for the children and patients who will be spared the wrath of their frustration.

As for me, chalk dust has settled in my veins.

Once I was a teenager, with the experience of being raised with seven kids all so close together, I had good credentials for babysitting. I was much sought after and loved it. I even traveled to Cape Cod with the Stack family to babysit.

One favorite afternoon comes to mind when three-year-old Billy, slow to use intelligible speech, pulled on my sleeve, led me to the refrigerator, and pointed to the top, asking, "Can I have some bosch?"

I looked up and saw the fudge container. Ah, I thought, a teachable moment. "Billy, say 'fudge,'" I directed.

He stared intently, hoping for his reward. "Bosch," he said with a wide grin.

I tried another tactic. "Say 'ff,'" I told him.

"Good, now 'uh,'" I said, mimicking the sound for him. "Great. Okay now say, 'ja.'"

He repeated each sound with accuracy.

"Good boy! Okay, Billy, ready? Now say them all together: 'f-uh-ja.'"

He smiled, ready for his triumph, green eyes looking into mine. "Bosch," he beamed.

Undaunted, I started the process over again. In the middle of it, he pulled on my sleeve once more and I felt a tug on my heart as he asked, "Can I have some?"

My days with these children were days of gold. So I was startled when, on October 17, 1961, Billy was diagnosed with mental retardation. Two days later, his little sister, eighteen-month-old Mary Beth, a violet-eyed beauty with dark ringlets, was gone, choked to death when playing on Billy's ride-on fire truck, her neck caught under the steering wheel. His diagnosis turned out to be incorrect, and hers a death that should never have been.

In early August, the summer before I left for convent, I was invited for a farewell visit with Billy's family on Cape Cod. His younger sister Eileen, just three months old when Mary Beth died—her blue eyes and curly black hair so reminiscent of her older sister's—became as precious. I watched both of them on the seashore of Cape Cod Bay tumbling in the waves, no speech needed to capture such joy. Billy's role is my life was precious, my choice of a college major in Speech Correction inspired by him.

Later that summer, I visited San Francisco with my sister Mary Jean. I walked the pier at Fisherman's Wharf where I bought a poster for my classroom: a tall man handing a red balloon to a child, captioned, "How much does joy cost?"

I returned to my second year teaching at the Foreman Center, a school for children with special needs. Jimmy, Paul, Judy, Carl, Carolee, Foch, and Christopher—all children with mild retardation—kept me on my toes as I learned on the job about discipline and classroom management. My poster was in place on my door. The film The Red Balloon became a class favorite, the almost-silent story leveling the playing field for total enjoyment by all.

One morning little Christopher, wide brown eyes looking up at me as I tied his shoe, said, "That was bery good, Miss Osta." This class had thrilled me since my first day. Diagnostic labels from Down's Syndrome to brain injury failed to describe the children's depth and beauty. It was 1968 and no law yet mandated services for these kids, yet through the vision of Superintendent Ken Harris and the Board of Cooperative Educational Services, programs were developed and tailored to meet their needs. Demand was growing; so was the Fairport campus, north of the Erie Canal.

The children become my teachers as I learned more about the syndromes and disabilities that had forced families to redefine their dreams. I watched and learned as thirteen-year-old Carl, with his gentle smile, worked to complete puzzles designed for three-year-olds. Dark-haired eight-year-old Judy could have been his younger sister, her narrow eyes smiling as she learned to pedal a tricycle. Jimmy's thick glasses slipped down on his nose as he talked into his hand, channeling Clark Kent. Ricky copied his name patiently, tracing the pattern I'd given him. These youngsters had no pretense, no guile. They accepted help, struggled to learn, occasionally misbehaved, accepted correction, and kept on growing.

When I had received my acceptance letter from Reverend Mother Agnes Cecelia with permission to enter the Sisters of Saint Joseph congregation, I was told I could continue to teach there after I become a postulant as long as Superintendent Ken Harris would give his okay. I'd been told that if he agreed, I would retain my convertible, continue to wear secular dress, and send my wages home to my mother. According to Canon Law, no exchange of finances or goods would occur until I received the habit, which was two years away.

Soon after I found myself waiting in Mr. Harris's office. He entered and sat across from me.

"To what do I owe the pleasure of this visit?" His dark hair was combed back, his black eyebrows raised in question.

"Well," I began, unfolding the letter, "I've got some news." I paused, took a deep breath, and blurted out the story. "In March I applied to become a Sister of Saint Joseph. I've recently been accepted." I gulped and thrust the letter toward him. "They've started a new program that allows postulants to keep their jobs and still enter. I wanted to make sure that was okay with you."

He took the letter and read it over. I waited, watching to see what line his eyes were reading. He looked up at me and said, "Well, how about that."

A smile crossed his full face as he adjusted his glasses. "Can you tell me a little bit more about it, or is it secret?"

I laughed and relaxed a bit. I didn't know him well, but from my initial interview and the faculty meetings he's chaired, I'd grown to like him. His response was so much in keeping with what I had seen of him: bright, winsome, curious. I took my time, explaining the newly designed program that allowed a two-year period before signing on for good.

"I'll take classes on the weekends and begin a full year of novitiate two years from now. That's when I would receive the habit."

I paused, took a breath, and charged on before Mr. Harris could say anything more. "I told them how much I like this job and they agreed that if you approved it, I could continue teaching here until then." I dropped my gaze and picked up the cold coffee cup and sipped from it.

"For free?" he asked.

I looked up in surprise and found his eyes playful.

We both laughed. I put my cup back down and waited. He uncrossed his legs and leaned forward.

"Well, I don't see any reason why you can't keep on teaching here. You won't have to take any vows from me, except obedience, unless I think of something else."

I smile, relief washing through me. He handed the letter back to me and, as I stood to leave, he stood and extended his hand. His gray-green eyes met mine. "Let me know how things are working out for you, will you? I'll be interested."

I thanked him and, before he could see the tears in my eyes, I left his office, giving his secretary a wave. I smiled all the way back to my classroom, thrilled to keep teaching through my first postulant year.

"Betty, can you come into my office?"

Sister Mary Rose, hair the color of salt and pepper showing from under her modified veil, asks how I am doing and if I am settling in all right. Then she gets to the point.

"Betty, I want to tell you about something I heard and what I think we should do about it."

Back in early October, as part of our two-year postulant program, our band began a six-week assignment on a mission—a convent—to give us an idea of what day-to-day living in religious community feels like. We'd be a part of the daily routine while continuing to keep up with our own jobs or studies.

Three of us were assigned to a parish in northeast Rochester that had a school run by Sisters of Saint Joseph. As with most schools run by the congregation, the convent superior served as the principal. Sister Mary Rose had been welcoming and proud as she lead us to our second-floor bedrooms, each with their own sink. We shared a large common lavatory down the hall.

Daily Mass, charges, meals, evening prayer, and community night were all a part of the routine. It felt like an easy adjustment.

Until this evening.

I settle into the cushioned chair in front of the desk in her first-floor office. Mary Rose stays on the leather chair behind her desk. Familiar adornments in this small room include a statue of Joseph, and the open window brings a gentle breeze, the light of the early evening soft.

In the next few minutes, Mary Rose tells me a story as fanciful as any I have ever heard. It had come from the principal of the congregation-run school for children with developmental disabilities. She told Mary Rose that the reason I hadn't been assigned to her school was because I chose not to go there, that I preferred to work with lay professionals.

I am aghast. Sister Mary Rose comforts me by confirming that from what she had learned of me in the past few weeks, I would be incapable of thinking or saying such a thing.

"But Betty, I think it would be wise to go visit and apologize."

Apologize for what? For something that's untrue, something I never said? I begin to speak, to tell her my reservations. "But Sister . . ."

She leans forward across the desk, twirling a pen between her fingers. "I know these Sisters and I think you would be wise to clear the record. They'd like to have you come over for a tour of the school and to get to know them. It would be a good time to meet with the superior and . . ."

"But Sister," I interrupt, "this is all made up. I was never even asked about going to their school. I started at the Foreman Center because it's where I was hired before I ever entered." I am frustrated and defensive, my stomach churning.

"I love teaching at the Forman Center but that doesn't mean I prefer it because they are any more 'professional' than the Sisters," I continue.

The Foreman Center teachers down the hall from me, Sharon and Mary, were fun and full of laughter. On a recent warm sunny Friday, my convertible top down, car still running, I scooted into the bank to cash my check. They were just coming out. We exchanged hellos as we passed one another. When I returned they were gone and so was my car. I discovered it parked at the far end of the lot, loud music blaring. As I pushed the buttons to turn off the obnoxious music, I discovered each one had been reset to that same station. They were nowhere in sight, but their handiwork had me laughing out loud.

Carol and Mary Anne, who worked in the Verbal Behavior Clinic across the hall from my classroom, were both Nazareth College graduates in speech correction and both working mothers who embodied realism and dedication. As top-notch clinicians, they were chosen for a pilot program with the University of Rochester's Dr. Stanley Sapone to use operant conditioning to "shape" the language patterns of children with mild-to-severe communication issues. The program was based on the work of B.F. Skinner and attempted to modify behaviors by reinforcing appropriate ones and extinguishing undesirable ones. Several of my students were candidates for the program.

To learn more about the program methods, I'd even enrolled in a course at the University of Rochester to study the methodology. I began by training a black and white rat I'd named Algernon as a nod to the book. My goal was to teach him to perform designated tasks and then push a bar to receive the reward of food pellets. I wore a big black glove the length of my arm and learned to handle him by holding him by the torso and gently transporting him to and from the cage. It was a major hurdle for me. Each session got easier, and as the semester comes to a close, we both succeeded: Algernon pushed the bar on cue and I remained consistent for him, handling him calmly despite any unfounded fears. This was a life lesson I hoped to carry with me.

The level of professional sharing that had developed among those of us working on the project was strong, and the bonds built spilled over to form personal friendships. The advances we saw in Angela and Faye, two tall, gangly ten-year-old twins who were severely delayed, were exhilarating. They could finally indicate hunger and toilet needs. We were thrilled.

I want to stay with this team where I feel so needed and supported.

"I know, dear," Mary Rose says in a placating tone, as if she could actually know how important the Forman Center is to me, and how unfair this is. She puts the pen down and leans back, settling into her position.

I feel helpless and trapped. My mind whirls around. A rumor like this—where could it have come from? Then I remember Maggie Gleason, a college classmate who had left in her sophomore year to work at this privately run school with the nuns, a move I had encouraged. But I haven't seen her in several years. Still, could she have said something?

"Let's call right now and set up the date. Is there any night you couldn't go?"

I reluctantly pull my calendar from my purse, my face burning, my hands trembling. I read off the teacher conference dates and my graduate class schedule.

"So we'll shoot for next Monday, okay?"

Before I can answer, she has the receiver in her hand and dials the number from memory. They must be good friends, I think. To my surprise, Mary Rose hands the phone to me. I put the black receiver to my ear. "Sister Angela? This is Betty Osta," I say, haltingly. My eyes search Mary Rose for clues about what to say next. I needn't have worried.

"Oh, Betty," Sister Angela says, "I saw Sister Mary Rose at the principal's meeting yesterday and told her how much we would like to have you over. We'd love to give you a tour of our school. How good that you're calling me."

The following week I am sitting in the parlor of the old brick building tucked in the middle of the inner city. I open by saying Sister Mary Rose told me of some unfortunate things I had supposedly said that weren't true. "I know the work you and the other Sisters do here is very well-regarded throughout the community." I intentionally stop short of apologizing.

Sister Angela smiles a too-sweet smile, a smile that tells me she doesn't believe a word I'm saying. I take a sip of the glass of water she has offered, wishing it were wine, and smile back.

Sister Angela says, "Sister Mary Rose and I go way back. We went to high school together before we entered. She's a marvel, isn't she?"

I heartily agree and feel satisfied that I've been true to myself while tucking away a lesson in convent politics.

6

THE BELL TOWER

THE SMELL OF THE CIGARETTE SMOKE draws me in and upward. I'd given up smoking a month before entering; there were no smoking nuns that I knew of. Now here I am, being invited to join in this clandestine adventure in a hidden-away spot in the uppermost part of the Motherhouse. Why not, I think. Be a part of the group and enjoy the moment.

As I climb higher, it grows darker. I find my way to the last stairway, which rises almost straight up like a ladder. I wonder who discovered this delightful getaway, high above the chants and daily prayers of the Motherhouse.

We are in the bell tower, the low, gauzy light adding to the mystery and the moment.

"You probably won't come up with us, will you?" Katie had challenged me the previous afternoon, her white nurse's uniform soiled after her day's work at the infirmary. I accepted the challenge.

Now Katie passes me a lit cigarette along with an unlit Lark. My brand. Its familiar brown filter tip urges me forward. I hold the filter between my lips that had earlier sung the Magnificat:

> *My soul doth magnify the Lord.*
> *... Because He that is mighty,*
> *hath done great things to me;*
> *and holy is His name.*

I hold the end of the lit cigarette to the end of the unlit Lark. I inhale and watch the tip of my cigarette fire up. The taste is familiar. I pass the first cigarette back to Karen.

I think of the words of the Magnificat, words I believe, trying to square them with what I am doing. I inhale again and feel smoke fill my lungs. I realize that the words are a part of my mission, my heart. Great things have been done for me and now it is my turn to stay a part of the world and proclaim the sacredness of it all. This act of smoking, I consider, is one way to stay a part of the world.

I take another drag of the cigarette and see Rita, a dark-haired beauty with a wry sense of humor, put her fingers to her pursed lips. "I think someone is coming," she whispers.

The four of us, dressed in secular clothes, look around at one another, the whites of our eyes big, our breathing shallow. Very few know about this spot above the fourth floor, hidden behind the small oak corner door that leads up the narrow, steep staircase to the bell tower. The early evening light leaks in around the rafters, yielding just enough visibility to see one another.

We hear the sound of the lower door opening, then footsteps on the stairway. I freeze, my eyes darting around to the others who look equally stricken. No one makes a sound. The last steps come closer. Finally, round-faced Peggy emerges; we all breathe again.

Peggy is the first-year novice who has shown Rita and Karen this hideout. Her black skirt, white blouse, and small black veil signify her status.

She sits down on one of the oak beams that serve as benches. *Ah,* I think, *this goes beyond our band.* I wonder how many others have come up here.

A conspiratorial nature surrounds us as we sit awkwardly on the beams. Peggy makes us laugh with her adventure of coming up unnoticed. "I dodged Pat and Marilyn, who wanted to go for a walk," she giggles. "I told them I had 'lofty' studying to do." I continue puffing my cigarette as we carry on sotto voce conversation that's more personal than the ordinary conversing we do.

We share stories of our journeys into the convent, tidbits about our families. We pledge to keep our meeting secret and not to return again until three nights from now, to avoid developing any pattern that could be traced. We're to leave after our chores in ten-minute intervals until we are all assembled. Peggy, who had learned of this place from a junior Sister, will tell only one other novice. Six, we decide, is a reasonable number to keep our club secluded and private.

Our next scheduled night arrives quickly. I am the second to arrive, just after Karen, our space beneath the rafters seemingly undisturbed since we last met. We sit crouched on beams that rest on wide floorboards, great massive iron bells a few feet above our heads. I reach behind a major oak beam that creates our corner to retrieve the gallon-sized blue Maxwell House coffee can that serves as our ashtray. I look inside to see several dozen discarded cigarette butts. This is a popular spot, I think, and wonder how we can ever empty out the can undetected.

As arranged, others arrive one at a time, in ten-to-fifteen-minute intervals. Katie doesn't come that night, her nursing shift most likely interfering.

This time the cigarette doesn't leave me dizzy. It tastes better and feels satisfying as I blow smoke up into the rafters.

I linger longer and have a third cigarette as Peggy answers

my questions about Kathleen, the first-year novice whom I had liked so much and had given me the advice to stay below the radar. One day she was gone. No goodbyes, just gone.

"What happened?" I ask as I pass the coffee can to Peggy.

"Nobody will say," she says, her blue eyes highlighted by cherry-red cheeks. "I think she was asked to leave."

My eyes widen, the smoke swirling around my head. "They can ask you to leave? Just like that? In this day and age?"

It's the early 1970s, and thousands around the country are leaving convents of their own will, making congregations like ours re-examine their programs. I am stunned to think they can afford to ask anyone to leave.

I've collected doubts like fireflies during these first months of being a postulant. I snuff out the cigarette in the bottom of the coffee can and slip away, down the steps and corridors back to my white-curtained cell. I open my breviary and read the evening prayers of compline, trying to make sense of them, attempting to believe in the power that prayer could bring people around the world together.

> *Be sober, be watchful!*
> *For your adversary the devil, as a roaring lion,*
> *goes about seeking someone to devour.*
> *Resist him, steadfast in your faith.*

That religious men and women around the world said these prayers in unison is impressive, but does it matter? And is there really a devil?

The next afternoon, a Saturday, I am summoned to Sister

Evangelist's office. As Director of Novices, her reputation as a tough woman precedes her. Her graying eyebrows match the forelock of hair that shows under her modified veil. Despite what many say of her gruff, no-nonsense manner, I like her. There is something real about her. She has come from Lima, the same small town south of Rochester where my mother had been born and where my aunt and uncle still live. It turns out that my Uncle Tom had worked with her father building silos.

As I look about her office, I wonder what could she want. I sit in a chair opposite her; she stays seated behind her desk. Her brown eyes look stern. I smile briefly and squirm in the chair.

"You wanted to see me, Sister?" I ask nervously.

"Yes," she says evenly, no smile or cordiality extended. "I've been talking with several of the other postulants as well."

Good, I think as I look around her office. She must be doing a survey. Maybe I'll get a chance to give my ideas about how things are going. I've been forming some definite opinions. I've wondered if during evening recreation we could introduce some popular music in our sing-along time: Simon and Garfunkel perhaps and move to include the Beatles and Diana Ross.

As I look over at her, I see above her a bronze crucifix, the figure of Christ affixed to narrow pieces of oak. Her desk is uncluttered, a plain brown leather blotter in the center, a black pen holder with matching notepad on one side and a black telephone on the other. To my right in an oak bookcase, a copy of Bonhoeffer's *Letters and Papers from Prison* catches my eye. On the wall above hangs a portrait of Our Lady of Perpetual Help. *Nicely done*, I think.

Sister Evangelist looks at me and I wait. I wonder if she is in charge of the Mistress of Postulants, Sister Maureen. Will I get to say how I think it's going, I wonder. Evangelist leans forward and stares right into my eyes. *Wow, this is serious.* "I want to know if you've been smoking," she says straight out.

I feel my face flush and know I am caught. I squirm in the straight-backed chair, wanting more than anything to escape. I look out the window, think a minute, then say, "Yes, Sister, I've smoked most of my life."

"Have you been with the others?"

Now things are getting dicey. I have been working in my job at the Foreman Center with access each day to cigarettes that I've successfully rejected, proud to embrace my new status as postulant. I am allowed to drive my own car. The deal remains the same—that once I receive the habit, the car will be sold to the congregation for a dollar. Up until now, I've been pretty much able to come and go as I've needed, being treated as the responsible twenty-three-year-old I am. Why now, I wonder, is there a question about smoking?

"The others, Sister?" I ask, feigning innocence and wondering how much she actually knows.

"The others who've been going to the bell tower," she says sternly.

I swallow hard. Oh, my God! She knows about the bell tower. What else does she know?

I feel myself shiver. What do I say? My mind races around and twice I look toward the door. Finally I look at her, her eyes studying me.

I relent. "Just twice I was there, Sister. Up 'til then, I had quit."

She stands, turns from me, and peers out the window that overlooks the lawn between the two wings of the motherhouse. The opposite wing is where the general councilors of the congregation and many of the older professed Sisters live.

With her back to me she says, "You do realize that smoking is not an option as a Sister, don't you?" Her hands are clasped behind her back, her black veil draping down past her shoulders. "As a postulant, you are asking to take the vows of poverty, chastity, and obedience. There's no room in there for smoking. Do I make myself clear?"

"Yes, Sister," I say, frozen now in place. What happens next? Will she give me a penance? Remove my car?

She turns toward me now, her soft-collared white blouse displaying the brass profession crucifix, her matching black jacket and skirt simple, attractive. "I expect any behavior like this to be ended. Is that understood?"

"Yes, Sister," I stammer. I start to stand. She steps toward me now, her eyes softer.

"I'm sure your mother expects more from you. And so do I."

I feel my lip quiver. "Yes, Sister," I say again, tears beginning. As I blink them back, I think of my mother sitting in the kitchen with Dad, her Canadian Club on the rocks, her Chesterfields within easy reach.

She nods toward the door, indicating I am dismissed. I practically run down the black and white linoleum hallway to the chapel. I genuflect, slip into one of the back pews, kneel, and put my head in my hands, biting my lip. Tears stream down my cheeks.

I whisper the words that are within me:
He that is mighty hath done great things to me.
Holy is His name!

7

WHAT A WAY TO SAY GOODBYE

SOON AFTER OUR BELL TOWER EVENT, Katie leaves. At least this time there is no secretive exit in the dark of night, as had happened in the past. We don't know why she's leaving, but least we know it is her decision. And at least she says goodbye, unlike the novice Kathleen I'd grown to like.

Because of her rheumatic heart, when she was little, maybe six or seven, Katie lived at Convalescent Hospital. That was probably the start of her calling to serve others as a nurse. Ironically, that same heart condition had served as a roadblock to her first attempts to enter the convent. She persevered and was finally accepted. Within four months, she leaves. We've still not talked about why. A different heart condition, I suspect.

I'd been sick with the flu when Katie was actually leaving. I heard her in the hall and called out to her, "Collins, you'd better get in here before you go too much further."

I didn't want to believe she'd actually leave me and not say goodbye. As I began to pull back the bedcovers to chase her down, she appeared in the doorway in her white starched uniform, blonde hair poking out from under her nurse cap, brown eyes staring at me.

"You didn't think you'd leave without a goodbye, did you?" I asked, wondering what I would do without this friend with whom I could argue, debate, smoke, laugh, and cry.

"Of course. I wouldn't leave without seeing you, but you do know I'm off duty, right?"

I laughed, hearing her standard answer for anyone looking for free medical advice.

She smiled as I pulled the covers back up.

"I'll be in touch with you, never fear, but meantime, don't say I never gave you anything." And with that she tossed a roll of surgical tape onto my bed and was gone.

Five months later I still miss her. I miss her humor. She'd put a spin on things that helped me relax. I wish I could think of just one to cheer me.

But good to her word, she does get back in touch. When she finally visits, we sit in the upstairs parlor, formally chatting like we are being watched. We catch up on details. She's working at Saint John's Home and she's getting an apartment. Her parents are happy to have her home for the time being.

There are things she does not say and things I do not ask. Our visits don't bring the comfort I'd hoped for. I sense she doesn't want to ask too much for fear of something. Disrupting me? Missing things? But we still joke and I remind her I have my surgical tape. "One day you'll be 'on duty' when I need you," I quip, referencing her classic "off duty" line. We don't say it, but we both recognize how awkward these visits are. After a few more, she stops coming.

Though I miss her, I am soon wrapped up in responsibility. I've been asked to head up the first-ever Monroe County Special Olympics. I've become acquainted with the Executive Director—newly appointed Dorothy Buehring Philips, a silver-haired, well-regarded woman from Albany—through my involvement with the New York State Teachers of the Mentally Handicapped. Dorothy doesn't give me much chance to say no, but I am hooked on the mission and her enthusiasm anyway. Eunice Shriver is the driving force, and Dorothy has a similar spirit.

My role as Area Education Coordinator means I work with all the Directors of Special Education for all the various school district facilities to organize the game site, participants, entertainment, and publicity. The local Jaycees are partners. As we divvy up the names of the many contacts to be made, I note that Sister Angela's name appears on my list—and I imagine I am still on hers.

A required meeting for all the county coordinators and state-level directors is held in Albany, and I must attend. Assistant Mistress of Novices Sister Joellen is assigned to accompany me as my prudent companion. Sisters don't travel alone, primarily for safety reasons. As part of a community, this proves to be one of the benefits. Joellen is very "with it," ten years younger than Elaine and part of the experimental dress program. She wears fashionable clothes and has a keen eye for style, as shown by her neatly tailored brown tweed suit and coordinating blouse and scarf. I am in my best navy suit. Neither of us wears a veil; nothing except our religious crosses distinguishes us as Sisters, though the two Jaycees we meet up with in Albany, who are Junior Chamber members from Monroe County, know we are Sisters.

Together we are wined and dined by Eric and Richard. Both men are generous and engaging. We revel in this bit of freedom, lingering over coffee and listening to the band play. I decline Richard's invitation to dance, but am oh so tempted.

8

FORMATION

"You wanted to see me, Sister?" I say respectfully as Sister Maureen looks up from her desk in the large open office. Both her light brown eyes and her matching hair, which is always in place, catch daylight from the tall windows that line the room. This summer solstice is a beauty. I feel a warm breeze come through the open window.

"Oh, yes, Betty, come in, please," she says, "and close the door, would you?"

She moves from behind the desk and motions me to one of the two chairs in the corner of the room, opposite the desk. The tangerine color of the upholstery brings an unexpected bit of 1960s flair to an otherwise sober room. I'm glad for the wooden arms that give me something to hold, sensing this isn't going to be an ordinary conversation.

The mahogany desk is forbidding in its central location. An exquisitely detailed Saint Joseph stands on the matching credenza on the near wall, the lily he holds impressive in its realism. Joseph, I am learning, is highly revered for his courage in accepting the role of father of Jesus. He is also seen as pure, thus the lily. I've still to sort out all these church icons and myths but I do appreciate the artistic rendering of the man for whom the congregation is named.

The beautiful alcove at my childhood church, Most Holy Rosary of the Immaculate Heart of Mary, is one such image that first stirred me. Elegant lettering around the bigger than life-size gleaming medal, all surrounded by shining green marble. It's always stood out for me when I think of the Immaculate Heart.

The opposite wall in Sister Maureen's office has a small bookcase with titles I don't recognize. On the top shelf a small radio plays classical music. From the little I know so far of Sister Maureen, she's shared that Mozart is her favorite composer. She even mentioned a special piece she'd like played at her funeral, "Ave Verum Corpus." She entered at the same age I did, twenty-three, working in business first. She's new to the job of director of postulants and to the Motherhouse staff.

I've yet to feel comfortable with Sister Maureen. Her face twitches and her gaze darts. She seems burdened by the responsibility of thirteen young women aspiring to religious life. Scheduling, counseling, listening, arranging mission experiences—all while living in community with us—has to be challenging. I try to be understanding.

The atmosphere in her office feels heavy. I've been here in the past for messages, occasional spiritual direction sessions, and with others for meetings, but never alone without an agenda, and never with the door shut.

"I wanted to update you," she says, fidgeting with her hands. "You might be aware that several postulants approached me last month, asking if it would be possible to get the habit sooner than the agreed-upon two-year program calls for."

Yes, I think, *I did hear rumor of that*, certain it would never be considered. The whole objective of this two-year program seemed wise to me: to stop so many from leaving by providing a longer time to discern before getting the habit and making such a big commitment.

Sister Maureen continues, her twitching intensifying. "The others felt they were ready and that they didn't need another year. After a lot of prayerful thought and meditation, Sister Evangelist, Sister Joellen, and I met with Reverend Mother and made the proposal. It has been agreed to offer the option."

Yikes.

I am silent. My first thought is that I am not ready to receive the habit. I'm still investigating. Most Sisters are choosing to wear contemporary dress. Give us time for this second year and we may not even end up with a reception ceremony with a veil.

My second thought is, Why the hurry? Is the congregation worried that delay will lead to more defections? Are they trying to stem the tide? Are the girls themselves afraid that they won't last through a two-year postulancy?

She continues. "I've spoken with Reverend Mother and wanted to let you know as soon as I could. She knows you were not in the group asking to receive the habit early. We've decided to let those postulants who want to get the habit a year early go ahead and start their novitiate this fall."

I'm listening but disbelieving. I wonder what Joellen, the assistant mistress of novices whom I was beginning to trust after several honest conversations, thought. Certainly she would agree this mutiny against the existing program is ill conceived and fraught with difficulties. Yet she and Sister Elaine were in on the conversation. Why did no one even ask me what I thought?

Before I can say anything, Sister Maureen continues. "Marnie will wait another year so she can finish her undergraduate Spanish studies. However, she'll continue to live with the novice group."

Sister Maureen's cheek twitches in staccato rhythm and she looks down at her hands. I'm still silent wondering where this will go next. Sister Maureen looks up at me and says, "Reverend Mother understands you have some psychological reservations and is in agreement that you can also have a second postulant year."

Whoa.

I take a deep breath and look past Sister Maureen to the towering trees beyond the windows, watching them bend with the breeze that blows them. Is that what I'm being asked to do? Since when, I wonder, do I have psychological reservations? And why do I have to be granted permission to continue in the program I signed up for? Wasn't this designed specifically as a two-year postulancy? Wasn't I instructed to tell my boss, Mr. Harris, that I'd be teaching for two years as a postulant? This change in the program is a mistake. But I remain silent.

Sister Maureen continues. "Because you do have your car already, Reverend Mother thinks it might work best if you simply continue to live right here at the Motherhouse for a time."

Sister Maureen pauses and I try to collect my thoughts. My breathing is shallow, my face heating up. I don't dare express any feelings that will give grounds for the notion of my psychological reservations.

I've often had a sense that I make Sister Maureen more nervous than she already is. In my meetings with her about my prayer life, I've never felt inspired by or confident with her assessments. She has told me often that prayer will be difficult. I tell her often that right now it isn't and for that I'm grateful.

However, I don't tell her of my cherished prayer moments, fearing she'll not understand and destroy what is so special to me. I keep to myself the times I slip into the area known as the Triduum, three stained-glass windows on the fourth floor that open to overlook the chapel. It's there I often end my evening, after Grand Silence has been invoked.

There I sink into a kneeling position on the priedieu, the wooden kneeler in front of the open window, and look down on the Celtic cross suspended above the altar. The view is majestic, the colors soft. What I know of prayer thus far comes easily.

I repeat the opening line, "O God, come to my assistance," and as my mind drifts, "I praise the Creator of all that is for my blessings, which are mine in abundance." Prayers of praise come easily and I try not to whine and beg for much assistance. Instead I remember the song of my youth and count my blessings before I sleep. I hum in my mind my song from my college days, appreciating so much the fact that it still brings me joy and peace.

> *Great is the Lord, worthy of praise;*
> *Tell all the nations God is King!*
> *Spread the news of His love!*
> *The Spirit of the Lord is upon me*
> *Because the Lord has anointed me.*
> *He has sent me to bring glad tidings*
> *To the lowly, to the lowly.*

The noises of these late evenings are eerie. Grand Silence forbids anymore conversation. Noises of doors creaking, shoes shuffling, and an occasional cough are all that can be heard. The smell of wax and incense lingers in the air. The crucifix, held by transparent wires above the marble altar, appears to float, catching the flicker of the sanctuary lamp as shadowy shafts of light dance about the walls and rafters. Often I am easily transported, with fears removed, and peace filling me. I'm sad that Sister Maureen feels the need to tell me that it won't always be this way.

I find the gift of this space away from others to be brilliant, as is much of the architecture of this magnificent structure. These stained-glass windows are an example, designed for access to the chapel for Sisters who lived in the fourth-floor infirmary before a separate building was erected, to hear Mass or other liturgical services.

Built by the Sisters of Saint Joseph in 1924, the Motherhouse stands as a tribute to the congregation's foresight and dedication. Architect Joseph P. Flynn, who I learned, went on to design several churches in the region as well as the Art Deco fire department at North and Andrews streets in downtown Rochester, adding compelling details to make this building not only one that would endure but one that would bring a dimension of beauty to those without and within.

It has been home for thousands of young women, who have studied, prayed, and gone out to spread the good news after being received into the congregation. The walls have stories, I'm sure.

Now I look around Sister Maureen's office and wonder how meetings went with the notorious Sister Hilda. What I'm experiencing now with Sister Maureen is nothing compared to the stories I've heard of postulants and novices in years past who've been dismissed or disciplined, leaving lasting emotional scars. Another era, I think. I hope.

Sister Maureen says a few more meaningless phrases and I stumble out of her office. I haven't been treated with overt harshness; still, I'm angry and hurt. I feel betrayed by them all: the band, the directors, and especially Reverend Mother. Psychological reservations indeed. Being left out of a decision like this without any chance to voice an opinion or hear the reasoning hurts. I walk down the stairs and out to the front driveway.

Where is Katie when I need her? I'm still not exactly sure why she left. I trust someday she'll be able to share the reasons. I'm guessing she's being respectful of what seems to be my decision to stay. I long to have her here. Her caring spirit might bind up my wounded one . . . even if she does insist she's "off duty."

9

DIRECTOR OF NOVICES

I'M BEING LEFT BEHIND to stay at the Motherhouse. I now come under the supervision of the much-feared Director of Novices, Sister Evangelist, who is now to be called by her baptismal name, Elaine. Because of our hometown connection, I'm hoping for the best.

On August 29, Sister Maureen, who doesn't choose to go back to her baptismal name, presides over the reception of the habit for seven of the remaining nine members of our band. Besides Katie, whose leaving rocked me, Celestine, Diana, and Carol have left before Christmas. It seemed easier somehow than when Katie left. Marnie and I sit on the side aisle in the Motherhouse chapel with Sister Joellen, Sister Elaine, and a few first-year novices.

The ceremony is simple, the music stirring. The seven postulants process down the aisle, their new veils and black clothing freshly pressed. They are about to become first-year novices. Each one has a radiance I hope is sustained. My mother's words come to me: "Clothes don't make the man." Or the nun, I think.

As the ceremony continues, my mind wanders to what sort of ceremony I might be a part of for my own reception. Would there even be a reception of the habit, as contemporary dress becomes more and more popular? I wouldn't mind contemporary dress. The whole idea of witnessing to Christ's love doesn't have to be shown through public dress, does it? Though for centuries that was the idea. Lots to sort out, I think. No wonder the upcoming governmental Chapter session is so important.

While the organist, Anne, who accompanies us at choir practice, plays the triumphal "Voluntary in D Major" and the new novices of my band process from the chapel out into the August heat, I think again about Katie, whose decision to leave still rocks me. We'd seen so many things the same way. I stand and turn to watch these seven and wonder. Are they somehow right—more spiritually in tune than I am? Am I missing something? I look at them in their radiance, surrounded by the joy of their families and the congregation. I feel alone and can only trust that I'm on the right path.

As the service ends and the recessional music isn't from *The Sound of Music*, I smile. The new novices and their families appear overjoyed, Terry's father, up from New York City, practically bursting his buttons. Her African American family brings a welcome depth to this band that feels right to me, reaching out beyond the Rochester diocese for new blood and new ideas. The families go off to a reception with their new nuns and I return to my cell and pull out my journal, my trusted source for working things through. What, I wonder, will a habit change? Anything at all?

Within a week, Sister Maureen and the seven newly minted novices, along with Marnie, move to a new location, the Mount Vernon Retreat Center. The building, donated by generous benefactors, sits behind Highland Hospital. It's a 1920s-built home with Arts and Crafts architectural influence, stained glass, an eat-in kitchen, ample bedrooms, a sitting porch, and enclosed private yard. It's perfect for classes, reflection, and quiet. Sister Hilda, the former and now-retired mistress of postulants, will live in residence with the novices and be a grandmotherly influence I hope, her own reign of terror well behind her, her reputation known by many former Sisters.

I am left behind and on my own. Sister Elaine assigns a new room for me on the second floor, across the hall from hers, a small one with a view of the front grounds, the tree-adorned landscape bringing bird song inside.

As planned, I go back to my job at the Foreman Center. Foch, Carolee, Faye, Angela, and Joanie return while Linda, Scott, and Michael join us. Sweet Carl has moved to Newark Developmental Center.

I learn from Sister Elaine that a new postulant will be coming in. Alice will be studying theology at the college and on her own schedule, much as I would.

I'm given sufficient leeway to manage my own schedule, my charges, and my ongoing project. In this redesign of the agreed-upon formation program, Sister Elaine will now be my teacher for formation classes, a Saturday schedule to be set up. My bell tower encounter with her is never mentioned, an assumption, I trust, that we've moved beyond it in this next phase. I do sense a new ease in our relationship, though initially it still feels awkward using her baptismal name Elaine instead of Evangelist.

I'm glad for this year to be with Elaine, who has the wisdom and experience to guide me as I go forward. A part of the original two-year design, as I imagined it, was to provide ample time to think about everything that might keep one from entering in the first place. Like Tom.

While at Saint Ambrose for those six weeks last fall, I'd discovered a favorite Sister, Sister Mel the parish assistant. She was close to my five-foot-two height and maybe five years older. I was immediately taken by her open spirit and warmth. She sought me out one night after supper to accompany her on her evening errand. We chatted comfortably as we walked into the school auditorium in search of Roy the custodian. She had a message for him and wanted me to meet him.

"Roy is one of those guys you only meet once in a while," she said as she opened the gymnasium door with her big ring of keys. "He's kind, competent, and has an unusual gift of perceptiveness. I've learned a lot since I've met him."

When we entered the school through the auditorium entrance, it was dark, except for a light from the hallway. A figure in black moving startled me. We moved through quickly. Eventually we found Roy in the custodian's office in the back of the school. He smiled when he saw Sister Mel.

"This is Sister Betty, a postulant staying with us at the convent for a few weeks," Sister Mel said as Roy extended his hand. His gray eyes were soft. Sister Mel said, "We went over to the gym first to find you."

Roy smiled broadly. "Did you see Father Jerry doing his fencing?"

"We sure did," Sister Mel said, and I was relieved to know who the dark figure was. "I'd forgotten he was there."

"It's his sister who's the poet in residence at Nazareth College, isn't it?" I asked. Francesca Guli's poetry, with its mix of sensuality, spirituality, and scholarly allusions, had suited us young Catholic college women perfectly.

"Yeah, it sure is," Roy replied, "and she's good. I just went to one of her readings last month."

I saw what Sister Mel meant about Roy. How many custodians out there went to poetry readings?

Roy addressed me. "Sister Betty? You know, I've got this friend in AA with me. He was in love with a woman who went into the convent. He's a neat guy. Just started a group for folks under thirty-five. He's a real go-getter."

I blinked to see if I was awake.

Roy continued, "Yeah, he talked to me a lot about this woman. He wanted to marry her, but he said it was pretty hard competing with God."

I swallowed hard. Sister Mel turned to leave and I turned to Roy. "I know AA is anonymous," I say, "but are you allowed to say your friend's first name?"

"Oh sure," Roy said, "It's Tom. Nice-looking guy too."

I turned to Sister Mel, then to Roy. "I'm pretty sure I know him."

10

TOM

TOM PULLED ME TOWARD HIM and I let myself slide into his embrace. We'd been dating since just after Christmas ,1967, my first year teaching, seeing each other every weekend. It was only mid-February and already I found myself falling for this engaging man with his Gregory Peck looks, winsome smile, and wicked sense of humor. He made me laugh out loud. He was taller than me by at least a foot, which I found enchanting. His spirit was light, our times together—mostly watching his favorite sport, hockey—fun and relaxing.

Often we met up with friends of his and he introduced me with funny names; "This is my friend Matilda." "I'm pleased to introduce you to Hilda." I laughed as we climbed to our seats. I learned about the game of hockey as the puck zipped by and goalie Bobby Perrault got creamed. I'd known nothing about the sport or our local team, the Rochester Amerks, until Tom. Now I learned what a violent game it was.

"See number eight right there?" Tom asked, his arm around me, directing my attention to the ice. "He just used his elbow to body check the man he's guarding." Before I could ask, Tom said, "He's getting a penalty. I knew he would." I watched the player skate to the bench. Tom stood in the bleachers with the other fans and applauded.

I continued to digest all I was learning and picked up the lingo: slap shot, power play, penalty shot. One of our players got a penalty and the crowd booed, certain the defending team was at fault. A fight broke out and the crowd roared. I turned to Tom and quipped, "I think all you guys go to these games just to watch the fights."

When Tom and I had first met at a springtime party two years earlier at the home of his cousin Therese, a high school classmate of mine, I'd found myself immediately attracted. He was easy to talk with, and interesting—and handsome, with his lean physique and smiling eyes.

He'd asked me out that same night to visit friends on Cross Lake. On the car ride there, as I listened to him, I'd been impressed with his maturity. Unlike high school boys I had dated, he was measured in his opinions.

After a half-dozen dates—visiting friends at Cross Lake, going to movies, playing miniature golf—I returned to Nazareth College and Tom was gone. No long-distance phone calls, no visits, no contact.

I wondered. I dreamed of him.

Then at a Christmas party at Therese's house, I spotted Tom. He was standing with his back to me as I entered the dining room. I was thrilled, and as he turned around I laughed out loud. His arm was in a sling and scrawled on it was: *YES, I BROKE MY ARM. I SIMPLY TRIPPED. NO FUNNY STORY. SORRY.* This fit my memory of him: funny, gentle, and clever. His eyes smiled when he spotted me again.

We discovered we were both working in Rochester: he at Gleason Works as a service engineer, I at the Foreman Center as a teacher. We had apartments: he with a roommate who was never there, I with my friend Mary Anne, who was only away one weekend a month. He said he'd call, and this time he did.

After that Friday's hockey game, Tom and I stayed in the car—Mary Anne was at our apartment and her boyfriend, Ed, was in town. Tom and I were content to hug and kiss some more. I was thoroughly enjoying his caresses and affection, happy to have the possibility of the love of this man, something that for me was a prerequisite to any decision about the convent. Before I could think about giving over my life to the vows of poverty, chastity, and obedience, I felt strongly I should know what I would be giving up. My high school forays were frivolous. This felt different.

I hadn't told Tom anything about my convent leanings. I'd already sent off the initial inquiry papers and application form before we met up again. The longer we dated, the more I was half-hoping that the convent thoughts would slip into the background. I enjoyed Tom's attention and companionship. He was gentle, with a certain air of mystery I found intriguing. I was finding myself more and more sexually attracted to him, and increasingly had to use concerted willpower when we kissed to pull away before I got too carried away.

As we dated, we grew closer together. He spoke openly about his faith and I did too. I told him of my passion for social justice and about the impact John Kennedy's death had on my life goals. He listened well. I was thrilled to be able to share these thoughts. Thrilled that he listened so attentively. He was becoming part of a dream, and yet . . .

Did I dare travel into this world with this man? What would become, then, of this lifelong struggle over whether or not to enter religious life? How would I know if I didn't try? Yet this man was too good to lose, wasn't he?

Dr. Tremblay, the college physician who had an office in the village of Pittsford, was one of the few who knew of my sleeplessness and anxiety, my dilemma about what choice to make. He prescribed Valium, a popular tranquilizer that has a calming effect. I took a few but didn't like the numb feeling that accompanied it, so I stopped taking it.

On weekends when Mary Anne was home, Tom and I parked in the back of the College Complex lot, away from the huge lights. Often I fought my desire to go beyond heavy petting. I gently sat up when I felt we might be going too far and untangled myself from Tom's embrace. I was thrilled with how understanding and gentle he was. We snuggled together and shared funny stories and childhood memories, comfortable in each other's arms. Once we even fell asleep in the front seat of his well-loved used Chevy.

That Friday night we didn't. Instead, I shared my plans for a Chicago visit with my brother Jim and his wife, Susan, during the February recess. He said he had some plans of his own, though he didn't say what. Valentine's Day was Wednesday. I'd found a card to mail to Tom. I wondered if he'd have one for me.

Curiously enough, Tom and I didn't usually date on Saturday nights. Once in a while doubts crept in. Was he dating someone besides me? I didn't ask. It seemed unfair to make any claim on him, uncertain as I still was of my own intentions.

"A whole week you'll be gone?" he asked and pushed out his bottom lip.

I laughed. "You'll just have to watch Bobby get beat up all by your lonesome," I jested as we said goodnight.

I began teaching at the Foreman Center though I was still quite unsettled. Tom was becoming a bigger part of my life, yet thoughts of the convent weren't fading as I'd hoped. I sought help in the confessional from a young priest I'd seen say Mass a couple of times. He was one of the assistants whose sermons were relevant and brief, his manner light. He also had what I deemed to be caring eyes. I thought he would be simpatico.

"Bless me, Father, for I have sinned. It's been two weeks since my last confession." The starting words I learned as a seven-year-old didn't seem to fit. I continued on my own. "Father, I'm dating a man I'm quite attracted to. We haven't talked of anything serious yet, but I'm ambivalent about continuing to date him because I've been thinking about going into the convent."

There, I'd said it aloud again, this time to a priest. I heard him shift on his chair, his voice closer to the darkened screen.

"How long have you had these thoughts of the convent?" he asked, his voice almost a whisper, secretive and gentle—just what I needed.

"Since childhood, Father," I said quietly, my face flushing in the dark. I told him of the years of avoiding this calling. I shared how Aunt Betty, who was a Sister of Saint Joseph and whom I'd been named after, had given me a nun doll one Christmas. I felt embarrassed by it and kept it sitting in the back of the glass china cabinet in my bedroom, her black and white habit haunting me. I confided that I prayed on my high school retreat to not have this vocation.

I didn't tell him that I didn't want to be locked away from the world—that I wanted to live out loud, not in a convent. I adjusted myself on the kneeler. Was I really talking about this to a priest?

"I've just talked for the first time with one of the Sisters from the College where I was in school." My voice cracked.

"Can you share your dilemma with the man you're dating?"

I paused. I wanted to ask, "Do I have to?" Yet I knew it was only fair. I didn't want to lead him on. But I didn't want to lose him either.

Instead I said, "I suppose so, Father."

"If you have a good relationship with him, this won't hurt it. You'll have to trust that."

I knew he was right and I knew I had to move off the dime, for Tom's sake and for my own.

That same week, I received a letter from the psychologist I visited as part of the application process. His recommendation was that I wait another year before entering the convent. He didn't outline why, except to say that more time would help to sort things out. At first I was devastated and frustrated. What good would that do, I wondered? Give me more time with Tom? Was that fair to him? Or to me?

I left on my February recess for Chicago, hoping to sort out my struggles. I felt unbalanced by the psychologist's recommendation, which I was unprepared for and was resisting. Yet at the same time, Tom's endearing presence was so tempting.

Jim and Susan had been supportive of my doing whatever I want to do. At dinner with Jim's colleague from Catholic Extension Lay Volunteers, Father Ricky Bell, we talked of their work in Henry Horner Projects, where unrest often erupted into violence. Their focus was helping residents get justice, whether by helping mothers get food stamps, enrolling children in schools, or mediating with gang members. It seemed so brave and so important—just what I felt the Church should be doing. What I should be doing.

Ricky was the celebrant at Susan and Jim's wedding a year earlier. His easy manner, brush-cut hairstyle, and horn-rimmed glasses gave him a sage appearance.

Jim arranged time for me alone with Ricky. After dinner, he sat and listened as I blurted out the whole dilemma.

"You know, Betty Anne," he said, "psychologists can't measure the human heart. You're the only one who can judge that." I felt relieved and let his words give me solace, if only for a while. I told him I was planning to talk to Tom when I got back.

"In all fairness, you have to, much as you don't want to," he said.

I agreed.

When I returned from Chicago, I found two letters in my mailbox. One acknowledged the receipt of my convent application and included an interview date for mid-March. My stomach fluttered. The other was a Valentine from Tom. My dilemma was succinctly encapsulated by one mail delivery.

Once back home, Tom and I went to our Friday night hockey game. I was happy to be with him again and was resolved and ready to tell him that night. Again we ran into friends of his at the game. He paused as he introduced me and surprised me this time as he said, "This is my dear friend Betty." I was delighted to have gained the status of "dear," not to speak of being introduced by my actual name. I sensed something was shifting in him.

We sat together in the stands and snuggled. He was more publicly affectionate than I remembered. Maybe he'd missed me more than I thought. On the way home, we kissed at every red light, sometimes more than once. I was speechless as we pulled into the parking lot. How could I begin? He turned the car off and before I could speak, he pulled me toward him and kissed me with great tenderness. I responded, wondering how I would ever start now. Then he held me close and whispered in my ear, "Will you marry me?"

I was dumbfounded. I hugged him to me, breathless, tears brimming.

This was what I'd been waiting for; this was the dream I'd longed for. A man who loved me and wanted to marry me, to share his life with me. I felt like crying with happiness. Then I sensed a pain in my chest, a heartache. Was this what I truly longed for, or what I'd been taught to long for? Like a movie with Cary Grant and Doris Day, I felt the romance, the proposal, and—off in the future—children. As I looked into the eyes of this real man, offering real love—a kind, funny, intelligent man, and handsome besides—my eyes filled with tears. Oh, how I didn't want to hurt him.

"Oh Tom," I sobbed, "how I wish I could." I struggled for the words I'd rehearsed while lying in bed thinking of this moment. "I have something I've wanted to tell you that can't wait any longer."

I sat back from him and held his hands in mine. I blurted it before I could chicken out: "I'm thinking of going into the convent." I didn't wait for his response but plunged further in. "I've been struggling with this decision since before we started seeing each other again. It's been so difficult because . . ."

I stopped and closed my eyes. I said a little prayer hoping he wouldn't hate me.

I opened my eyes and saw his smile, the one that made his eyes crinkle in the corners.

"I've been wanting to talk to you about this for so long, but was so afraid I'd lose you," I said through my tears.

He freed his hands and held my shoulders squarely. "You can't lose me. Not that easily."

I breathed deeply, feeling so relieved.

"I respect your struggle," he said evenly. "I wish you had a different dream that included me. But if this is important to you, you need to follow it."

I nodded slowly, wiping tears away.

After a few minutes, Tom sat back and said, "I have some news of my own to share with you, but not tonight. When can we see each other again? I want to hear more about your decision and your plans, okay? I can still see you for a while, right?"

"Oh yes," I say exuberantly, "oh yes!"

He kissed me and I returned his kiss, wondering if I had any idea what I was doing.

I was curious about what Tom wanted to share. The week slid by as I wondered. He seemed so easily supportive of my decision. Letting me go that easily—I was glad to feel less guilty about hurting him, but, he hadn't even put up a struggle. I wondered what was going on for him.

The next time we saw each other, I greeted him at the door, charmed by how his blue-green shirt highlighted his hazel eyes. His manner was smooth as he leaned down to kiss and hug me. I'd prepared lunch, so we sat at the round table my roommate Mary Ann had bought and painted black.

I was eager to hear what he had to share and wondered how to help him begin. I didn't have to. As I served the lemonade and sat down, he reached across the table, took my hands in his, and looked directly into my eyes.

"Remember the woman I told you about from work? Alice?"

Oh no, here it comes, I thought. Another woman. His backup plan. No wonder he'd taken my news about going into the convent so easily.

"Yes," I answered tentatively. "I haven't met her, have I?"

"No, you haven't. I hope someday you will. She's my sponsor. I'm an alcoholic. She's helping me get grounded in AA. She's a wonderful woman."

I gulped.

"You're a what?" I said, as I tightened my grasp on his hands, jaw dropping, mind racing. I had heard about falling-down drunk people who needed hospitalization. My mother's childhood friend Betty Tubbs was an alcoholic who had gone away to "dry out." She never had a drink again.

I'd done my own share of drinking during college at the Pittsford Hotel Stephany, our gathering place for beer and playing pool. I'd managed a few hangovers and vowed never again. But an alcoholic? Not being able to stop?

"I'm an alcoholic," he said again, his eyes holding my gaze. "I mean I'm a recovering alcoholic. That's what I'm learning to understand." He released my hands and I pushed the chair back.

"I don't understand," I stammered. We'd had an occasional beer or drink but never anything that seemed excessive to me. "When did you discover this? I can't believe I didn't notice anything."

I was miffed at myself, and also feeling a little betrayed. I got up and fussed with lunch, hoping for some time, searching for relief from this thunderbolt. I picked up the two plates, with their tuna sandwiches on bread made by monks at the nearby Abbey of the Genesee monastery in Piffard. The neat brown-rimmed edges of the pottery plates were a welcome order amidst the chaos I was feeling. I tried to act casual, but my hand shook as I placed the plates on the table.

"Do you remember when I'd introduce you with funny names?" Tom asked, as I brought the pitcher of lemonade back to the table. I nodded.

"I did that because I couldn't remember your name. I've been having blackouts since I was a teenager."

I shook my head in disbelief, a calm settling over me as I realized the depth of this conversation, and how my affection for him was deepening.

Tom told me of his journey, of years of difficulties, starting as a teenager when the older guys would give him beer. He spoke of car rides when he'd end up in unfamiliar places, of nights when he didn't remember anything, and days when he'd arrive at work unshaven from the night before.

"Alice is like my guardian angel. Her perceptiveness has helped save my life," he said.

"I see. How old is she?" I asked.

He immediately got what I was driving at and grinned. "Oh, she's about fifty, with gray hair and the wisdom that can go with it. She approached me because she recognized the signs," he said as he took another bite of his sandwich.

I didn't ask what the signs were.

"I stopped drinking on February first. I can't tell you how good it feels," he said, and reached for the second half of his sandwich.

"I began going to the program the week you were away in Chicago. And if things go right, I'll be helping to start a group for people under thirty-five." His eyes were sparkling as he described his plans and the wonderful people he was meeting. I could see his joy and sense his pride.

We moved to the living room and sat on the small rose brocade love seat, another of Mary Ann's contributions. Over coffee and cookies, I told him I felt embarrassed that I never noticed. He consoled me and told me he was very characteristic of good alcoholics, clever at hiding his drinking.

As we continued to talk, I was reminded of how we never went out on Saturday nights, something I had often wondered about. Now I asked. He assured me this was very deliberate because Saturday was devoted to serious drinking.

I was learning about Tom's world and it reassured me that perhaps I'd made the right choice. We both were on a journey.

The afternoon wore into early evening, and as we stood at the door, Tom looked down at me and said, "If it's okay, I'd like to still get together with you," and here his hazel eyes crinkled, "at least, while we can."

"I wouldn't have it any other way," I replied. We hugged and he was gone. I blinked away the tears. There would be time enough for more tears, I thought, but not yet.

11

THE ANNUNCIATION

As I drove the familiar roads toward East Avenue, I noted the melting black snow that lined the curbs, temperatures finally rising above freezing. It was Monday, March 25, the Feast of the Annunciation, the day when the Angel Gabriel declared unto Mary that she would conceive and bear a child.

It was also the day of my interview to enter the Sisters of Saint Joseph. I was to meet with Sister Mary Ann at the Motherhouse. I was certain we'd have no talk of child bearing.

I pulled on the massive oak door and climbed the short flight of stone stairs to the main floor. I found Sister Mary Ann's office easily, her open door assuring me I had the right place. She was taller than I by a few inches, and beneath her modified white cap and black veil, I saw a warm smile and bright brown eyes. What showed of her dark hair didn't have any gray. Her easy conversation helped calm my anxiety. She invited me to sit and chatted about her nieces whose pictures were on the bookshelf behind her.

I shifted in my chair, trying to get comfortable as she opened a folder on her desk. "I've reviewed your application along with your transcripts; your high school transcripts arrived this week. Your grades indicate you excelled in English."

I flushed.

"It says here," she continued, "that your work was published in a high school journal." I nodded, no comment.

I was remembering my disappointment when I found that Sister Saint Matthew, who submitted the essay, had made minor changes without asking me.

She asked about my classmates. I told her many were from my neighborhood, and that there were sixty-three in my graduating class. "Some of us still get together once in a while," I said.

Then she shifted the topic to the application papers I had mailed in weeks earlier. I watched as she looked through the folder that probably contained Mr. Hauser's recommendation. "Everything seems to be in order," she smiled. "And about Mr. Hauser's recommendation..." I squirmed. "It still isn't clear to me what good his idea of waiting another year would do. This process is good for the candidates and for the congregation, too." She paused and put the folder down.

"The testing Mr. Hauser does in his hour-long evaluation can't take everything into account." I shifted in my chair, remembering his small face and soft voice, remembering the stick-figure self-portrait drawing I did. And I knew enough of psychological testing to know that it was only one part of the battery of tests.

"After all," Sister Mary Ann continued, "man proposes, but God disposes." A familiar quote from Thomas à Kempis.

I forced a smile, not sure what to expect.

Sister Mary Ann looked directly up at me from the papers in front of her. "In your case," she said, "with your current job at the Foreman Center, your good physical..."

I held my breath.

"We think you'll make a fine postulant."

I exhaled, my face relaxing into a real smile. I'd been

accepted!

I would have hated waiting another year. I would like to say I was relieved, yet I was not quite certain how I felt except scared. I was aware that this was a big step.

Sister Mary Ann stood up and came around the desk. I stood too. She offered a hug. I felt her arms around me and breathed deeply and hopefully. Was this the right fit? I wanted it to be, but still I wondered. Still I had doubts.

As she walked me back toward the great massive oak door, she reassured me that I still had time to think it over.

"The final papers will be mailed after Reverend Mother reviews them. It will be another month or so. You have plenty of time to digest all this. Enjoy it and trust the process. It'll be fine."

As she pushed the door open, she raised her eyebrows and added with a smile, "Do come back when you can stay longer."

I chuckled as door closed behind me. I stepped into the crisp March air and thought about Tom. I was so glad I'd finally shared this with him. I was eager to tell him how the interview had gone. We had plans to meet up in a few weeks.

Before that time came, on the first Thursday of April, Dr. Martin Luther King Jr. was shot to death.

I was numb. This man preached the word of God—like Gandhi, he preached non-violence. Familiar feelings of rage and betrayal made me restless, unable to make sense of what was happening in the world. I followed the television broadcasts and sobbed, went to work and wondered. I was shaken but felt stronger in my decision. Prayer and hope must be the way.

I felt thrilled to see Tom again. We hugged longer than usual, clinging together in hope. He reiterated his support of my decision.

"You know I'd like you to be a part of my future. But I don't dare compete with God." I laughed and felt more serene.

We saw each other a half dozen more times, filling the spaces with affectionate and honest talk. His program in AA was going well; his feet were on the ground. We were both moving forward with our plans.

We decided to have a "last supper" that would include a steak dinner and time at the swimming pool, a benefit of the College Complex apartments. I hoped for a clear June day and extra time to say all I'd stored up. But before I got a chance, storm clouds darkened the days.

Just two months after Dr. King's assassination, on another first Thursday, Senator Robert F. Kennedy was killed. The world felt like it had gone mad. I was angry and frozen. Sleep didn't come easily. I was grateful that I'd made my decision; my resolve grew stronger than ever. I must answer John Kennedy's call.

Tom and I did have our last supper, and the day was picture perfect. We dangled our feet in the pool in silence for a while, the weight of the world looming alongside the weight of our diminishing time together. We talked about his program; I told him I'd received all the papers.

"You've certainly made this decision a lot more difficult," I said, splashing his feet with water and smiling up at him.

His comfortable nature eased me, and my ease at sharing things with him surprised me. We bantered back and forth. I was thankful there was no one else around as Tom reached over and kissed me.

"It's been a pleasure," he said. I looked at his handsome face lit by the afternoon sun.

I stared out at the silky blue water of the pool. "You know, you once said to me that unless I try this time in the convent, I'll be haunted the rest of my life."

"So this is my fault?" he laughed. "Maybe I shouldn't be so understanding."

He told me more about his under-thirty-five group that he'd be starting over the summer. His excitement was palpable, his hazel eyes shining with a light I hadn't seen before. He was meeting people with stories similar to his and finding strength to stay sober. He told me that his job situation had improved and he was thinking about going back to school for more education.

"I can actually remember things from day to day," he said at one point, referencing the sobriety he now experienced. "Oh, and I've been down to see Mom and Dad. They send their best to you."

I'd met his parents on several occasions. Most recently I noted that Tom got his sharp wit and green eyes from his mother. His father, a gentle man with a full head of white hair, was attentive and interesting, telling of their recent trip to Aruba.

Later, at my apartment, over a broiled Delmonico steak dinner that Tom praised, we talked of other dreams. More schooling was on Tom's agenda, his plans including classes at Monroe Community College. I told him of my upcoming trip with my older sister Mary Jean to San Francisco, which was her gift to me before I entered the convent.

We lapsed into comfortable silences, words not necessary.

I presented Tom with a book: Prayers by Michel Quoist, a volume I'd found comforting and inspiring.

"I've marked a prayer called 'Help Me to Say Yes,'" I told him. "I think we share a common struggle. See if you don't agree."

He appeared touched, his eyes growing moist. He presented me with a Hallmark book about friendship. A giant chasm had closed.

I'd received far more than I'd ever imagined. I'd fallen in love with a wonderful man who would go on to fill the world with the same kind of love I hoped to. The tears were joyful as we hugged, for what I imagined would be the last time.

I watched as he walked up the stairs to the parking lot. The line from the song, "Hello, Young Lovers" from *The King and I* runs through my head as I watch him go. I hum it feeling so fortunate that I've had a love of my own.

But even after all that, the single question still haunted me: Is this religious life, with its ancient traditions and potential for a relevant future, truly what I wanted?

PART TWO

There is only one happiness in life, to love and be loved.

–George Sand

12

SURPRISE NIGHT

FOR THOSE OF US LIVING at the Motherhouse over the summer, the directors propose a new twist: Surprise Night. The concept is simple. Each Sister, novice, and postulant is responsible for planning a surprise for a different Saturday night. It's to include dinner and an activity. The reason, though never explicitly stated, is to give the group of twenty-year-old women a way to enjoy summer Saturday nights—the classic date night.

My idea, when my turn arrives, comes directly from the era: fondue! At the two fondue dinners I attended prior to entering the convent, I remember being charmed by the small cubes of red beef and bread chunks speared on sticks and dipped into hot, bubbly oil. One of the two parties stands out in memory because it took an extraordinarily long time for us all to be fed, as the oil was not hot enough.

I have devised a simple solution. I've decided to heat the oil early so it will be ready for our tabletop sharing. My plan is to serve the fondue supper at six and follow it up with two movies of the Madeline books that are based in an old house in Paris, where twelve little girls lived in two straight lines, the smallest one, Madeline.

French Sisters tend to the children in the Madeline books. Since the Sisters of Saint Joseph originated in Le Puy, France, I feel I've made a strong connection for the evening's entertainment. And Madeline's spunky personality along with her irrepressible and mischievous nature makes her seem a perfect performer for an evening of fun.

During the week, I make arrangements to get a film projector from one of the classrooms. I contact the public library and arrange to pick up the films on Friday afternoon, just after I stop for groceries. I even borrow two fondue pots from former work colleagues who are delighted to contribute to a night of fun for the nuns.

From my window, the Saturday July morning dawns brightly, the birdsongs especially cheerful. I'm determined to one day learn their songs, differentiating one from another.

After Lauds, Mass, breakfast in the refectory, and completing my morning charge of setting tables, I head straight to the fourth-floor kitchenette. I pull the cellophane-wrapped beef from the refrigerator. Burdette's Meat Market has been a great resource in helping me get the right cut and grade of meat, tiny lean, white rivers of fat running through it. I'm pleased. I find the wooden cutting board and begin to the slice the meat into bite-sized chunks. The knife glides easily through the sinewy material, the large ceramic bowl filling up more quickly than I expect, the thin blue stripe around the top of the bowl almost covered with the uncooked beef.

Next I cube two large loaves of Italian bread into appropriate-sized chunks, putting them in a breadbasket I've lined with a paper napkin. I pull a sturdy oval blue bowl from the wooden dish cupboard and fill it as I cut up vegetables— broccoli, carrots, green peppers, and white mushrooms. In the center I tuck a bowl of French onion dip. With the final addition of cheddar cheese and crackers on a tray, I think I am ready for the evening. I've even set the table with some

Madeline quotes at each place, a sampling of my favorites that I planned to ask each Sister to read when we started. Madeline who believes even though she's very small that inside she's very tall. And Miss Clavel, who afraid of a disaster, ran fast and faster.

After lunch, I return to the kitchenette. I fill a medium-sized saucepan three quarters of the way to the top with oil, set it on the electric burner, and turn it to low. This, I think, will ensure that the oil will be hot enough. I'm satisfied that everything else is in order and go down to my room on the second floor. I sit on the edge of my bed, neatly made since early morning, and review the Madeline books that are on the bed stand, confident that this little character will help make the evening one of surprise and delight.

I take time to complete another reading from the blue book about the congregation for my formation class and then change into a clean blouse and skirt for the evening event. I check the time and decide to return to the fourth floor. Dinner is scheduled for five-thirty so we won't interfere with the silent retreat. Over one hundred Sisters are gathered to attend the retreat, an experience I have learned is based on the spiritual exercises of Saint Ignatius. There is no talking from morning to night. The retreat master, a priest I'm not familiar with, gives lectures and instruction. No conversation accompanies them. The participants come and go in silence, a practice that helps clear the mind and open the soul. The house has been pleasantly quiet without the ordinary hustle, bustle, and buzz.

It's early but I think it won't hurt to set up the projector and make sure the films are ready to go. As I stroll down the hall, one of the novices, Kathy stops me and says, "I thought you might want to know. There's smoke coming from the kitchenette."

"Oh," I say with confidence, "that's the oil!" I'm glad to know the heating process is working, if a little ahead of schedule. I scurry down the hallway, which is highly polished from an industrial buffing machine applied to it earlier, one of the many "charges" accomplished for the day. As I enter the community room and open the adjoining door to the kitchen, I can see what Kathy means. A light fog envelops the room. I immediately turn the oil off and open the window to air the room.

As I turn back to the stove, the four-quart aluminum pan, which is three-quarters full of oil, bursts into flame. I stand back aghast. The flames are hot, red and orange and high. Quickly I search for something that will cover the pot, hoping to extinguish the flames. No luck. I have chosen the largest of the saucepans, never considering the need for a lid.

I have vague knowledge about oil fires and try to remember if baking soda is the right agent. I know there is a red fire extinguisher in the hallway. Something makes me think it might not be the right kind. I study the situation and think about moving the pan, which is precariously close to the wooden cabinet that holds the dishes and glassware. The red flames force me back. I wonder if a blanket would work.

I am acutely aware of the more than one hundred professed Sisters, the ones who are on a silent retreat, and I don't want any alarms disturbing them.

Aha, I'll just call the fire department and see what they advise.

I go into the office across the hall where there is a general use phone. On the desk, I find a list with emergency phone numbers taped in place and call the Pittsford Fire Department.

"Hello," I say in as calm a voice as I can muster, "this is Sister Betty from the Sisters of Saint Joseph Motherhouse on East Avenue."

The male voice on the other end is quietly receptive to my call. "Yes, Sister," he says, "how can I help you?"

I'm calmed immediately, knowing that help is at hand. I proceed to tell him my dilemma.

"I've got a pan of oil that's caught fire and I'm hoping you'll be able to help me figure out how to extinguish it."

He confirms our address and offers to send a fire truck.

"I don't necessarily need a fire truck," I say. "You see, there's over one hundred Sisters on silent retreat here, so if you can just help me figure out how to put the fire out, I think that will be enough." The voice on the other end continues to be soothing and asks me to explain. "You see, it's in a pan that's near a wooden cabinet and there's no lid for the pan and I'm on the fourth floor of the building."

He asks if there's an elevator, and if I can carry the pan out of the building.

My knees beginning to shake. "Yes, there's an elevator, but the flames are pretty high. I don't think I can carry it safely. There's a red fire extinguisher."

"Don't use it," he says. "That will make it worse."

"Okay. Well, what can I do? You see, with the retreat going on, I really want to avoid any fire trucks coming. Can you send just a station wagon?"

"They're already on the way," he says. "We automatically send them when a call comes in."

I feel an alarm go off within me, my heart pounding in my

ears, my stomach churning. "How soon will they be here?" There's a new level of panic in my voice.

I'm about to ask if they can come without using sirens—but it's too late! Through the open windows, I hear the familiar whine, distant but growing.

"Uh, thank you, officer, I'd better go now!"

I return the black handset to the receiver, take a deep breath, and brace myself.

I dash into the hallway and head for the stairs, taking them three at time, hoping to meet the trucks as they arrive, hoping to ask them to be quiet.

As I round the third set of stairs heading to the first floor, I turn to look down the main hallway, its polished black and white tiles gleaming, hoping no one has been disturbed. A sea of moving black and white greets my glance as it advances toward the doorway. I have no idea what tipped them off, but I realize the retreat is silent no more. My eyes dim momentarily and I whisper a forbidden expletive. Like Miss Clavel, afraid of a disaster, I ran fast and faster. I know I am too late to keep a lid on anything.

I look into the yard and see not one but two big red fire trucks, ladders and hoses in place. There's also a small station wagon. Others are ahead of me on the steps of the building, directing the firemen. I confirm it is the fourth floor. I step aside as one after another, five firemen, clad in brown rubber suits, hats, and boots, troop up the stairs, tan hoses unfurling from their great folds. No one speaks. They move quickly. I follow back up the stairs to the kitchenette and arrive in time to see one of the firemen spray foamy liquid from a yellow canister into the red, orange, and black flames licking up out of the pan. Flames leap to the floor; the fireman sprays once again. I note the charring of the wooden cabinet once the fire has been extinguished. Well, my initial fear was not unfounded.

As I look about me, I notice smoke has enveloped the community room and the dining room that are located on either side of the kitchen. I watch as the firemen lift the pan and, along with their hoses, move toward the doorway.

I follow them to the hallway. I'm numb, not knowing what I feel. I ask about fire extinguishers and am assured that using the red one could have caused the fire to spread. "You did the right thing by calling us, Sister," the red-faced lieutenant says as he leaves.

I see Sister Elaine heading down the hallway toward me. Suddenly I realize that I am surrounded by most of the women for whom I was preparing dinner. I stand transfixed and speechless as I fight back tears. Finally I whisper to anyone close enough to hear, "Surprise!"

Once the firemen have all left and some of the other novices have cleaned out the kitchen a bit, Elaine leads me to one of the visitor's parlors for a while to gather my wits. Within a short time, my tears now dried, she comes in and asks if I think I could continue and put the dinner on. I feel like someone just asked me to get on the horse that had thrown me. But I do it. With help from the others, we watch the films first and enjoy the fondue second, oil heated in small pans and absolutely hot enough. The bread and beef are a great combination, the veggies a perfect complement. The evening is actually enjoyable, and I, the mischief-maker, feel embraced by forgiveness, love, and appreciation.

13

CHOIR

I AM IN THE TRIDUUM, that favored prayer spot of mine that overlooks the chapel. It also serves as a fourth-story passageway between two sides of the Motherhouse, between professed Sisters and those in formation. I never tire of this majestic view, as calming as ocean waves, the eternal truth sheltered on the altar, the gold tabernacle holding the center of the Catholic faith: the host that represents the body of Christ.

I am aware of the growing movement in the Church that says, "We are the Body of Christ." I ponder the notion that we can bring our behaviors into a more perfect reflection of our beliefs. I have far to go to even approach the goodness I imagine possible.

The noises of the evening I once found eerie are now comforting, the soles of shoes worn by the souls of the faithful below who pray—for what, I don't know. These women keep coming back, each finding her own pew, each one's breviary tattered from use. They are representative of this congregational faith I am attracted to. And yet.

What, I sigh, am I doing here? I am living in two worlds, maybe three. I yearn for some silence, and yet am afraid of it. I yearn for the freedom to pray alone without the scrutiny of theirs and I am finally beginning to wonder if I know how to pray. Sister Maureen's prophecy.

I long for action, not convinced that prayer can do what service can. I'm impatient and growing tired.

I direct my eyes to the prayer of the divine office.

Hear me when I call, O God of my righteousness: thou hast set me at liberty when I was in trouble; ... O Lord, lift me up: the light of thy countenance upon us. Thou hast put gladness in my heart...

I read the prayer that goes all the way back to the fourth psalm of David, knowing that I am part of worldwide prayer of religious men and women. I put my head in my hands. I sigh into the quiet. Can I really do this?

I am still recovering from Surprise Night, insurance adjustors fortunately providing enough money to do a much-needed makeover of the entire space because of the extensive smoke damage.

My charge to clean the pool, which gets me out of doors, is a continual joy, and the friends I am making in the congregation are comforting. I'm not sure what is plaguing me. Exhaustion overtakes my desire for prayer, communion, answers. I tiptoe out of the Triduum and down the highly polished floors to my room, eager for sleep. I pull my pajamas from the hook behind the door, brush my teeth at the sink in the corner, and crawl into bed.

Sleep comes easily. The morning bell rings sooner than I wish. I rise, put on my robe, and patter to the marble lavatory that echoes each sound. Murmurings of "Praise be Jesus" can be heard. I make sure not to make eye contact so I don't have to enter into the forced salutation. There are no mirrors—one less distraction as I ready myself. My choice of clothing is limited but so far I still wear street clothing, though the day of receiving the habit is coming closer. I rush down the four flights of stairs to the chapel, the tall pendant lights all lit, a different view than the one I had last night. The sound will soon be different too.

I find my way to my pew, genuflect—remembering to make it a deep bend of the right knee—and move into place on the brown padded kneeler. I reach down on the shelf below the seat just above the kneeler and retrieve my breviary. Lauds has begun.

> *Show me your mercy at daybreak,*
> *Because of my trust in you,*
> *Tell me the way I should follow,*
> *For I lift up my soul towards you.*

With a rich, firm chord, the organ intones the first notes of this morning's Mass and Monsignor Schnacky enters the altar from the sacristy, the small room off to the left where he has robed himself in his vestments. Song lifts into the arches and rafters. Each Sister, young, old, believer, doubter, saint, and sinner, has been trained over the years in weekly choir practice, much of it Sister Flora's music.

I look forward to the weekly choir practice sessions that are held in a classroom on the lower level. Sister Flora's advanced years don't show as she listens with her trained ear to our attempts to sing her songs. She knows what she has written and she knows what it should sound like. So again and again, I hear her say to Anne, who is the accompanist and a second-year novice, "Stop, Sister. Stop."

I wouldn't trade places with Anne for the world.

We stand silently as she scolds us for our vocal failings, our botched attempts to sing the notes she's written. I want her to let us go on. I can't hear what's missing. I only hear the majestic sound of this collective force of voices.

With each successive practice I attend, I have become more steeled to Sister Flora's tirades, knowing they will pass and the music will go on. But this night is different from the others. Sister Flora is more agitated and screams at poor Anne too often. I become unsettled, anger bubbling up.

"Sister, stop right now. Stop! I said stop!" Flora hollers. Anne looks up innocently, her hands off the keyboard. Sister Flora whirls around, her veil catching upon her shoulder, looks out at us all, and shouts, "Sisters, I told you to reach a climax!"

Silence fills the room. I can't resist. I glance around the room, looking for laughter, someone else who can join in this ultimate comedy. No one? Not anyone who catches the absurdity, the hilarity of this moment? I spot Sheila, a music major and magnificent vocalist. Our eyes meet and we smile. The rest of the postulants, novices, and junior Sisters, aged between eighteen and twenty-four, look somberly ahead. I bite my lip to stifle my laughter—and my dismay.

Anne resumes playing; the musical phrase again attempted. We must have reached the longed-for climax, for we are summarily dismissed.

I file with the others out the door and catch up with Sheila. "Are we the only two to get that?" I ask, my voice laced with disappointment.

"'Fraid so," she whispers as we reached the hallway. "I'm trying to start a campaign in the johns to add an alternative to the 'Praise be Jesus.' An occasional 'Go to Hell.' What do you think?"

We giggle and go to our separate stairways.

14

GENERAL CHAPTER

I HOLD TWO FOUR-BY-SIX INDEX CARDS in my hands, glancing at them as I read out in a voice strong enough to be heard by even the oldest Sisters. I've been selected from the dozen or so Sisters in the formation program to represent the views of the younger religious at this gathering of General Chapter delegates.

The convening of a General Chapter is not undertaken lightly, and this one, the first I have been a part of, is no exception. Sisters convene in the late afternoon and evenings after their own roles as teachers, principals, nurses, and parish workers are completed. The assembly of elected delegates struggles to address how to implement Vatican II changes.

The Vatican II Council seeks to address centuries of social change and scientific and technical discovery during which the Church has held the line without thoroughly examining what is the baby and what is just dirty bathwater. Both clergy and laity have felt the tension of living in a modern world and a medieval church. "Aggiornamento," a word that means "bringing up to date," becomes a key word as this new wave continues. Christians from outside the Catholic Church have been invited to the Council. Bold thinkers like the French Dominican cardinal and theologian Yves Congar become influential in moving the agenda of Christian unity. The quest for the right path to this hotly debated ecumenism becomes the topic of the day. Reverend Edward Schillebeeckx, who helped prepare the New Dutch Catechism, helped carry the Vatican Council's message of ecumenism. I am thrilled that work of the Council to restore unity among all Christians remains in the forefront.

But it goes even further. The hope of Vatican II and the promise of openness in the words of Lumen gentium (light of the nations), one of the principal documents of the Second Vatican Council, declare:

> *Those also can attain to salvation who through no fault of their own do not know the Gospel of Christ or His Church, yet sincerely seek God and moved by grace strive by their deeds to do His will as it is known to them through the dictates of conscience. Nor does Divine Providence deny the helps necessary for salvation to those who, without blame on their part, have not yet arrived at an explicit knowledge of God and with His grace strive to live a good life.*
> *—Lumen gentia 16*

This is it in a nutshell for me.

I have accepted the request that came from several of the Chapter delegates to speak as a representative for the few younger Sisters who are still in the congregation. I am twenty-six years old. Within the past year, four of the thirteen women I entered with have left, their reasons not shared publicly. Four other women have entered, two from other communities where they found questions without answers.

Our formation has no common bonds, our programs

individualized, our philosophies disparate, our experiences varied. We don't have activities that bind us together as did the larger bands of novices from the past. We are unique and individual, forging new pathways, trusting in the results.

I have labored over what to say, cautious not to be too radical and yet careful not to cop out by sidestepping an emerging vision that calls for more relevance. It's the summer of 1970 and being authentic is very important.

"Religious life in the year 2001," I begin, "will differ in many respects from the religious life we are experiencing today. Much of what we are struggling with now in terms of definition and resolution will become a part of history. And all we struggle with now will take its part in creating the future."

I take a breath and steady my shaking knees. This lecture hall at the congregation's Nazareth Academy, a girls' high school near Kodak's industrial park on Lake Avenue, provides an ideal setup. The chamber with its three-tiered seating gives everyone an eagle eye's view of everyone else. The Sisters present in this assembly have been elected by their peers to sit on this General Chapter. They all seem attentive as I speak.

"This realization helps many of us, as young members of a traditional institution, to place proper emphasis on the history of the congregation. The more fully we comprehend this past in all its implications, the more sensitively we can live in the present and the more fully we can work for the future."

I know from the classes I am taking during these days in formation that a General Chapter is a big deal, its roots in the ninth century with Saint Benedict of Aniane. This concept of governance for religious orders eventually was made canonical by the Fourth Lateran Council in 1215, which dealt with discipline issues among clergy and religious orders partly through these General Chapter meetings for electing the next general or superior of the order, appointing or electing other officials, settling matters of business and discipline, hearing appeals as needed, and, in some cases, sanctioning changes in the constitution. A tall order.

This chapter has drawn more than seventy women, many wearing the modified habit with the small veil, black skirts and white blouses, black blazers, or dresses. This chapter is momentous because the times are. Each delegate's election has been prayed over by the entire congregation. There's no smoke, but it feels as important as the selection of a pope. It will go on for several weeks of evenings and weekend sessions, attendance by observers permitted, each day's agenda public and professionally executed. The congregation is taking its place in being a part of the world and inviting the world to witness their deliberations.

I am more than a month away from receiving the modified habit. The lines regarding dress are in a state of flux. While a few older Sisters still come to the meetings of the Chapter in their traditional habit—of linen and serge with large rosary beads—they aren't in attendance at today's assembly. Today is about the future. In addition to the modified habits—a shortened veil and headdress and black and white attire—a significant number of nuns, many from the college, are wearing what is still called "experimental dress." The hope is that clothing in step with one's contemporaries will help us be more engaged and accepted in secular settings. I remember from my blue book studies of the congregation's history that this actually has historical precedent: the original habit was not far different from simple dress of the people of its times.

Currently, makeup and jewelry are not included in the mix,

except for the small specially designed pewter cross that was voted in as an option at the previous Chapter.

Although some older Sisters cling to their habits, others who have lived in religious life for more than twenty-five years chomp at the bit to dress more like their secular peers. Sister John Mary, a vivacious, round-faced woman in her mid-forties, comes to breakfast on a muggy August morning in sandals with no stockings—unheard of until that moment! I am filled with hope.

The chapter room is stuffy, air-conditioning not an option in this upper auditorium at Nazareth Academy. Still I don't remove my light green blazer. I have dressed conservatively enough not to be considered too bold. I am aware that the voices of young Sisters don't carry much weight, yet ours are important and thoughtful voices, the voices of my generation, and I hope we can be heard. I have learned that the louder voices are the eager Sisters in their thirties and forties who have been serving in parishes and hospitals around the Rochester diocese, in Selma, Alabama, and in Brazil. It is this age group who see the real need for change. They see the sorrows of the streets and witness the violence in the villages. They know there is anger in this new age. They have seen poverty and its consequences, incest and domestic abuse first hand. Becoming relevant for them is not a nicety but rather a necessity. As much as we younger Sisters wish to have a voice in this congregation's deliberations, these women are determined to have a voice in today's Church. There is no time to lose in gaining a foothold in communities that are desperately in need of what these religious women can bring to them.

I look around the room at the gray-haired wise ones and the

dark-haired hopeful ones, some with veils and some without.

"Living sensitively in the present," I declare, "will be a demand in every age, and in our age we continually realize the need for this. This age of renewal that religious life has been evolving through has taught us much about religious living."

I realize I am not saying anything too much, working hard to capture the half dozen or so older Sisters so they can hear the words I am speaking without writing the ideas off as too faddish.

I continue. "We have worked together at being less judgmental of others and their motives." I recall the instincts that I am praying to stifle at every turn. As I wash dishes, scrub floors, use the industrial-sized buffing machine on the massive terrazzo floors, I hold quiet counsel in my head. All my readings and contemplation have led me forward. I am not to be concerned with someone else's behavior. I am only responsible for mine. I long to see change happen and don't know if this is the way. I long to see silence around all levels of social injustices ended and more challenge brought to maintaining decorum. More sandals and bare legs. More real emotion not suppressed and subdued. Let this group of women challenge authority, think out loud, and love their enemies. I want to scream out with urgency that together we may be able to make a remarkable difference. Instead I go on with measured tones and stick to the script, my four-by-six cards looking a bit more tattered as I shift them in my sweaty palms.

"We have stretched ourselves to accept things that at one time we were certain we could not. We have grasped the notion of becoming and have affirmed through our Chapter enactments our desire to continue always to become."

I am using the language of the day, laced with words of Corita Kent, who recently left the Sisters of the Immaculate Heart of Mary in Los Angeles where her classes were an avant-garde mecca for groundbreaking artists of the time. I find her mixing of the sacred and secular thrilling. Her friendship with the Berrigan brothers raises her credibility even higher. I trust her words, as many do. "Damn everything but the circus!" is one of her popular posters seen in several convent bedrooms. It is a reference to a poem by e.e. cummings that rants against grimness and timidity, and valorizes risk-taking and joy. Corita has given hope to a growing number who wonder if religious life needs to be as stuffy as the air in this room. "Find a place you trust and then try trusting it for a while," she says. Many of us are doing just that.

I sneak in a few more phrases to urge movement forward. "We are moving away from black and white truth and are opening our minds as a congregation, a Church, and a world to a broader vision. We realize we can no longer document the truth."

Though it feels like I am a stand-in selected by some who may think our generation has something to offer, I trust I am not a voice in the wilderness. I have talked with many Sisters, and I have found a ground swell for change. War protests are swirling about us, lives are being lost daily while we debate what to wear. Does it really matter? How long can we go on not making a difference?

"The implications of not being able to document truth range all the way from being open to Buddhism, to listening openly to support for abortion. Somewhere between these two we find the implication of being open to a different approach to living out a Christian commitment."

I look around at the women I admire, women who are musicians like Alice Rose, whose voice brings tears when she sings and hope when she speaks, and theologians like Margaret Joan, whose gentle persistent faith is echoed in every class she teaches. These philosophers and cooks, teachers and nurses and hairdressers are women who are serious about making a go of it and making this congregation one they can be proud of, even as the bombings continue in Hanoi. The world is changing and so must we. I decide it's time to call forth a sage that speaks to us all, and for us as younger Sisters.

"It is the challenge of such implications that impels so many of us today. We are able to live without certainty in great hope. Chardin describes this very experience in his Divine Milieu: 'What is happening under our eyes within the mass of peoples? What is the cause for this disorder in society, this uneasy agitation, these swelling waves, these whirling and mingling currents and these turbulent and formidable new impulses? Mankind is visibly passing through a crisis of growth. Mankind is becoming dimly aware of its shortcomings and its capacities .... It sees the universe growing luminous like the horizon just before sunrise. It has a sense of premonition and of expectation.'"

We younger religious are not great in number nor are we united. Our differences are strengths as we help the congregation figure out what avenues are open. Our disunity can also be distressing; we may be missing out on one of the great joys of living in religious community. I know I cannot really speak for all of my band, yet I continue as if we were one:

"The hope we experience for the future of religious life is

what has prompted us to enter. The vision and energy that we have we feel we must, together as women, channel to a deeper awareness of Christ. We trust together the changes that yet must come to make a meaningful future for tomorrow that will include our vision."

I am done. I pick up the index cards and return to my seat. There is no applause. Applause doesn't belong in the reflective atmosphere of Chapter. As the break comes for the morning session, several of the women I have come to admire thank me. I nod but feel I played it too safe, that I talked around the edges of what so many hoped for. I'm not authorized by the newest novices to call for radical changes. Yet some others I know hope for a radical opening up of the rules and routines, to make the impossible possible, making room for those of us who would like to be able to follow the Daniel Berrigans of the Church to prison if necessary.

I stand, looking over the elected members of the General Chapter, old and young, liberal and conservative, happy and sad, grouchy and placid. These are the women determining the future. I wish I could start my remarks over again but know that I can't. And even if I could, what would I say that would make a difference?

It's 1970. Six hundred thousand attend the largest rock festival ever on the Isle of Wight. The first gay pride marches have been held in New York City, Chicago, Los Angeles, and San Francisco. One hundred thousand people are demonstrating against the Vietnam War. I'm a postulant in an order that is seeking to address the challenges, longings, and hopes of this era.

And Richard Nixon is in the White House. For now.

15

THE INTERVIEW

"LET'S WALK," Sister Elaine says when I appear as requested at her office door. We head down the hallway and out the side door, sunlight bathing us when the huge oak door yields to our push. As we move down the gray concrete steps to the paved driveway, Elaine turns to the right and I follow her across to the front lawn, the recently cut grass smelling of summer. A light breeze cools the air and as we walk toward an opening in the woods across the lawn, the fragrances of spring accompany us.

"I wanted to see you," Elaine begins, "because it's time to discuss your readiness to receive the habit."

I gulp as we make our way down the small pathway and back around to the other end of the lawn.

Elaine glances in my direction and continues her trek a few paces ahead of me where the path narrows. The grounds are in their glory, bushes bursting with blossoms, leaves in towering trees rhythmically swinging as if to an unheard melody. I breathe in the sweetness of the smells, waiting for the next part, the part about sacrifice and piety, about poverty, chastity, and obedience. Sister Maureen has always said that prayer is hard. Despite moments of feeling stuck or weary, I've rejected that posture. I've struggled with belief, wrestled with various notions of a deity, and questioned the relevance of religious community, yet my prayer life, as I define it, is rich and amazingly comforting. Comforting not because I hear guidance, voices, or answers, but because I am at peace. I am doing my best to live fully, honestly, and openly amidst the constraints of community. I have struggled to keep alive the friendships I had before I entered, aware that the tightrope of being in can cause a tension that feels wrong to me. I am trying to live a life dedicated to service, to be there for others, not get away from them. I feel guilty at times for the luxury that is mine to sit and contemplate, write, read, and remember.

I have grown to trust Sister Elaine, whose blend of sensitivity and sternness I appreciate. It is the same combination I have grown up with. My mother, though a bit older than Elaine, had some of the same Sisters at Saint Rose of Lima School—Sister Hermine—the one they both speak fondly of.

I've become aware that my mother's warmth doesn't include hugging or too many words of affection. Her familiar admonitions, "Don't wear your heart on your sleeve," "Don't be melodramatic," and "Don't make mountains out of molehills," fit the same kind of demeanor Elaine displays. Elaine's response to my Surprise Night fiasco had comforted me in an old world way, by neither scolding me nor overtly consoling me, but rather giving me privacy to collect myself and then asking me to go back into the fray. This way she allowed me to regain my dignity and self-respect and pull off a successful evening despite everything. Elaine's warmth could be seen in ways unexpected. Her rendition of "Sleep, Kentucky Babe," hummed as if her lips were a trumpet, brings squeals of delight at evening recreation. It's joyful to observe how tenderly she treats her father, whose face she mirrors— gray hair, brown eyes, and pink skin—hers pulsating pride, eyes shining and focused on him as he fulfills the random requests she asks him for: fixing chairs and railings, adding shelves and hooks, creating new order—all with little effort, his professional carpentry skills fully intact despite his years.

As we walk together this afternoon, I realize how much I have grown to care for her. Our Lima connection is a strong foundation, and the pain of her disapproval during the Bell Tower incident has been pushed to the background by her deftly nurturing handling of the Surprise Night fire.

She pauses in the shade of the pine trees on the south side of the massive building.

"Since your second year as a postulant is almost over, it's time to talk about your reception."

I feel my chest tighten. *My reception*, I think. *Wow.* At least I'm entering at a time when reception ceremonies no longer mean shaving our heads, donning wedding gowns as a bride of Christ, and receiving a habit made of heavy serge, a scapular, a starched cornet, underskirt, under veil, giumpes, a cincture around the waist with five knots to remind one of the wounds of Jesus, and oversized rosary beads.

This was the garb for most Sisters I knew in the past, their heads completely hidden. The ceremony of today is far different. The new small headdress—the Bergdorf Goodman–designed white band with a veil attached—is one I've thankfully grown to like the look of. The ceremony is symbolic, service, dedication, and devotion central themes. At least that's what I think about. Service to the wider world, I try to remember, is central to the ritual, and something I easily and fully buy into.

The black veil, a black dress, shoes, and some accent of white to highlight the headband make for an attractive look. As a parochial school survivor who wore uniforms from age six on, I am aware of the yards of individuality that could be attained by the strategic use of length, belt tightening, and the placement of the dickie-collared blouse.

I can still see my mother dutifully altering my first-grade uniform to what she thought was the popular length, having trusted my supposed best friend from across the street over me to advise her. I suffered through the embarrassment for the entire school year, the skirt too short, with too little hem left to be lengthened.

Here I am thinking about yet another uniform, a habit symbolizing a life to be lived in religious community.

This step in the formation program marks the beginning of a new relationship between the congregation and me. As a postulant (the Latin *postulāre* means "to ask"), I have asked for admission for the past two years. Now, if I receive the habit, the congregation accepts my request and receives me into their community.

As we walk down the small gravel roadway that leads to French Road, trees that border the road shimmer. The only sound besides that of our shoes scraping along the gravel is the thumping of my heart beating overtime. I try to catch my breath. I'm uncomfortable with the silence, afraid of what I know I must say.

During this past year, I've discovered Elaine to be gentle and real, able to deal honestly with whatever seems to come along. I feel ready to be honest with her, no matter what she asks. I tell myself that this will be a defining moment where I can come clean about who I really am, about what I really believe. It's a risk worth taking, I tell myself. I find I'm holding my breath as we walk up the slight elevation of the road.

"So do you think you are ready to receive the habit,

knowing that it symbolizes an important step toward taking your vows?"

Vows.

Poverty, chastity, obedience.

I've been studying them in class with Elaine. Poverty seems the easy one. We've discussed it enough and I'm attracted to the simplicity of it. Letting go and freeing myself of possessions to serve others more fully. Poverty of spirit is something I'm eager to explore.

We haven't discussed the other two in much detail yet, nor am I in a hurry to do so. Long walks with Fionna, a novice older in religion than I who's become a trusted friend, have given me much food for thought regarding letting go of the possibility of sex. We've explored the life of Gandhi, his sublimation theory valid to us both. Mastery over one's passions. Obedience, so far, doesn't seem an issue.

We've arrived at the gate by the road. It's open and though traffic is light, we step aside for possible cars. From this vantage point, we're overlooking fields on our left, fields that are green ripples of wheat sown last autumn by the Briody family. Mr. Briody, the robust father of eight, has been a college employee for generations. During my days as an undergraduate, I remember his name being paged over the PA system hourly by Sister Teresa Ann, whose nasal twang gave it a homey air as she called him: "Mr. Briody, Mr. Briody, please call the main office, Mr. Briody."

There's something I must say.

I smile and try to breathe deeply. I feel drawn into the earth, a kinship with my mother's family of farm people. I feel somehow a truth and strength emerging. I turn and look directly at Elaine, her eyes open and expectant. "I don't think I can receive the habit. I don't think it's right that I stay."

We have already begun the journey back and I find no comfort as she walks ahead. She pauses a moment and then turns to me and says, "Tell me why you feel that way?"

I struggle for a minute to gain back that burst of strength and finally the words tumble out, ideas I've been thinking about and writing about for the last two years. I tell her of the readings, my attraction to the ideas of Daniel Berrigan, my fascination with Hans Küng, the Swiss theologian consultant to Vatican II who openly questions the concept of infallibility. She listens fully, never interrupting, her pace slow enough that I can gather my thoughts. Then she stops me and turns to me, "Do you believe in Jesus Christ?"

We've reached the pathway now to the north entrance of the building where we started. We've come full circle. Instead of answering her question, I tell her my belief. "I don't think I can commit myself to an order or a religion that doesn't have room for Jews. It's too exclusive, too narrow. I don't really think that the Jesus I believe in, who was a Jew, would approve."

Elaine pauses at the concrete steps and makes no move to go up them. I'm guessing we've been walking more than a half hour. No cars are about and no one seems to be around. Still I feel self-conscious and exposed. I've told my truth.

Now Elaine's gaze meets mine.

"Those are the right questions to be asking." Her brown eyes shine softly with understanding . . . and perhaps even pride? "There's no reason to leave because you're thinking and wrestling with such thoughts and ideas. That's precisely what you should be doing. That's what you are being called to do."

I fight back tears. "Really?" I ask, unbelieving, my eyes wide, my heart racing. "The doubts are okay? I've never dared say them out loud."

Elaine glances toward the college and says, "Your studies have served you well. That's the job of a liberal education. And you will serve well as a member of this congregation if you decide to. We can't be sure of all the answers anymore. We have to live the questions. You're already doing that!"

I feel a flutter of excitement ripple through me. Elaine puts her hand on my arm and says, "It's a calling. Listen and see if it's one you dare to answer."

16

RECEPTION

I AWAKE EARLY, STAND, STRETCH, and move to the window of my little bedroom. It's Saturday, September 12, the feast of the Holy Name of Mary, a gray and cloudy day, no trace of blue peeking through. My small desk is tidied in readiness, papers piled neatly, books stacked, pens and pencils in a Nazareth College mug.

I look over at the headdress I've hung on the handle of the closet door. The black veil is pressed and pinned neatly into place over the white band. Its newness is evident in its crispness. I wonder how long that will last. I head for the shower thinking about my family coming this afternoon to the reception ceremony and worry for my hair since, after today, only the front will show. I'll make a big wave in it. My mother likes that.

At breakfast in the refectory, several offer congratulations and good luck. Marnie is nowhere to be seen. I sit with a few novices who offer idle chatter. I'm distracted. I've not attended the morning Mass. This afternoon we will have our own, Marnie and me and our families with our invitation-only group.

I go to chapel after breakfast and open my breviary to Lauds, the Morning Prayer. I'm pleased to find it's one of my favorites:

*Sing to the Lord a new song of praise
in the assembly of the faithful.
Let them praise his name in festive dance,
Let them sing praise to him with timbrel and harp.*

Prayers of praise are what I believe in. I breathe in deeply. I am glad for this quiet before the events of the day unfold; glad to reflect on this next phase of commitment. A calling? That's what Elaine has named it. I don't know for sure, but I am willing to go forward trusting that this is what is right for now.

I slip my breviary back in the shelf and try to calm myself. Images from the film *The Sound of Music* flash through my mind. Maria marching down the aisle in a wedding gown, shorn hair ready for receiving the veil. Triumphal music, a Wagnerian march, crowds its way in and scenes of wedding gowns and hair cutting loom up unbidden. As quickly as they appear, I erase them.

I am consoled that having one's hair clipped by an electric razor is no longer a part of this ritual. I never ask where the bridal gowns came from or what happened to them after the ceremony. The marriage-to-Christ symbolism is not mentioned.

I leave the chapel before any other films play in my mind. I go to my room, and sit for another few minutes craving guidance. I reach for *Gift from the Sea*. It's not on the best religious books of the year list, but I love the depth of it and the setting of it at the sea. I flip open the book randomly, confident I will find a passage worth contemplating. I am not disappointed:

Simplification of the outward life is not enough. It is merely the outside ... I am looking at the outside of a shell, the outside of my life—the shell. The final answer, I know, is always inside. But the outside can give a clue, can help one to find the inside answer.

I reread Sister Elaine's note, explaining she can't be at the ceremony. She knows, she says, that some of the traditional words may rub against the grain. I'm so grateful she understands. Today I will go forward addressing the outside as I live into finding the inside answer.

The assigned time arrives. Marnie and I meet up on the fourth floor where we've been told to stay put. Others will see our families into the fourth-floor solarium that we use as a chapel. We are to take time to ready ourselves physically and spiritually. Well, Anne Morrow Lindbergh has helped with the spiritual part. As to the physical, I'm in my white blouse and black jumper that I sewed from scratch, a traditional postulant task.

Sewing the jumper convinced me that a career as a seamstress is not one I care to pursue. With the help of Elaine amidst tears of frustration, I finally completed the project and am proud to wear it today.

I chose a simple jumper with a button affixed at the top of each shoulder strap. The button box had plenty of choices and I found not one but two gold anchors. That would do it. They were in honor of my brother Tom, who had recently finished his tour of duty in Vietnam aboard the aircraft carrier *USS Franklin D. Roosevelt*. His time in the midst of the Gulf of Tonkin surrounded by naval destroyers can't have been easy.

SAVING FAITH: A MEMOIR OF COURAGE, CONVICTION, AND A CALLING

He reported in one letter that he saw his company commander shot down. My heart aches for him and I hope he notices the buttons.

Father Reinhart, the Motherhouse chaplain, greets us in our makeshift green room as he puts on his vestments, the alb and rope cincture first, the chasuble atop them. His fatherly appearance, slightly balding dark hair, soft voice, and kind eyes are reassuring as he tells us he will invite us in just after the welcome, as the opening hymn is being sung.

Sister Maureen appears just as Father Reinhart finishes. She compliments us on our attire, Marnie's black dress with white cuffs good looking. She checks our veils and, with her nod of approval, we place them on. I feel excited. Yet I do wonder, with so much talk afoot of contemporary dress, how long we will actually wear these veils.

The strumming of the guitar chords to the tune of "Whiskey in the Jar" serves as a fine processional hymn. Talented Diana, a second-year novice, has written a biblical verse to the tune that works well. "Yahweh is my shepherd and there's nothing I shall want."

Marnie and I follow Sister Maureen and process into the room, taking our places in the first row. I glance around and smile when I spot my mother and father, and younger sister Kathleen—no Tom to be seen.

As the Mass progresses, Marnie and I are called forward. In a simple ritual, Father Reinhart asks us to repeat after him the words of our commitment to enter into the novitiate year in the Sisters of Saint Joseph of Rochester. He asks Sister Maureen, as representative of the congregation, if these two women are accepted as novices. Her answer in the affirmative is followed by another hymn, this one from John Michael Talbot, "Yes, Lord, Yes!" Father Reinhart blesses Marnie and me and then all assembled.

We are in an upper chamber like Our Lord at his Last Supper. Our Mass is completed. And now I will go in peace, eager to be with my parents at dinner at The Maplewood, a favorite spot since my college days. Sister Maureen will accompany Marnie's family and my friend Sister Joellen will join us. It won't be a last supper, but rather a new first.

I wonder what it will feel like to go in public wearing this new veil. I am about to find out.

17

NOVITIATE

I AWAKE BEFORE THE MORNING BELLS and sit up in bed. The sight of the veil hanging from the doorknob makes me smile. I did it. I'm officially a novice. This is the year I get to "drop out" and "go within" to see whether this life is really for me. Time will be plentiful for prayer as I retreat from the teaching work and learn more about the congregation and the vows that I am moving toward.

After returning from the lavatory, I dress in my new black and whites and look in the small mirror over the sink in my room. I push my hair in place and pick up my veil and put it on, careful to leave a wave in my hair that shows. "The new nun," I laugh inwardly, pleased with how well the "hat" fits and how easy it is to put on and take off. I adjust the back to make sure it's not tangled and smile into the mirror. I'm ready to begin my novitiate year.

I make my way down the familiar black and white hallway to the chapel. I feel new. I feel different today at Mass as I stand and kneel, aware that from the back of the chapel, I look like all the rest of the Sisters, blending into the black and white tableau I have observed for so many years. This morning I open my breviary and listen as Sister Marie Emily, the Motherhouse Superior, leads us in the familiar versicle: "O God come to my assistance."

In my new status as novice, I will be added to a schedule

and take a turn leading morning lauds, a strong incentive to be punctual.

This morning after Mass I find a new place in the refectory, my veil giving me a new freedom to join in at other tables. Nothing before barred me from them but my own reticence. I sit with Sister Agnes Ruth, one of the Central Administrative team here at the motherhouse, who talks happily of her years as superintendent of the Catholic schools, no small job.

I ask about her work in the diocesan office.

"You know," she says, a piece of toast in her hand, "so much of what went on that was noteworthy was confidential, but there are some wonderful tales I could tell. Working for Bishop Kearney was a treat. He was exactly how he was when you met him. No guile, no pretense. Generous and open. Now Bishop Sheen, that's another story."

Fulton Sheen was a prominent man, practically the inventor of televangelism. His assignment to Rochester was a bit of an exile placed upon him by those who thought he was getting too big for his cassock. I smile and can only imagine what dealing with bishops must be like. I find it inspiring that these religious women in the early decades of the nineteenth century—before women held such positions of power in a male dominated society—started and ran institutions. Nazareth College, Nazareth Academy, Nazareth Hall, Saint Agnes High School, St. Joseph's Hospital in Elmira, and St. Ann's Home in Rochester are among the list of their well-respected and well-run schools and institutions in the Diocese of Rochester, others scattered throughout the eight thousand miles and twelve counties it covered. Strong missions in Selma, Alabama, and Brazil add to their collective accomplishments.

These have been women in charge, women with skills who

are respected leaders at a time when their counterparts have been relegated to lower pay with fewer choices: housewife, nurse, or teacher. This common bond of standing on the shoulders of such giants is unifying. I look forward to other tales.

I've now been included with the other novices for classes, meals, common prayer, and recreation. I have time on my own for personal prayer, spiritual reading, charges, and silence. I now follow the daily schedule, the horarium, without going to work, my day free for contemplation and prayer. It's like a vacation.

Our common recreation is held on the first floor, a huge room divided into smaller areas of comfort. Tables and workspace are provided for projects and studying. My favorite area is the living room space where we often sing. One of the second-year novices, Toby, writes songs that are often sung in harmony, the folk songs of the seventies not lost on this group of young women. Sheila, whose friendship started in choir practice, is studying voice at the college. I prize her skill and attend as many of her recitals as I can, her specialty the aria, "Un Bel Di Vedremo " from Puccini's *Madama Butterfly*. I leave enchanted and encouraged that talent such as hers is being nurtured.

I have finally relinquished the keys to my white convertible, which is now community property. Sister Elaine was gentle as she directed me to hang the keys up on a hook where other car keys dwell. A line on the signup sheet is added to include the convertible. It becomes a popular choice, and is not always available when I need a car. I amaze myself with how little this disturbs me.

This past week, five new postulants have entered and form

a new band. They come under the direction of Sister Maureen and have their own schedule and activities. We share common meals and, of course, charges.

At breakfast one morning I sit with a new a postulant who has come from another order in Erie, Pennsylvania. Her name is Kathy. I'm curious about the switch but don't ask. Instead I ask of her Erie order, "What was eerie about it?"

She laughs and we talk of other things. She's bright and attractive, her height and dark hair reminding me of a great blue heron, standing alert and ready for action at any time.

"Do you know what charges you have yet?" I ask. She's been assigned kitchen duty with Sister Julia. "Oh," I smile and ask, "doing what?"

She shrugs and says, "Shining the stainless steel. I did the same thing in Pennsylvania. What is it with these kitchen czars?" We both laugh and I'm relieved to know it wasn't just me who thought it bizarre.

My new charge as a novice is specials cook. I'm to report by four o'clock p.m. and prepare dinners for Sisters who have special dietary needs. Sister Marie Emily meets with me in the little kitchen on the basement level, approximately under the kitchen where Father Rhinehart's meals are prepared. She goes over the list of names and the procedure. Tonight's dinner is roasted chicken. Sister Rosario can't have poultry so she needs a hamburger. Sister Saint Francis likes a pork chop once in a while. She doesn't eat poultry either. A few others are diabetic and need protein and extra vegetables. The cottage cheese is for two who are on weight loss diets, and toast is for one of the Sisters who has an ulcer. I'm simply to prepare the food, put it on small trays, and set it on a stainless steel (there it is again) cart. Then I wheel it into the dining room and place it near the entrance. Those who have ordered something special will come take it off the cart. The orders vary by day according to what needs arise based on the main menu.

I delve into the task first by looking to see what's available and cleaning the kitchen, which is already near spotless. After I shine the faucet and wipe down the counters (Sister Julia must have rubbed off on me), I check the refrigerator for ingredients and find ground meat and pork chops ready for tonight. There's also cottage cheese and white bread for the toast requested.

I don't think it will take an hour and a half to do this job tonight, but each day I arrive punctually. On my first day, I bring with me a decoration for the wall over the sink, a world map saved from an issue of National Geographic. I pin it up deliberately and ceremoniously to bring a visual perspective to this time of service. Rochester is barely visible. Nothing can be that important. It also reminds me that in this world, everything is sacred.

As I pull the hamburger out of the refrigerator, Sister Saint Francis stops by to visit. Her name is on the list for a pork chop.

"So you're the new specials cook, huh?" she says. She is shorter than my five feet two inches and her habit, with the new veil, covers a bit of girth.

I smile and introduce myself.

"I'm Betty Osta. Glad you stopped by." I invite her to sit at the small table and am glad she accepts the cup of tea I offer. I continue shaping the ground meat into patties and setting cottage cheese onto the salad plates.

"You know any good jokes?" she asks. Before I can answer

she asks, "Would you like to hear one?"

"I'd love to," I reply as I turn on the burner to cook the hamburgers and check on the pork chop that's already in the oven.

"Well," she says, "this is one my father told me and I've always loved it." She settles back. "You see there was this little boy in school whose name is Jesus. He's a sweet little boy but when it comes to singing, he's loud and off key. Sister tells him to sing softer but he's proud and always bellows out the song."

She pauses and takes a sip of the tea I've made for her. "Well, word comes that the bishop is going to be visiting the school and each class should be prepared to perform something."

She glances up to see if I'm with her. I smile and she continues.

"Sister has the children prepare a special version of the 'Ave Maria.' She encourages Jesus to sing softly and all seems to be going well. But when the bishop arrives in Jesus's class, before Sister can start the song, the bishop asks, 'Who would like to sing a song for me?' Jesus jumps up and waves his hand wildly. Sister anxiously calls out, 'Jesus, you can't sing.' The bishop turns to her and says, 'Christ, Sister, give him a chance.'"

I chuckle and tell her next time she comes, I'll have one for her. I finish stocking the cart, and Sister Saint Francis walks down with me and shows me where to position it by the door, my new helper.

I watch as Sisters come by and take their dinners from the cart, glad for the success of my first evening of specials. After dinner, I ask Sister Rosario, who can be a bit dour, about the hamburger.

"One of the best I've had. What'd you do to it?"

Since I hadn't been instructed to jazz it up, I whisper, "I

mixed in some Italian dressing! Shall I do it again?"

"Please," she nods.

As the weeks progress, I find I am enjoying my private novitiate classes with Sister Elaine. She often reads from congregational documents or assigns readings to me and we discuss them.

One conversation I savor is on poverty. I've already let go of the car and before I entered let go of almost everything I'd accumulated: clothing, books, a cherished typewriter on which I'd begun writing as a teenager. I offer most of my religious statues and my nun doll to my younger sister, Kathleen, something to remember me by, I tell her facetiously. I let go of my letters, note cards, and all the papers I'd written for college classes (a move I will ultimately regret).

In this talk, I'm turned around as we discuss the Sisters in Selma who have asked not to live in the plush convent house the bishop has arranged for them.

I'm engaged by their sense of choosing personal discomfort and acting on their belief. Elaine shares another perspective. She speaks of a poverty of spirit that doesn't get trapped in the externals of material things.

"The cost to the diocese for them to live in simpler living quarters is higher now. The house the bishop offered was already a diocesan property."

This perspective is new to me and one I need to think more about. I'm not sure what else is in store for me during this year, but I'm glad to have started.

I remember the Rilke quote: "Beginnings in themselves are always so beautiful."

Now I take inspiration from another of Rilke's missives from *Letters to a Young Poet*:

> *I beg you . . . to have patience with everything unresolved in your heart and try to love the questions themselves as if they were locked rooms or books written in a very foreign language. Don't search for the answers, which could not be given to you now, because you would not be able to live them. And the point is, to live everything. Live the questions now. Perhaps then, someday far in the future, you will gradually, without even noticing it, live your way into the answer . . .*

I hope it works.

18

RELEVANCE

"How are you doing?" Sister Mary Clare asks, her silver and gray tweed suit highlighting the silver in her hair. She wears the small pewter Celtic cross, the congregational design now a common choice among the Sisters. She's the instructor for the course in learning disabilities that I am auditing during my novitiate time.

I smile shyly, adjust my veil, and answer, "I'm glad to be here."

We are walking into Smyth Hall on the college campus. Sister Mary Clare has been a champion of mine since my undergraduate days when I took classes from her: Phonetics, Speech Pathology, Methods of Speech Diagnosis, and my favorite: Seminar in Language Disorders. She's intelligent and compassionate, a combination that attracts me. I understand the unspoken parts of her question. "How are you doing as a novice in this sea of ever-changing tides?" And I trust she hears the unspoken part of my answer, "I'm glad to be here, happy to be learning from you again, happy to be 'in the world.'"

"I've just returned from a six-week mission experience where I lived at Saint Thomas More Parish on East Avenue." We have reached her classroom door, and I hold it open for her

Clare's dark eyes smile as she sweeps into her room to

prepare for her students. She clearly feels privileged to induct bright young minds and caring hearts into her beloved vocation. They will be the teachers of speech for those who long for that very fundamental skill—to communicate clearly.

"Isn't Sister Elizabeth Mary wonderful?" she asks. I nod as we part ways, she to the front of the classroom and me to the back. I let the paying students sit up closer and get their money's worth.

My take on Sister Elizabeth Mary is the same as Clare's. She's a solid, peace-filled woman, whose lovely open face matches the character I observe. She serves as the superior of the convent on prestigious East Avenue and as principal of the elementary school, a common practice for parish schools and convents of the time.

Over my six weeks at Thomas More, under Elizabeth Mary's guidance, I observe a community of Sisters, content in their ministry and supported by the pastor, Father Francis J. Pegnam, a retired Navy officer. It's easy to imagine his bald head covered by an officer's cap. His parish runs smoothly, as if he were the commanding officer. He's well regarded. Evidently he was able to steer the parish through rough waters in its beginning days when a Court of Appeals decision finally granted the parish leaders the right to build the parish school in this exclusive neighborhood.

It's a pretty campus, the brick and glass buildings attractive, trees forming protective archways, many preserved from the days when William A. E. Drescher, assistant treasurer and director of the Bausch & Lomb Optical Company of Rochester owned the home on the property. One of the stipulations for the gift to the parish was stewardship of the house that is now the convent, a detail well attended to.

In my time in the mansion turned convent, I patter up and down the servants' back stairs to and from my room, imagining myself living in this gracious home in its heyday. I more easily identify with the role of servant than lady of the house. As I stand at the bottom of the staircase that dominates the front hall, I suppress the desire to climb up the plush oriental stair runner and slide down the magnificent curved, polished oak railing.

My own home in Syracuse, though smaller, borders on this charm, with a reception hall and wood-paneled dining room, the house built in the early 1920s. Still, my childhood neighborhood is more mixed than this one that has magnificent homes lining the whole avenue.

This East Avenue house has a circular drive that adds to the regal feel. I wonder if studying the vow of poverty may have something to do with my awareness of the splendor and my discomfort in it.

My friend Sheila, of choir night fame, lives at the convent and teaches music in the parish school. Besides teaching, she has become involved in the life of the parish, working with the choir director one evening a week. We share a concern about the wealth that surrounds us, but say little.

I am studying from a text written by Dr. Samuel A. Kirk, who in 1963 first used the term "learning disability." He identified many failing students who were not mentally retarded, yet were plagued with learning difficulties caused by neurological disorders. His newly released book, *Educating Exceptional Children*, identifies strategies and specific regimens of training that can help children who previously had been left to the shadows. I'm enthralled.

My class time with Sister Mary Clare is precious. She helps

me understand better the developmental delays of students I've encountered, and I find her style of teaching engaging. She shares stories from her own experiences. One I particularly cherish is about Dr. Albert Murphy Jr., a nationally recognized psychologist and expert in speech disorders from Boston University, where she had studied. His work was intense and included serving as the president of the Massachusetts Speech-Language Hearing Association and as consultant to the Massachusetts and Rhode Island Departments of Education and Mental Health, the Joseph P. Kennedy Jr. Hospital, and several other national organizations. She tells of Dr. Murphy's weekly appointments with Dr. Jrbu. His secretary has been alerted that these were sacrosanct appointments, not ever to be disturbed, never to be cancelled.

With a gleam in her eye, Clare tells us that only after many years did the secretary learn that the appointments, which took place on hiking trails, harbors, or in parks with Dr. Jrbu were appointments kept by and for Dr. Albert Murphy Jr.'s Boston University alias, Dr. Jr. B U. They were his secret to preserving a time alone to collect himself and reflect.

Another hero Clare introduces us to, Dr. Burton Blatt, started a campaign for the rights of people with developmental disabilities. Clare arranges for him to come speak to our class.

"Baby seals," he tells us, "are treated better than babies born with disabilities." He's a short man, slightly balding with a wry sense of humor and an appropriate outrage that I find compelling. In his book, *Christmas in Purgatory*, he portrayed life inside mental institutions and facilities. He had asked friends across the nation to let him into the back wards of their institutions and took along Fred Kaplan, a colleague with a hidden camera. They published the results and brought to national attention the abuse that people with intellectual disabilities were subjected to in many of the country's facilities. His colleagues called him, not angry, but scared. "Burt, that's not my place, is it?" And Burt replied evenly, "Don't you think you ought to go look?"

My days are blessed with stimulating educational discourse such as Clare's class. Additionally, I am free to choose my own readings, Berrigan and Bonhoeffer still on my favorites list. I read about prisons and join in the common prayer. I read about protests and demonstrations and sit in the garden and pray and write. I do my best to meditate. I tend to my charges. I cook the specials dinners, buff hallways, and keep the swimming pool bug-free. I talk to the priests who are available for confessions and counseling. I'm not dissatisfied, but I am restless.

I am being given time, plenty of time, to learn about the congregation, prayer life, even educational advances, as well as the mysteries of myself.

Sister Elaine continues to be my other teacher, moving me towards greater understanding of the order and of my own spiritual journey. I'm to finish reading the little blue congregational history from cover to cover.

I dutifully go off on a balmy spring day, daffodils waving in the wind, sunshine lighting the soil so it gleams. I wear a jacket despite the sixty-degree temperature and sunshine. I bring the blue book with me, determined to see how it speaks to today.

I find my bench, a place to perch while I check for relevance. I'm certain I can talk with Elaine about my findings. She has encouraged this level of inquiry and I am thrilled with the freedom to keep exploring. The bench faces the college, the sun directly above. I pull my black jacket tighter and open the book.

I'm growing to admire these women who have radiated out from Le Puy, France. I am especially thrilled to read the charge the bishop sent them out with:

> As he gave to each a brass-bound crucifix, the Bishop said, "Receive, my child, the Cross of Our Lord Jesus Christ. Wear it openly on your breast; bear it bravely; carry it down the ways of pain, into homes of fever, into the warrens of the poor; bear it to far-off lands. Especially endeavor to carry it faithfully in your heart."

I'm so glad to find relevance in the founders of this congregation, delighted to discover no need to discard the past. These folks have set the standard. They've had relevance all along. Hospitals, nursing homes, foreign missions, the poor. These women are following a mission that's been in place for more than three hundred years. I'm but a speck on the long line of historical significance.

I read on to learn more about Le Puy, a city of twenty thousand in the South of France. The descriptions are luscious, the presence of a "colossal statue, fifty-five feet tall of Our Lady of France," makes me curious to visit and see if it's still in place. I flip ahead in the book and find a black and white photograph of the Motherhouse. The only trees that surround it are small evergreens. I look around me at the now-towering evergreens that are easily fifty years old. These women had vision and patience. I have much to learn.

I try to quell the impatience I feel to get going. At least I am learning new things each day. I remember Rilke's admonition to live the questions. Can I?

Then one day Father Murphy gives a retreat. We are sitting in sunlight in the community room, chairs in a circle. There are more than a dozen of us. Father Murphy's bushy eyebrows and balding pate give him an aura of monastic credibility. He presents an author, Rabbi Abraham Heschel, then reads the title of his book: *God in Search of Man: A Philosophy of Judaism.*

I beam inwardly. Yes. Yes. I needn't worry. The God I'm learning to know won't let me go astray. He will search and search until I am found. Even if I don't know I'm lost.

I breathe deeply and listen for more.

19

PROMISES AND VOWS

SISTER FIONNA—A JUNIOR SISTER who has already taken first vows—walks down the back road with me for one of our talks. I value her wisdom. We have an easy familiarity, coming as we do from similar families. She has as many brothers as I have, and our parents share friends in common. The day is clear, our pace invigorating, and I tell her of the new choice I'm being offered. Taking promises instead of first vows. It's a less binding commitment, yet still in preparation for perpetual profession.

Her silence and deep listening thrill me. She walks ahead of me by a bit. I note her brown-rimmed glasses sitting lightly on her freckled nose, her pink cheeks and auburn hair covered by the small black veil. Instead of giving me any comment about my impending choice, she turns toward me and asks, "Do you really believe what we're doing can make a difference?"

I'm startled. I watch the red-winged blackbirds dive into the fields, their sputtering chatter filling the air. Until now, Fionna has always seemed to have the answers. Though she's a year or two younger in age, she's older "in religion" by two years, a distinction I've come to learn carries status. I'm used to my own self-doubts, but coming from her they seem shocking.

As we continue our walk, the potholed black asphalt

beneath our feet creates bubbles of tar in the heat of the summer day. We dodge them as we walk up toward French Road. Modern ranch homes are visible as we crest the hill bordering the fields that surround the 1924 Motherhouse and the accompanying college campus.

"I'm surprised to hear you ask the question about making a difference," I say as we turn back down the hill. "Want to hear what you told me a few months ago?"

Fionna pauses along the way and pulls some Queen Anne's lace from the fields that line the roadway. As she twirls it in her fingers, she asks, "Did you used to color this when you were a kid?"

I stoop and pick a stalk of my own, remembering the milk bottles full of food coloring–tinted water that turned the heads of these gracious flowers blue, red, green, or yellow. "My neighbor used to. I always liked them the way they were."

She moves ahead on the road, turns, and walks backwards, facing me. "Okay, what was it I said about making a difference?" Her lips are turned up in a wry smile.

"You told me," I say as I watch her turn back to walk beside me on the road, "that if Gandhi could make a difference in his simple gesture of non-violence and in his commitment to sublimation, so could we."

I recall the earlier conversation clearly. I was stunned with the notion that the celibacy I was contemplating could be framed in such a powerful way. Sublimation, as I understood it, was overcoming sexual desire, replacing it with service and prayer.

I have thought about celibacy enough to know it is a big consideration in approaching commitment to this way of life. Throughout my dating years, I resisted sexual intercourse. I even resisted it with Tom, difficult as it was. My younger sister was from the next generation that didn't value such a stance. I did. Raised in the fifties and in the Catholic Church, my choices seemed at one time clear. Sex before marriage was a sin. Now I am on the cusp of vowing to live celibately in the seventies, in the midst of a sexual revolution. Women, so long repressed in so many ways, are slowly becoming freer to do all kinds of things, professionally and sexually. Still, those of my high school and college classmates who experienced sex outside of marriage usually got married if a pregnancy resulted. As far as I knew.

Fionna turns to me, then smiles. "I said that, huh?"

I nod.

We walk on in silence. I'm still anxious about the notion of chastity. I'm okay with poverty, actually attracted to the idea of it. Being one of seven siblings, I never got a chance to amass too much stuff. Stuff got handed down to me, and I likewise handed it on. It was easy to discard college books and papers, sneakers, loafers, shirts, jeans, and jewelry, things I wouldn't be using in the future. I had given my treasured Mickey Mouse watch to my younger sister Kathleen several Christmases ago.

I shared with Fionna the wonderful conversations I had had with Sister Elaine about poverty. Fionna knew I had already sold my car to the congregation for a dollar.

"The goal," Sister Elaine had said, "is poverty of spirit, something we are espousing to attain, an openness if you will."

I tell Fionna of my one prized possession. I keep it at my family's home. A small cedar chest jewelry box with a tiny gold lock.

"I guess I could live without it, but it's a gift from my godmother Ceil Herbein who died when I was twelve." As we round the corner to the road toward the Motherhouse, I think of the contents of the small cedar chest: my high school classmates' pictures with good luck messages written on the back; a brown scapula from a retreat when I was a senior; a tiny blue rosary in a cotton matchbox from Ceil; a silver ID bracelet engraved with my name, B-E-T-T-Y, carefully spaced in big letters, a gift from my mother who saw me admiring it in the jewelry case when we were Christmas shopping for the others. Another treasure from Mom was a gold Hamilton watch with a black cord band. It was inscribed with the year 1947, her fortieth birthday.

"How did your godmother die?"

"Tuberculosis," I tell her, remembering I'd never been allowed to visit Ceil in the Mount Morris Sanatorium where she was a patient, but how devoted she was to writing and sending me tiny gifts, like the matchbox rosary.

I don't tell Fionna about letting go of my Sea Biscuit horse racing game, my Nancy Drew books or my plasticine statues of the children at Fatima. I no longer feel the need to treat these small surrenders as sacrifices. I like the idea of streamlining my possessions. I have even let go of my Smith-Corona typewriter, knowing that writing will always be a part of my life, I reluctantly let go of this hand-me-down typewriter from Mrs. Stack, whose children I babysat. She's a writer too, with stories published in Redbook.

Fionna's voice draws me back with another question.

"Do you fully agree with the Gandhi idea? About sublimation and service?"

Twilight is descending and casting a mystical light through the grounds and up the sidewalk to the motherhouse. Reds and golds shine from the stained glass windows of the chapel.

Before I can answer, the bell rings for vespers. We scurry down the walk. I'm not sure what I would answer if we had more time. For now I feel saved by the bell.

In my classes with Sister Elaine, I'm learning about the vow of obedience. While Reverend Mothers and convent superiors are still in charge, theologians like Bernhard Häring are influencing the thinking with ideas that are seeping into religious congregations. The "new" Christian is seen as co-responsible for community. Our newly released Values in Faith document, which replaces the old Constitution, states that each member of the community has access to the same Spirit of Truth as does the superior.

These are radical changes from the 1958 Constitutions:

By the vow of obedience the Sisters consecrate to God their own will and bind themselves to obey their lawful Superiors in all that directly concerns the observance of the vows and of the Constitutions.

I feel fortunate to be entering religious community at a time when blind obedience is being forsaken.

The Gandhi notion of sublimation that Fionna has introduced into my thinking stays with me as I ponder celibacy. It is a foundation for Catholic religious life—consecrated virginity, an individual and direct love of Christ that embraces God and neighbor; one that allows service to the whole church. Celibacy is meant to allow a more universal love to take the place of love focused mainly on a physically intimate life partner, to free one to follow one's calling to God.

I don't know if I can do it.

It's a big jump, this notion of being "free" from one form of human love, trusting in the gifts of the Spirit to be able to give back to the same world that our Savior has redeemed.

I'm grateful for my memories of being turned on: in backseats and front seats of cars, petted and fondled within the bounds of necking. My discovery one college summer of French kissing with a boy I hardly knew opened a whole new range of feelings and possibilities. Yet I was raised in an era when the woman was responsible for not overexciting the male. Not exactly a fair equation.

One particular weekend evening in the front seat of a car with Brian, a boy I really cared for, stands out in memory.

His oak brown brush cut always had just the right amount of Vitalis. His tortoise shell glasses made him look smart. He was short and adorable. We had been dating for over a year. We adopted "Baby Blue" by The Echoes as our song, even though neither of us had blue eyes. His initials, BB, made the song perfect for us. Dancing to it was always a thrill.

That particular evening, after a lengthy time of kissing and hugging and touching, I knew I'd better stop before I could no longer resist. I sat up, straightened myself, and declared, "We've got to stop. I'm thinking of going into the convent."

Brian was silent.

I laugh now to think of it and applaud him for his restraint. If I was planning on going into the convent, what was I doing with him in the front seat of a car? Thankfully, he never asked. I wouldn't have had an answer.

As a young woman in my early twenties, I wonder if I know enough to let go of the possibility of intercourse for a lifetime. Many have, but at what cost? I remember one of Father Shannon's comments in senior Theology class. When asked by a young woman how long intercourse takes, he answered, "If you're trying to get something, only a few minutes. If you're trying to give something, a lifetime."

As I ponder taking this next step, I wonder if I can ever fully realize what I'm getting myself into and what it is I'm letting go of.

I'm fortunate to be able to attend several Chapter sessions during this novitiate year. I empathize with the older Sisters whose traditions and routines and dress are being disrupted with these changes. These older Sisters have lived lives in vowed obedience and now their security in that life is challenged. They may still vow obedience but it doesn't mean they have to like the changes that are afoot. As the old habits give way, hemlines grow shorter and hair grows longer, and many Sisters change back to their baptismal names, these older women wonder if there is still room for them and their habits of a lifetime in the new congregations. Meanwhile, for me, the changes may not be coming fast enough. And so I wonder if there's room for me.

Gratefully, I am present when Sister Dorothy Agnes, an older and sincere woman with sea-blue eyes, wavy white hair, and a ready smile approaches the microphone. She looks about the room and begins:

"Sisters, this time-honored, venerable tradition, this brass-bound crucifix coming to us from Father Médaille himself, is a lasting symbol of who we have been and who we may yet become."

She is speaking of the profession cross, traditionally given upon final profession and that many believe has outlived its relevance. There is some rustling among the delegates and finally a middle-aged Sister responds, "Sister, I too value the brass-bound crucifix and cherish mine but I must tell you, it has no history or meaning to the incoming Sisters. It has no place in their lives."

Obviously distressed, her hands trembling a bit, Dorothy Agnes, the former college registrar, responds, her voice quivering: "Well, Sisters, couldn't we just give it to them as a gift?"

I'm pleased to witness these moments, to observe these religious women as they struggle with the changes that affect their lives and the lives of those who follow them. Their sensitivity with each point of view and their striving for openness to differing opinions speaks well of who they are. I'm intrigued enough to want to learn more about the process of making promises.

20

FINALLY

"YOU MUSTN'T WHISTLE, DEAR," my aunt told me as I skipped down the stairs toward her on one of her rare visits to our home in Syracuse. She added the weight of religious guilt to her admonition: "It makes the Blessed Mother cry."

Cry, I thought, *over whistling?* The Blessed Mother must be stronger than that. The certainty in Sister Betty's voice told me she thought she was right. And that to be a lady, I mustn't whistle. What she didn't know is that I'd been a tomboy most of my youth and a happy one. So I whistled.

Besides the ordinary whistle of pursed lips used for singing tunes and making comments of approval, my brother Jim taught me to whistle a big strong "boy" whistle by pulling my lower lip in and breathing out in a short blast. I cherish the skill and have found it invaluable when corralling children, signaling my location, or getting someone's attention when needed.

I'm tempted to let out an appreciative whistle now as we drive down North Goodman Street in Rochester. I see children skipping rope as we turn onto Bay Street. We pass the Bay Goodman Pizza decorated with graffiti on one side of the building. I see the corner dry cleaner's sign half off the hooks. The Lincoln First Bank next to it looks out of place, its paint crisp, the brick clean.

I'm falling in love as we drive past the old houses with

proud porches that now sag, their spindles, like broken teeth, missing from railings. I count three that are boarded up. The patch of worn grass between the sidewalk and the street is littered with pop cans, discarded candy wrappers, tipped over garbage cans, and empty whiskey and beer bottles. A child glances up as we pass. He sits on a tricycle, eyes vacant, clothes raggedy. Next door to him a man sits on the stoop wearing an undershirt, a cigarette between his fingers. His look is as vacant as the child's.

This is where I long to be. It's happening. I'm in the midst of the inner city. I will live here among the people. I've been assigned to a mission: Saint Francis Xavier, 314 Bay Street. This neighborhood isn't one of the worst, I've been told. Joseph Avenue and Clinton Avenue are far worse, streets central to so much of the 1964 riots. In giving me the news of my assignment, Sister Elaine is confident. "You will find new dimensions of Christ's love in the people there. Trust yourself and them. It will be a good start."

These, I tell myself as I look around the streets, are the people I want to learn from. These are the people who know a truth I want to discover. Their faith amidst so much turmoil mystifies me. "The Mission Hymn" comes to mind, the one I sang as I walked through the tunnels as a college student, the one I clung to as I was deciding to enter the convent, the one we sang as I received the habit. I whistle it softly under my breath as we drive into the parking lot.

Great is the Lord, Worthy of Praise,
Tell all the nations God is King.
Spread the good news of his love.

Two novices, Christine and Mary, are delivering me lock, stock, and barrel to my first mission. I gawk at the huge brick building and continue listening to the hymn in my mind:

The spirit of the Lord is upon me,
Because the Lord has anointed me,
He has sent me to bring glad tidings,
to the lowly, to the lowly.

I'm not in agreement with the "lowly" line, but I am certain there is good news to bring. I feel blessed and relieved. I climb the crumbling cement steps to the front door while Chris and Mary bring my two bags and box onto the porch. They wish me luck and, with a hug from each of them, they leave me on the doorstep and drive off. I ring the doorbell.

Two blue suitcases replace the small black footlocker I entered with three years ago. My secular clothing, including the green plaid suit I wore when I entered, are long gone, given to charity and replaced by three black skirts, the black jumper with the gold anchor buttons, six white blouses, two pair of black shoes, sufficient undergarments, and blue and pink pajamas. All are neatly packed in the bigger of the two bags. A smaller matching bag holds some toiletries and a few mementos, the cardboard box books and papers. Poverty here I come.

A round-faced, bespectacled woman answers the door. "You must be Elizabeth Osta. We've been expecting you," she says as she opens the door wide and picks up the small bag. She's stocky and seems wary, and I don't get a feeling of welcome from her. "I'm Sister Marie Walter, the house superior and principal," she says. She steps aside as I carry the bigger suitcase into a hallway that is not unlike the one I remember from my childhood home—high ceilings with a staircase and newel post of polished oak. Rooms off each side of the hallway are framed with oak trim. A worn flowered carpet lines the hardwood floors. After I retrieve the box from the porch, Sister Marie Walter locks the door behind me.

"The other Sisters should be back shortly. This is the last of summer break for some of them," she offers as she moves toward the bottom of the Victorian-style stairway, her hand resting on its beaded newel post. It's not as gracious as the staircase at Saint Thomas More that reminded me of Loretta Young's sweeping entrance on her television shows, but its shiny finish is impressive.

I'm not certain what to make of Marie Walter. I feel like I've interrupted her. Maybe I have.

It's August 30, 1971, a Monday afternoon. Three years exactly since the date I entered the convent. It seems light years since I was in my shared apartment with Mary Ann, dating dear Tom, and teaching at the Foreman Center. Now several years later, I am starting anew yet again. School begins a week from tomorrow, on September 7. I'm to teach junior high: seventh and eighth graders. My stomach churns each time I think of it. My background is with little ones. Junior high kids can be brutal. I remember how nasty our eighth-grade class was to one of our classmates, calling him names behind his back and excluding him from activities. And that was at a parochial school.

I glance into the room on the left, a small parlor with several green upholstered straight-backed chairs and a small mahogany table and Tiffany-like lamp in front of the porch window. The sitting room on the right has a reasonably sized television, several worn beige recliners, a brown plaid sofa, and a few inexpensive wood end tables. The decor is simple, even a bit dowdy, with gold drapes covering the windows. Sister Marie Walter picks up the small bag and indicates I should follow. As we ascend the ten steps to the landing, I note a three-foot tall statue of Saint Joseph sitting on the ledge in front of a huge stained glass window. I feel a sudden amazement. This is the Joseph of the Sisters. I'd not given much thought to him. Yet here he is, greeting me on my first day, his carpenter's square in one hand and a lily in the other. I wink as I walk by him, comforted by his presence. I know enough not to whistle.

The room to which I'm assigned is on the parking lot side of the building, overlooking the relatively new single-story school. I wonder how new it actually is. I noticed the old school as I came up the porch stairs, another story to learn.

The room is painted yellow, a wrought iron bed on the left, a six-drawer dresser opposite. The small sink on that same wall has a mirrored metal medicine cabinet above it. The closet door is slightly open and plenty of hangers dangle inside. A small oak desk and matching chair sit next to the entrance. I already have ideas of how to rearrange things. Sister Marie Walter puts the small bag on the bed and moves to the doorway. She seems uncomfortable in making small talk.

"One of the other Sisters assigned to teach here is Sister Elizabeth," she says matter-of-factly. "She's teaching second grade. We've decided it will be less confusing if you're known as Sister Betty."

I swallow hard. I had thought I'd be called Sister Elizabeth Anne. I wonder how Sister Elizabeth feels about it. No conversation about this, I guess. Obedience? Hmm.

"You'll be able to get into your classroom by Wednesday. The floors are just about all done." She turns to leave and then turns back again. "Supper will be at six o'clock. I'll be downstairs if you need anything."

I manage to say thank you and Marie Walter nods and leaves. I feel overwhelmed and all of a sudden very tired. I want to close the door and plunk down on the bed, but I don't want to appear unfriendly. I hear her go down the stairs and am glad to be alone to absorb the reality of this new mission. I pull the small suitcase off my bed and stretch out on it.

"Tell all the nations God is King." I whistle. I'm on my first mission.

"Maria, do we each teach our own religion class?" I ask after dinner one of my first nights. Sister Maria, a redhead about five years older than I, is my "grade partner." It doesn't take me long to learn that she and Sister Marie Walter are good friends. They do the grocery shopping together and do other errands together as well and many decisions seem made by the two of them. No openings for newcomer input. I suspect I'll find other issues are out of my control and even beyond influencing.

She looks up in answer to my question and nods, "Yes, you'll teach your own homeroom religion, math, reading, English, spelling, geography, and science. We switch for art and music. I'll teach the art and you teach the music."

She smiles and I cringe. I love music but haven't a clue how to teach it. And I haven't the least notion about eighth-grade math. *Ugh*, I think, but I smile back.

The other Sisters as I meet them are friendly and supportive.

My first favorite is Dorothy, meticulously groomed, no silver hair out of place from beneath her veil. She has a quiet voice but her eyes betray strength at her core. She's offered much-needed help already, showing me where supplies are kept and how the daily routines work.

"I can show you where things are before the kiddos start in. Once they're in, time disappears." She goes on to confirming my suspicion that she is a bit of a powerhouse. "I was able to get a desk to bring to the little Reyes boy down the street. I found it at the public school. They were getting rid of it."

Dorothy's own sister, Ann Elizabeth, is also an SSJ, missioned at a neighboring inner-city parish, Saint Bridget's. She's helped Dorothy do her bulletin boards and Dorothy returns the favor, solicitous of her older sister, whose childhood birth defect has left her with a significant limp.

Sister Marlene teaches fourth grade, a woman as uncomplicated as her mousy brown hair. She oozes dedication to children. "The Rivera girl is going to be as bright as her brother, I can tell already. Her reading marks are above grade level," she reports at dinner one evening. Her dark eyes shine as she speaks.

Sister Rosa teaches the fifth grade and has been at it for a good length of time. She doesn't say much. She has two sisters in the congregation and is well seasoned in community living. I wonder what has transpired in the past between her and Sister Marie Walter. Neither lets on, but through what they don't say, I sense a distance.

Sister Elizabeth, whose name has determined my moniker, teaches the little ones, their classroom located in the old school. She is full of fun and has an open manner. She lives in a different convent on Riverside Street, an elegant area near Maplewood Park. This is another new trend: Sisters can choose their living arrangements.

Our daily community life includes morning prayer, Lauds, said in the small chapel that is tucked in an alcove beneath the stairs. This time of prayer together is optional, as are many of daily activities that were previously required, emblematic of the changes that still are reverberating through the church. Morning Mass at 7:30 is in the ornate old church next door that smells of wax and incense.

The pastor, Father Joseph Beatini, extends a warm welcome after Mass. He's robust and follows in the footsteps of Monsignor Moffett who was known for his sympathy for children. At report card time, Monsignor Moffett often ignored the recommendation of retention and promoted children slated to remain behind. Oral history from older parishioners recounts that it became such a problem that Sisters and teachers who had students they felt should be retained had them sit in the coat closet during report cards until the good Monsignor left the classroom.

Barbara, a recently widowed long-time parishioner with children who have graduated from Saint Francis, is hired to prepare our daily lunch. We are able to have a nutritious meal while the children have their lunch and Barbara is able to have a part-time job with some financial benefit. She's a round, warm woman who easily becomes a part of our community. At the end of the school day, one of us is charged with evening meal preparation, generally served at six o'clock. Simple fare usually includes meat, a starch, and a vegetable. Dishes and cleanup are often accompanied by spirited conversation and occasionally songs sung in harmony, the nonsensical campfire round "One Bottle of Pop" the most popular. It becomes a favorite time for me.

Evening meetings, whether school board, parish council, or community boards, often follow. Studying, grading papers, and preparation for the next day's classes adequately fill the available time until Vespers, which are said at 9 p.m. in the chapel; Marie Walter as house coordinator serves as the designated leader. A weekly house meeting where the business of living together is discussed is also accompanied by a prayer service. Financial reports, updates on house needs, and time to air issues like use of the car and grocery shopping make their way onto the agenda.

I'm acclimating to this house and to this parish and neighborhood. The church holds a prominent place in the landscape of the community and has since its formation in 1888. As I learn more from the parishioners and the children and their parents, I find myself glad to be here, to be a part of this history. Finally!

21

FIGHT AND SWING

I decide to walk the neighborhood as one way to get to know the Saint Francis Xavier parish families and the families of the school children. The parish is within a few miles of six other parishes: Saint Andrews, Saint Philip Neri, Holy Redeemer, Saint Michael's, Saint Bridget's, and Mount Carmel, all with schools that offer an alternative to public schools—that is, for those families who can afford the ever-climbing tuition.

I meander down the tree-lined Teresa Street next to the church. I pass Englert and go over Hempel, the cottage-style houses similar in construction, yards close together, children clustered on porches.

I turn the corner to Coleman Terrace where several of my students live, the houses closer together, yards less tidy. Ultimately I walk to Clifford Avenue and into the small grocery store that has votive candles and *arroz y frijoles*, the Puerto Rican staple, rice and beans.

I have little money to spend but decide to treat myself to a Mounds candy bar as a way of participating. The middle-aged clerk smiles as she brushes her dark hair back from her face and watches behind me for the next customer. I return the smile as I take back the change from my dollar bill. As I go out into the light of the early evening, I decide to go back through Crombie Street to Bay Street, making a full square of my walk.

The simple houses, modest clapboard-covered one- or two-story dwellings with small porches close to the sidewalk, are home to some remaining immigrant families from Italy. They originally built this parish on streets with German names due to an earlier wave of immigrants who went on to establish nearby Saint Michael's church on Clinton Avenue.

In recent years, Latino families from Puerto Rico as well as African Americans from Florida, Alabama, and other Southern states have joined the Italian immigrants. These new families, although already American citizens, are also immigrants who have left their homes to avoid poverty and oppression, or to find opportunity. Like each wave of immigrants, they endure a shaky welcome.

Memories of the 1964 Rochester riots that horrified the city, the state, and the nation linger in the neighborhood; barred store windows are just one of the many reminders on Joseph and Clinton Avenues, the center of much of the chaos only a few blocks from our parish church on Bay Street. Worse are the businesses, which have pulled up stakes or closed altogether.

Only six years ago, I was working in a Syracuse inner-city park, unaffected by and unaware of the turmoil that rocked Rochester. Now I learn bits and pieces from neighbors about the arrest that triggered three days of rioting.

Gray-haired Elizabeth and her friend David live across the street in an old Victorian home that has seen better days. They say it started with an intoxicated nineteen-year-old black teen at a street dance who resisted arrest for disorderly conduct. He shouted that he was being beaten by police, evoking support from the crowd. The police called for backup, bringing in a K-9 team dog reminiscent of Southern anti-civil rights tactics.

That response ignited fury and fumes that spilled over from Joseph Avenue and Nassau Street to the opposite side of the city the following night. Police Chief William Lombard was unable to bring order (his own car tipped over by the unruly mob when he came to investigate) and called for the National Guard. With no local authority able to control the crowds, Governor Rockefeller eventually sent them in after two days of rioting and looting.

The stories became national, the wounds local and lasting. What were once close-knit parishes start to lose significant membership as the younger generation who can afford to move out to the suburbs. Redlining by banks brings property values down, and the incoming darker-skinned immigrants from the South and Puerto Rico are in any case discriminated against for getting loans, so more and more properties become less well-maintained rentals or even are abandoned. New tensions develop between the older white residents and the new black residents moving in.

Some semblance of community is restored to these neighborhoods thanks to many church and civic groups and organizations that have responded to the need. I join weekly meetings of neighborhood churches that have banded together headed by Lutheran Pastor Tim.

I hear more about Father P. David Finks, who has been appointed by Bishop Sheen to be Episcopal Vicar for Urban Ministry. His work with Saul Alinsky in the formation of the FIGHT organization (Freedom, Independence, God, Honor, Today) has brought the promise of creating their own progress to the dispossessed black residents of the city, who until now have struggled to obtain decent housing and have been kept from good-paying jobs at Kodak and elsewhere.

Metro-Act, which started as "Friends of Fight," brings allies from the white community into the fight against discrimination, while leaving FIGHT to black leadership. Metro-Act meetings serve as another strength and hope, led by Jack Skvorak, a former priest from Saint Francis Xavier Parish. His wife, Mary, a former SSJ, taught in the school. They are an inspiring couple, united in their passion to make a difference.

The school has a solid group of parents who volunteer setting up bake sales and assisting as guides for open houses and parent conference nights. The Italian women bake pizzelles; others bring cakes and brownies. I enjoy the time available to chat with them, some of them parishioners since their own youth, and many who have proudly graduated from the "old school."

My classroom is the first one on the right, with a wall of windows that look out onto the next-door neighbor's home. Green blackboards cover the front and back of the room, with a coat closet lining the hallway side.

I've been encouraged to apply for a grant by another one of the dynamic mix of women at the convent. Sister Aileen, college professor and historian turned activist, helps identify a funding source. The proposal I submit is successful, and with the funds, the Sixteenth Ward Interracial Neighborhood Group (SWING) is formed. The money provides funds for an after-school club for children from the whole neighborhood and not just from the school. Around a dozen children are regulars. A key activity for our SWING grant is a fall cleanup of the school and parish grounds. With the eighth-grade boys leading the charge, Charles, James, Clint, Brian, and Alfonso rake and sweep and haul garbage to the dumpster. The girls—Jenny, Donna, Diana, Denise, Cathy, and Robin—help direct activities and provide games and stories for young children and their siblings, all of them proud to be a part of this initiative. I am thrilled to watch children from black, Hispanic, and white families work together as one. Great indeed is the Lord.

At one of our class meetings, we decide to put on a Christmas play. With the energy and cooperation of this group of teenagers, a production of Dickens's *A Christmas Carol* is chosen. Lanky and cooperative Charles agrees to play Scrooge. We are equally blessed with Duncan who ably takes the role as narrator and holds the whole performance together. I get laryngitis. Exhausting and exhilarating play rehearsals fill the Fall. These young people get the idea of drama and pledge to make this an event to remember. Jenny, Cathy, Diana, Robin, and Denise become the production crew and keep the boys in tow. Brian, a math whiz and teaching assistant, works on staging and provides his little brother to play Tiny Tim.

By the night of the event, students have decorated the school hall with green and red construction paper chains. Posters advertising the event that have been placed at church and in local stores are now reposted around the walls. Students act as ushers. Parents, aunts, uncles, grandparents, brothers, and sisters fill the auditorium. Our custodian, Donald, has placed sufficient chairs, certain we won't fill them.

Duncan welcomes the families to our class's version of the classic Charles Dickens tale. Proud parents of all races listen attentively as the assistant pastor, Father Bayer, is introduced and offers a blessing that is inclusive of the many religions represented and is full of praise for the young people whose hard work has made this play possible.

The lights dim, a hush hovers, and Duncan, our narrator, begins. "Once upon a time—of all the good days in the year, on Christmas Eve—old Scrooge sat busy in his counting-house." Charles is bent over a makeshift desk borrowed from an unused "old school" classroom. Bright, funny, sometimes smart-alecky Clint plays Scrooge's nephew. "A merry Christmas, Uncle!"

Scrooge continues, "Bah! Humbug!"

The nephew responds, "Christmas a humbug, Uncle! You don't mean that, I am sure?"

Scrooge rises to the challenge. "I do. Out upon merry Christmas! If I had my will, every idiot who goes about with 'Merry Christmas' on his lips should be boiled with his own pudding. He should!"

A squeal of delight comes from the children in attendance.

We're off and running.

I watch from the side of the auditorium, my eyes brimming with tears. The fears and admonitions from Sister Marie Walter, Maria, and Rosa, the ones who've been here the longest—about parents not liking their children mixing with other ethnicities, the idea that the actors wouldn't show up, that the effort would be sabotaged in some way—dwindle as each scene unfolds. At the standing ovation, I'm called forward by Jenny, the stage manager, and presented with a bouquet of red carnations. These flowers belong to these blossoming students who teach me hope. I'm speechless, not even able to whistle.

It's been almost four months since I started this mission, yet I feel like I've known these kids all my life. Could it be I've found my place?

22

CHANGES

LAST FALL, ELEVEN AREA PARISHES joined together to form the Council of Inner City Parishes (CICP) in answer to the bishop's challenge to reconsider their mission to the poor. Increasing expenses of education and dwindling dollars begged the question. The Diocesan Office of Human Development even suggested this might be a time to look at alternative missions for inner-city parishes, instead of education.

Their first decision was to create a regional junior high school at the former Saint Michael's elementary school. The decision to separate the seventh and eighth graders from the parish schools brought tears and anger from families and lay faculty. Our role as participants in the process was to support the decision.

Sister David Mary, our congregational regional coordinator and a woman I had admired from afar, came to visit. She would be interviewing all of us working in the school to determine changes for the coming year.

Our dinner with David Mary was pleasant, with pockets of pure joy. Her charming demeanor and sharp interpersonal skills had led her through leadership roles and several principal positions to this administrative office for congregation. She called each of us by name, knew some personal detail, and listened to stories we told of school children, families, and our own lives.

"Dorothy, how's Anne Elizabeth doing after her fall? I hope she's back up and at 'em?" David Mary asked, her genuine concern apparent.

After dinner and before the interviews began, we sat in the community room and I was urged by a few to tell the snake family story. I had told it at other events to great laughter, its tongue-twisting challenges revolving around two key words repeated in rapid succession, "pit" and "hiss." Listeners were often spellbound, waiting for a mistake as I told the adventures of Mrs. Snake and her snake kids hissing in their pit and later hissing in Mrs. Pott;s pit while their mother was away.

As I started out, I looked for the laughing eyes that usually accompanied the opening lines. However, David Mary's eyes narrowed, no laughter in sight. It took me a minute to realize I'd had a slip of the lip. I stopped, David Mary's scowl daunting. Quick apologies and laughter followed, and I was encouraged to start again. The usual laughter followed as I deftly ended the story with Mrs. Snake's closing line: "Why, I remember Mrs. Pott when she didn't have a pit to hiss in."

Tensions were relieved, providing a fine opening to our individual interviews.

"How do you think the principal is doing?" David Mary asked point blank when it was my turn to talk with her. We were settled in the sparsely decorated upstairs front bedroom room reserved for guests.

I was wary. How truthful did I dare to be? I cared about this urban school and its survival. I cared about these children, whose parents needed as much help as they did in some cases. I didn't want to whine.

David Mary's kind eyes and attentive countenance helped calm my fears. I shared a few instances where I felt I could have had more support for the grant I'd been awarded.

"I had to have the students wash the floors and arrange the furniture for every meeting we had. I was told that there would be no extra staff support and that I was on my own."

I spoke with candor and though I felt a twinge of guilt, I was also relieved to tell what I knew might be helpful for the inner-city school to survive. David Mary had been a principal of a neighboring urban school and certainly knew the struggles.

I didn't talk about the favoritism Marie Walter showed to Maria. Maybe others would broach that one. I'd said enough.

Our June graduation of eighth graders is emotional. It is the last time Saint Francis Xavier School will graduate an eighth-grade class from its elementary school. Father Beatini speaks lovingly to the thirty-nine students, telling them to carry their heads high. "You are graduating from a school that has been in existence since 1888. We only wish we could be here longer so you could send your children here."

A party held the evening before graduation in the school hall included the reading of the class history by Robin, a star student. Her brown skin glowed, her black hair piled high with a purple ribbon. Her mother beamed from the front row. Her speech exceeded the dry recital of facts I had expected from a class history:

> *Good evening, Father Beatini, Sister Marie Walter, faculty, parents and friends. This speech is about the history of our class. The majority of our class came to Saint Francis in 1963. At this time our Principal was Sister Frances Mary. In 1964 we received a real treat, Sister Marie Walter, as our new principal. We've put*

her through hardships, and depressed moments ... but since she is such a cool principal, she glided with us. Our class has always had disagreements ... but we try to our best ability to forget them and live a better future. There is only one reason why we were able to forget and forgive. One person is responsible for all our successes (but we won't say anything about our failures) and that is Sister Betty. We've cut her on her last string but she always managed to mend it . . ..

I'm thrilled with the acknowledgement, thrilled that this class has come together so fully. I care deeply about these young people and they know it. The difficult times are indeed covered over by the stars of the class: James, Clint, Duncan, Brian, Vincent, Charles, Robert, Diana, Lydia, Cathy, Donna, Jenny, Angela, Sarah, and Robin. The others, like supporting actors, deserve rewards for their ability to go along and get along. My fears of teaching seventh and eighth graders weren't entirely unfounded, but the gift of that year will be a joy for many years to come.

During the week after the June graduation, new assignments for next year were announced. Marlene, Dorothy, Ursuline, and Aileen are staying. So am I. Two others, Rosa and Maria, are reassigned, as is Marie Walter. A new principal will be coming to Saint Francis Xavier, Sister Janice. Grade assignments will be determined during the summer months. Not much is said about the changes. More examples of obedience?

I finish a three-day retreat at the Motherhouse with Father Murphy, who's become a comforting spiritual leader. And eagerly I leave for a family vacation to a favorite place in Bancroft, Ontario.

Herschel Fishing Club on Baptiste Lake, three hours northwest of Kingston, Ontario, is a resort owned by Niagara Mohawk Power Corporation. It's on a pine tree–studded half-acre island. As a company executive, my father is entitled to go. For many years he and my mother have entertained friends there. And for years my mother has urged him to share this with his children. He's finally agreed. It's a true vacation for her. Meals are served, fishing boats take us to the best spots, and chipmunks roam the island, all to our delight.

In our comfortable lodge with green-shingled siding, we gather on the screened-in porch overlooking Baptiste Lake for our opening dinner together. Aunt Veronica, my mother's older sister, and Eldred O'Shea, Dad's friend and best man from their wedding and a favorite with us kids, also join us.

Over dessert, my brother John announces his engagement to dark-haired Nancy, who has come as his guest. Comfortable chairs and sofas surround the massive stone fireplace that dominates the main living room, with a stuffed moose head mounted above the mantel. Carved into the wood of the mantel three words served as the relaxation spot's motto: It Doesn't Matter.

I think of company executives, getting away from it all, gaining wisdom from these three words. Yet I wonder. My zeal says that it must matter. Here I am luxuriating on a Canadian island with people cooking my meals, no plans except relaxation, reading, and wandering in nature. How surreal this experience is compared to the lives of the families I have begun to befriend. Families whose interests are as simple as surviving another day; as simple as finding food for each meal, repairing children's clothing so it will hold for another school year, finding ways to keep cool in the sweltering summer days of urban Rochester. How can I reconcile this luxury with the life I am moving into? Where is the balance of retreat and contemplation in this world of poverty I am entering? I wonder.

I continue to search for answers in the writings of Daniel Berrigan. "It is humanly impossible," he writes of Dietrich Bonhoeffer's observations and his own experiences, "for a man to act alone and still act well."

Is that why I choose community? I continue to hope. I also retreat to Anne Morrow Lindbergh's *Gift from the Sea* who wisdom doesn't disappoint as she suggests finding a balance between solitude and communion, between retreat and return."

I begin to unwind, sleep, and ultimately relax into these moments and take full pleasure in the chance to catch up on what my siblings are doing. John talks of his work as a real estate agent, but his upcoming marriage is his preoccupation; my older sister Mary Jean's work as a reservationist for American Airlines gives her free airline tickets. I've been a happy recipient. Jim's career as a social worker in Chicago is closer to my interest, his work in the inner city akin to what I hope to do. His wife, Susan, and their one-year-old daughter, Kathleen Mary, provide great joy, as we each get time with her in our new roles as aunts and uncles. Tom's recent return from a four-year stint in the Navy is a subject for conversation, though he has yet to say much about his time in Vietnam. Mark's pride in his recently acquired landscape design degree from Danville College is evident. Kathleen works as social worker in inner-city Rochester at Baden Street Settlement House, an agency that has strong connections to the community adjacent to Francis Xavier.

I catch some fish, play cards, read, and relax, happy to be among them and finally settle down. It's good to be here.

I am rested and renewed when I return to Rochester, ready, I hope, for what is yet to come.

In the sultry days of late August, the school yard quiet and the streets still, Dorothy, Marlene, Aileen, and I welcome the newly assigned Sisters with a special prayer service. We've cleaned the house from top to bottom, rooms ready and gleaming. Aileen leads the singing, new voices adding to our chorus.

The change feels refreshing.

As new principal, Janice has created a welcoming environment for families and faculty. She's in her late thirties, with sculpted features and a regal Roman nose. Her physical grace and presence, combined with an engaging personality and sincere interest in the people, pave the way for success. Under her leadership, I've been reassigned from junior high to teach first grade, my favorite age group.

Anne Marie is to be vice-principal; Clare will teach at the newly formed Saint Michael's Junior High, while Peg, Pat, and Barb will teach at Nazareth Academy. Two new cars will be available to accommodate these changes.

The following evening after dinner, we have our first house meeting together. Janice leads us in prayer. We review rules and expectations and set aside Tuesdays for our community night. At the end, she hands out a card to each of us with that Rilke quote, the one that keeps haunting me:

> *And the point is, to live everything. Live the questions now. Perhaps you will then gradually, without*

noticing it, live along some distant day into the answer.

Something good is happening and I sigh with relief. Of all the new Sisters who have arrived, I quickly develop a fondness for Clare, a no-nonsense woman with short blonde hair, quick wit, and realism, the same traits that I suspect make her a strong junior high teacher. I find myself looking forward to each day and feel a new sense of community with these women as we share daily chores, sing as we dry dishes, and do what we are vowing to do: live life celibately in community.

The dream is fuzzy. Cottony images float past me. The dull sound of a long bell rings. I wipe the sleep from my eyes and lean up on my elbows, listening. The noise from outside the window has stopped. I look at the clock. It's 8:35. I jump out of bed and peer out the window onto the playground. It's empty. Not even a straggler. Oh my God. The sound was the playground bell. The noise stopped because the children have gone into the building. I splash water on my face, rinse my mouth, and climb into my black and whites, today a skirt and blouse. I dart down the stairs, my breathing shallow, heart pounding. Maybe the back door will be unlocked and I can skid into place. I skitter across the pavement, the mild fall day casting sunshine on the leaves that color the trees. Birds sing their songs. I reach the door and pull. It opens. Alleluia. I take the four steps up two at a time. I glance down to my classroom door. There stands the new principal, Sister Janice. I feel my face color as red as the autumn leaves, my stomach tightening with knots. She smiles and hands me a cup of coffee, black, just the way I like it. "I thought this might help you get started. They've said morning prayers and are now doing their seatwork. They've been good."

I'm still holding my breath, unsure of what to do. Hug her? Bend down and beg forgiveness? It's only October and I've overslept again, but this time beats all others. In the past, I've slipped into the pew for morning Mass a bit late, or slid into the school building without breakfast on several occasions, but never have I missed the morning bells.

I stammer thanks and take the coffee. I see laughter in Janice's chocolate-brown eyes. I step into my first-grade classroom and sigh. Just as she said, the children are busy with their seatwork. On the blackboard is a duck cartoon character and a list of words to be copied. The children smile up at me and Johnny raises his hand. "Should we draw that duck, too?" he asks innocently. I feel relief wash over me. "If you've finished your words, you can," I reply.

What a difference a year makes. A lot has happened in this past year. While my students finish their seatwork, I sip the coffee Janice gave me, delighted at how refreshing her manner is, direct but light. Her kindness in caring for my students when I overslept has brought her into hero status for me, a reminder of goodness.

I've been blessed again and again. I glance out at the sun shining through my classroom window, children working diligently. I feel tears of gratitude. I put down the coffee and prepare for our daily letter lesson. We are on to the twelfth letter, "L": Luck, Laughter, and Love.

23

CIRCLE MEETING

I CONTINUE TO MARVEL as I stand before the classroom full of six-year-olds. Their industry as they struggle to print their names is commendable. Latino, African American, and European American faces are bent over papers, pencils poised, exuding energy.

Two boys in the front row, recent immigrants from Italy, Egidio Carteri and Louis Novelli, join this first-grade class with very little ability to speak or understand English. Their parents nod hopefully when they drop them off and go to jobs at Hickey Freeman where they will use their skills to sew tailored suits that only the wealthy can afford.

These two dark-eyed boys immediately take me in; Egidio's wavy licorice-black hair accentuate his olive skin and deeply set eyes; Louie's closely cropped brown hair and petite frame give him a pixie look, his eyes curious with a bit of devilment. Both wear clean, neatly pressed clothing, indicative of the pride of the place they have come from and of their parents' occupations. I struggle to control their attachment to each other, their whispering often accompanied by giggles. They are on the verge of being class clowns and I have no Italian fluency to help cross the language barrier.

Fellow student Whitey Santana, named after his father Blanco, agrees to help them learn basic English vocabulary. Whitey's family has come from San Juan, Puerto Rico, his

English and Spanish both fluent. I watch as he teaches them the word for "bathroom" by using the Spanish word "baño" pronounced identically with the Italian word "bagno." "Bathroom: baño." They smile and nod, recognition evident.

Egidio and Louie are learning a bit more English, but continue to talk to each other in Italian, their misbehavior and giggling escalating.

I've been a part of a grant to take Berlitz Spanish, which has helped me connect with many Latino families, but I now need some help with Italian.

I seek counsel from my friend Sister Joellen's mother, Josephina, who emigrated herself from Italy as a young woman. She recounts the frustration and difficulty she first encountered in America, neighbors shunning her for her accent. It was her Jewish neighbor who made an effort to talk with her and became a lifelong friend. She's happy to help.

I tell her of my need to get the boys under control. She suggests two statements and teaches me to say them. *Stai seduto and stai quieto.*

I ask what it is I'm learning. "They will understand this," she says with a twinkle. "It's not a request; it's a command. They mean 'sit down' and 'be quiet.'"

I can hardly wait for an opportunity to try out my new secret weapon. Ample opportunity is provided the next class day. After the morning bell, the students stand for prayer and the pledge of allegiance. This morning I choose Egidio to be flag bearer. He has the honor and responsibility of holding the flag as the pledge is recited. I listen as the students chant in unison, "one nation, under God." I still remember the pride instilled in 1954 by my own fourth-grade teacher as we learned the new pledge that for the first time included the words "under God."

As the pledge ends, Egidio returns the flag to me and I turn to put it back in the bracket on the wood-framed chalkboard. I hear a giggle and spin around to see Egidio taking a bow. He has understood his role. The clowning around is good for his language development so I let it pass.

This morning's lesson is on feelings. We learn the words mad, glad, and sad. I invite children to come up and illustrate the oval shapes on the board with faces that match the feeling word written underneath.

Dominic, whose older brother Vincent I taught in eighth grade, volunteers to do our glad picture. He stands at the board, his blond Buster Brown haircut needing a trim, and draws a broad smile with a few teeth, the middle two missing. Sandy-haired Ronnie Ricketts, possibly the smallest child in the class, illustrates the sad face with eyes that have tears coming out. Louie ably draws a mad face whose lips are drawn into a very expressive pout. He returns to his seat with a smug look on his face.

I explain the next part of the lesson by encouraging the children to think of a time when they were mad, sad, or glad. "Put your head down and remember what that feeling was. When you have it in your mind's eye, get ready draw us a picture," I tell them. "When you are done, bring your desk to the circle and get ready to have us guess which feeling you've illustrated."

The children come up row by row and choose their color of construction paper. Johnny is the first one done, his picture not very detailed. One of the brightest children in class, he can be a handful unless directed. I encourage him to put his name on the paper and write what he wants to say about his picture on the back before he tells the story. This buys me some time as I walk up and down the aisles, checking the progress of the work. Angela has a bicycle that she's sitting on with a big smile. Our guess on hers will be easy.

As I bend over Brenda's work, I hear a squeal from the front of the room. Egidio and Louie are both out of their seats in front of the class, making "feeling faces." I stifle my laugh and go for stern as I near them. They see my "feeling face" and freeze.

I narrow my eyes and lean down toward them. In a loud whisper I say: "*Stai seduto, stai quieto.*"

Without a moment wasted, both boys return to their seats. They look at each other and back at me. They know now that I know. How long it will last I don't know but I am eager to report to Josephina the story of my success.

As the children finish their pictures, I'm grateful to see that they smoothly transition, clearing their desks, sliding them into position in the circle and then each climbing up to sit on the front of their own desk. We've practiced for the first several weeks and now they seem to have the hang of it.

We are about to start our "circle meeting," a concept introduced by Dr. William Glasser in his *Schools Without Failure* program. Each child gets a chance to express himself or herself with no fear of being ridiculed or disagreed with. The children have learned this is a special time for all of us.

My doubt as to whether or not the children were too young to benefit from the concept of the meeting was answered in one of our first sessions. Leon, our school psychologist, sat in on each session and I was so glad not to have been the only adult to hear the responses to the question that day: "Which one do you think is deeper, a hole or loneliness?" I reminded the students that there were no right or wrong answers and we went around the circle. As they thought and spoke, the children's legs swung and their hands twitched. I marveled—not for the first time—that anyone had ever thought that training young students to always keep still ever was an aid to their education. Leon and I listened as the children give thoughtful answers. "I think a hole is deeper, 'cause you look deep into it." "A hole is definitely deeper because it is in the ground." Then Dominic said, "I think that loneliness is deeper because if you're in a hole, at least you have dirt around you. When you're lonely, there's nothing around you."

Leon and I raised our eyebrows, smiled, and exchanged a glance. It was a deep answer that neither of us would forget.

I'm pleased to be a part of this program, pleased with the innovative ideas that are a part of the curriculum, the change from rows and regimens to a bit of fantasy and feelings. As the end of this circle meeting nears, children get to share their feelings drawings. After several glad faces that were easy to identify and one sad face that accompanied a pet turtle with an RIP sign on it, Johnny holds his paper in front of him and waits. All we can see are two prominent slashes and little marks covering his pink construction paper picture. Wispy, barely discernible marks are in the background. He swings his feet back and forth, a sour puss on him that might have been a clue. Finally we all give up.

He sits straighter on his desk, puts down his pencil, and says, "Actually, this is a mad picture. And it really happened. It's a picture of a drive-in movie we got to go to. The mad part is that the windshield wipers were broken and it rained real hard for the whole movie." We clap for him and are glad to see him smile.

As I collect the pictures and the children move their desks

back into rows, I look up at the crucifix, a fixture in most every parochial school classroom. I recall the tale of the youngster whose parents had taken him to so many schools where he continued to misbehave until they finally took him to a Catholic school where his behavior was no problem. His father asked the principal what they had done to get him in line so easily. The principal was bewildered and said they'd never had a problem with him since day one. She suggested they interview the child. She sent for him and invited him to join them in their meeting. "Joshua, every school you've been to reports you had a great deal of trouble controlling your behavior. Your father wants to know, and I want to know, too, what difference did this school make?" Joshua pointed to the crucifix. "When I saw that little boy up there, I knew this school meant business."

I wonder what impact the parochial education we are fighting so hard to preserve has on the children we teach. I wonder if their future will be more solid because of the religious values we are able to add to our curriculum.

As if in answer to my own question, a scene from the last school year comes to mind. One April morning, the entire school was evacuated into the church, the result of phoned-in bomb scare. Roll call for each class was held. All of a sudden, Angelo, one of Maria's eighth-grade students, appeared, sitting by himself in the back corner. When roll call was completed, he hadn't been there. Then he was. His mother, one of the widows of the parish, was up in front of the statue of Our Lady saying a rosary, the vigil lights flickering in front of her. She didn't understand until later what we learned about her son by his tardy arrival. She had been here praying. He had been home making a phone call. But he came to church. To see?

Because it was safe? The police told us later it was one of the telltale signs of bomb scare perpetrators. They need to see the action.

Father Beatini was gentle with Angelo who was an only son, his father dead since he was nine, his mother still mourning. His suspension included counseling. The intimate connection of church, school, and family seemed to have contributed to a better outcome. Still, I wonder: will church matter for him in his life? For any of these children? For Egidio, Louie, Whitey, Ronnie, Dominic, or Johnny? I can only hope.

24

THE NEWS

WITH THE LIST IN HAND, I'm off for my turn at grocery shopping, a chance to get a few items I find special while getting supplies for the week.

As I drive to Hudson Avenue Wegman's, the closest large supermarket in the area, I find myself singing "Oh What a Beautiful Morning," for it truly is. The sun, not a dependable visitor to Rochester, is glinting off parked cars. People are raking last fall's leaf litter off yards and green grass is sprouting up in patches. The first thing I see as I enter the store is a bounty of fragrant white lilies, Easter just around the corner.

I am reminded of the one that Dad will give Mom this Easter, as he does each year. I drink in the aroma as I walk by and am transported to our family kitchen with its six-foot long gray and white Formica table that accommodated the seven of us when we moved from Buffalo to Syracuse in 1950, my sister Kathleen just a baby then. Memories of hidden Easter baskets and Easter breakfasts at the Hotel Syracuse after Mass flood my mind. I'll visit next week—if there's a car available, another aspect of community living to which I'm learning to adapt.

We share two cars among the eight of us. Aileen has a designated car, provided by the ministry foundation she is working for. She's generous in loaning it, but by rights can't put it up for general sign-out. It's also not in great shape, so it's not one I'd consider for highway travel.

As I roam the orderly aisles with my cart, I find the ordinary staples easy enough to pick up: cereal, eggs, butter, and milk. I find my way to the produce section, fresh fruits and vegetables in abundance. I choose iceberg lettuce and fresh spinach, along with carrots and broccoli, some of my favorites.

I look at the listed meats and find the bologna for sandwiches and the pork chops that are Rosa's specialty. She must be cooking this week. I also pick up a package of chicken breasts that could have been requested by any number of folks who are cooking, as chicken is a popular meal.

I'm responsible for tomorrow's dinner. Since it's Palm Sunday, I'm preparing roast leg of lamb. Happily I procure a decent-sized one, along with fist-sized new potatoes, my Irish American mother's influence. Peas and mint jelly complete the list. I also pick up a few things not on the list, including soda pop, pretzels, and chocolate ice cream for dessert.

As I go down the next aisle toward the cashier, I stroll past the beer and pull down a six-pack of Genesee. Why not, I think. No one at the convent has ever said much about alcohol and this might prove to be a treat.

As I dole out the cash at the payment queue, I think about the fortune these bags of groceries provide, healthy meals for the week. Many of the suburban customers around me enjoy the same security. Not so for many of our neighborhood children and their families. While many from our school come from families that can afford tuition and groceries, others attend the neighboring public schools where absent fathers and food stamps are the norm. To add to the problem, supermarkets are starting to close their inner-city stores, leaving only more expensive corner stores with limited access to fresh and nutritious food.

I lug the bags out and into the trunk of the white Chevrolet Impala. It's a used car from Hallman Chevrolet where the congregation has negotiated an arrangement. These cars are assigned from the Motherhouse while Sisters in wealthier parishes often have cars provided for them by the parish. Ours is not a wealthy parish.

As I turn on the car, the radio also clicks back on, and I am jolted by the headline on the news. "Nazareth College president to step down."

Then I smile. The announcer goes on: "Sister Helen Daniel Malone, president of the small liberal arts college since 1960, is stepping down, her tenure one of growth and success." Her image comes to mind—her porcelain skin, sensitive face, attentive eyes, and easy smile. I'd learned as a college freshman she had given up a career on Broadway to enter the convent. Such is her grandeur. When she moves, it is with charm and elegance. She has been one of my father's favorites since I first attended Nazareth College and she addressed the parents.

"My dear," he said to me after her talk, "she speaks as I imagine the Blessed Mother herself would speak. I could listen to her for hours." His admiration never wavered.

Over my years at the College, as I became more familiar with Sister Helen Daniel, I understood what Dad meant. She has a way of being present, eyes never wandering or looking away. An aura of holiness surrounded her.

She founded the Speech Correction program in the late 1950s, the program I enrolled in. By my sophomore year, she invited Dominican Father James Loughery to become an instructor. We nicknamed him Father Love, his white habit unusual in the sea of black-robed instructors. Much of his teaching was about the importance of the therapist's relationship beyond the clinical skills with clients or students. It should be centered on love. He proclaimed love was the essence of a successful therapeutic relationship. We were taught well.

At our senior ring ceremony, I snapped a photo of Sister Helen Daniel and Father Loughery, she in her black dress and veil, he in his classic white habit. They were holding hands. It comes as no surprise that she might be leaving. And this is why I am smiling, though I feel the loss to the College. Because, though the radio announcement is silent on the matter, I surmise—in fact I am hoping—that she might be planning to marry Father Loughery. As I drive back toward home, spring flowers catch my eye; crocuses lining gardens, daffodils bursting forth. I think about the news and about coming home to a gaggle of women gossiping. I cringe to think of anyone besmirching Helen Daniel.

As I haul the groceries into the house through the back door, I smile as I walk past the exterior door of the oversized icebox, no longer in use, the refrigerator now covering the interior portion where the opening was. Imagining this grand old home with ice deliveries back in its heyday makes me wonder if there are photos, something I'd love to discover. I find myself humming "Amazing Grace" as I fill the fridge with the newly purchased foods. I slide the spaghetti, crackers, and chips onto the open shelves. Rosa saunters in—not to help, that's my job this week—and gets a cup of coffee and sits. "Did you hear the news?" she says.

With my back to her as I put the eggs away, I ask, "What news?"

"It's on the radio today but I heard it from John Joseph yesterday." Rosa has a sister in the congregation who lives at a neighboring convent. "Helen Daniel is leaving the college."

"Oh, yes, I did hear that." I reply with no further comment.

I hear footsteps on the back stairs, and Marlene chimes in. "I heard that too. What do you think?" she asks eagerly. I've finished putting the food away, but I shift a few things to look busy.

Ursuline, who has been in the front room reading, now joins in the conjecture. "Well, I suppose she'll go off with that priest she's always with."

I turn now to see the three of them, standing in what I think may be judgment of this fine woman who has given more than her share to hundreds of families and to the community at large, helping create a college that is a vibrant and vital part of the community. Under her vision, the Arts Center has become a permanent asset for what I imagine will be years to come.

Whether being the invited guest to say the benediction at the Susan B. Anthony celebration or speaking to the Rosary Society at Saint Joseph's Church in Rush, New York, on the apostolate of women, this woman is true. There is no guile about her and I cannot bear this conversation and certainly won't sustain the speculation. Holding the empty egg carton in my hand, I quietly say of this fifty-plus-year-old icon, "Did you hear she was pregnant too?"

The gasps are enough to satisfy me. I put the carton in the garbage and go upstairs to write a note of appreciation to Helen Daniel.

25

MUSIC, ECUMENISM, AND THE POPES

I WAS RAISED IN A MUSICAL FAMILY. Sing-alongs had always been frequent, with the family gathered around my older sister Mary Jean accompanying on the family piano. My father's love for music filled our home with recordings of guitarist Les Paul accompanied by his wife, Mary Ford, the smooth, mellow vocals of Perry Como, and his beloved *Student Prince* by Sigmund Romberg, performed by Mario Lanza. This particular record contained a new song written for the movie version, "I'll Walk with God," that reflected my father's fast faith in a God who was personally accessible to him and would never leave him.

Now, as I let the music of the liturgies fill me, I feel such blessings. I quip in one phone call home to Dad that I get to sing in a three-part opera before breakfast each morning.

As I observe the changes in the Church that are opening the doors to other faiths, I recall my first lesson in ecumenism that occurred when I was a child. Our next-door neighbors, the McAllisters, were Unitarian, one of the few non-Catholic families on our street of twenty houses or so. I was seven years old when eight-year-old Susan McAllister, nicknamed Webbie, asked to borrow my catechism. I said no, because it was only for Catholics. Webbie had dark inquisitive eyes and curly black hair. I was closer to her red-haired sister Joanie, two years older than I. I was always kind to Webbie, but her asking for my catechism was just too much, so I said no.

When the doorbell rang one night after supper, I answered it to find Webbie standing there with my catechism in hand. I summoned all the seven-year-old fury I could muster. "How'd you get my catechism? That's just for Catholics."

Webbie looked past me, her freckled face lit by the dim domed light in the small tiled vestibule.

I felt a gentle hand on my shoulder and heard my mother say, "Thanks for returning it, dear. Did you enjoy reading it?"

My mother reached across the chasm I was about to create and effectively helped me unlearn what I was being schooled to do. The seeds for my ecumenical beliefs were planted early. In a single incident, my mother taught me that Webbie, her sisters Joanie and Patty, her parents Jack and Polly, and all Unitarians—even the Behns, the Jewish family down the street—are saved. What a great relief. I didn't have to be the guardian of the church doors.

While my mother schooled me with her progressive outlook, I sometimes found my father on the opposite spectrum. At an Easter dinner with the family, eager to share my college theology learning, I opened a conversation once we'd said grace and the lamb was served. "Dad, isn't it fascinating that even though Pope John XXIII was already seventy-seven when he was elected by the cardinals, they never thought he'd do so much to open up the Church? He was to be a transition pope, but look what he's done. And in such a short time."

Dad had been a Knight of Columbus and attended annual retreats at Christ the King Retreat House in Syracuse. His attendance at daily Mass and generous contributions to the

Most Holy Rosary were signs of his devotion to his Church. I was not prepared for his reaction. He slammed his fork down and pounded the table with his fist, the crystal glassware singing as he proclaimed, "I don't know what they're teaching you at the liberal bubble-headed school up there, but no man elects a pope." His brown eyes surveyed the seven of us for argument. There was none. I stayed silent. "Not until there's white smoke is the pope elected," he stated definitively. "It's God who chooses the pope, not strategists and politicians."

Dad's political leanings were conservative, his religious beliefs passionate. I knew not to argue.

As a child I had been taught, like Dad had been, that the Holy Ghost was the elector of the pope, white smoke and all. The cardinals were just intermediaries. I knew Dad hadn't had any updated theology like I had. And I also knew I was not the one to bring it to him. I could only hope he'd be able to hear it from the altar—what he considered a credible source who hadn't gone to any liberal, bubble-headed school.

I can still see the bronze portrait of Pope Pius XII on the wall outside my childhood bedroom. I see his thin face, papal hat, and dour eyes, one of which, I learn as I grow older, was blind to the horrors of the Holocaust that swirled around him before I was born. By the time I was thirteen, I learned in school of his chronic hiccups. We prayed for him daily. I knew little of the papacy or politics of Rome, but I did know from personal experience how painful hiccups were. I got them whenever I was tickled or my brother made me laugh. The pope was included in our family evening prayer time, asking, ""or a speedy recovery or a peaceful death."

By October of eighth grade, Pope Pius XII died the peaceful death we'd prayed for.

His successor, Pope John XXIII, Angelo Giuseppe Roncalli, astounded the world. Born in 1881, ten years after my Grandmother Donegan, he didn't bring arrogance or pretension to his position. His father was a sharecropper. He carried the simplicity of his family background, along with faith, hope, and love, letting the world see that the greatest of these indeed is love.

As I told my father, it was seen that throughout his tenure he did more than was anticipated in his role as a transition pope. I learned so much more about him after his June 3, 1968, death than I ever did in high school.

It was the credible Sister Mary Lourdes, my freshman Theology teacher, who first taught me about Pope John XXIII. Her smile had a saintliness to it. Her garb at the time included the old habit, her starched white coronet wrapping her face gently, not unlike a bonnet, the veil and underveil pinned in place to form an apex on the tall white band that covered her forehead. Though the starched headdress gave her theological gravitas, it was her manner—her gentle and joyous smile and vibrant voice laced with kindness—that brought her teachings to life. As she spoke of Pope John XXIII, she said what for me became a favorite line: "God is good, girls, God is good."

Sister Mary Lourdes taught us that it was Pope John XXIII who convened the Second Vatican Council in 1959, proclaimed it was time to "open the windows" of the Church and let in some fresh air.

Pope Pius IX, almost about a hundred years earlier, had convened the First Vatican Council. Papal infallibility was established but not without controversy. The main topic was never addressed: the rising influence of rationalism, liberalism, and materialism. The Council was cut short when the Italian Army entered Rome at the end of the Italian unification.

The task for the Second Vatican Council was daunting. Its goal was to address centuries of social change and scientific and technical discovery during which the Church had held the line without thoroughly examining what was the baby and what was just dirty bathwater. The growing tension of a medieval Church living in a modern world gave rise to great anxiety among clergy and laity alike.

"Aggiornamento," a word that means "bringing up to date," became a key word as this new Council began. Christians from outside the Catholic Church were invited to the Council. Bold thinkers like the French Dominican cardinal and theologian Yves Congar become influential in moving forward the agenda of Christian unity. The quest for the right path to this hotly debated ecumenism became the topic of the day. They could have asked my mother for advice.

In Pope John XXIII's first public address, he expressed his concern for reunion with separated Christians and for world peace. In response, President John F. Kennedy wrote to him upon the opening of the Second Vatican Council in October 1962 assuring him that "people all over the world have found renewed confidence and courage in the welcome thought that the Fathers of the Council . . . will give special attention to the grave economic and social problems which daily press upon suffering humanity in all parts of the world, but more particularly, in the economically underdeveloped nations."

The Italian people called Pope John XXIII *il Papa buono*,

the good Pope. At one point during his reign, the man who ultimately would be his successor, Cardinal Giovanni Montini (Pope Paul VI), remarked, "this holy old boy doesn't realize what a hornet's nest he's stirring up."

Realize it or not, "this holy old boy" set the Church on fire with a new energy and vitality. He made an opening through which I could envision myself serving.

His influence gave promise and the whole world seemed to resonate with this good man. Upon his death on June 3, 1963, a newspaper cartoon showed the Earth shrouded in mourning with a single tear dropping, the caption, "A death in the family."

Only five months later President John F. Kennedy, another man of hope, was gone.

26

FROM SHREWSBURY TO PROMISES

AT A BRIEF MEETING IN HER OFFICE, Sister Maureen shares the news that Marnie and I will be going on a silent retreat for a week in July to prepare for making promises. Marnie seems pleased, a smile crossing her face. I feel scared, my breathing getting shallow. Maybe flabbergasted better describes my state, my eyes darting around the room for some verification that this is really happening.

They're sending me on a silent retreat? Me, who got a D in deportment on my report card for talking too much?

My only other retreat experience was senior year in high school, at Stella Maris Retreat Center on Skaneateles Lake, east of Syracuse. It was a lovely old mansion in an idyllic setting. That retreat for high school seniors was far from silent, thirty-two of us full of giggles. Stories and secrets filled the secluded dorm rooms with laughter and suspense as we conspired not to get caught for our transgressions, real and imagined.

I worried throughout that retreat that I would hear a call to be a nun, something I didn't want any part of. I was relieved at the end that there had been no voices or bells signaling me to another life. Instead I gladly went off to pursue my studies in speech correction at Nazareth College.

Yet here I am, nine years later, in the convent being sent on a silent retreat in preparation for making promises. Wow.

I needn't have worried so about the silent part of the retreat. I love it. Other than polite "would you pass the butter" comments, the silence is complete, and delicious. I don't want to talk to anyone. I want to listen to see what I hear.

Calvary Retreat Center, a simple, modern building in Shrewsbury, Massachusetts, overlooks a remote valley not far from Worcester. It's run by the Passionist Fathers and seems secluded enough to be in Outer Mongolia. The grounds are hidden away in hills and valleys that seem endless, beauty everywhere. Interaction with the outside world is not encouraged or facilitated in any way.

The vast skies that overlook the valley can be seen from the dining room where our meals are taken. Rich green and gold fields comprise the hillside and, even in the heat of these late July days, a morning mist hangs over the floor of the valley lending a mystical quality to the scene.

The idea of having a retreat master who is a priest from the Passionist religious order, whose goal, like the SSJs, is living in community, makes sense to me. The seven days speed by. Talks on forgiveness, generosity, and solitude get me thinking. In between sessions, I sit on the stone wall and look into the chasm in the terrain. I write thoughts and questions. Can the secular and sacred merge? Will I be able to bridge the gap of the holy that is remote with the holy that is everywhere? These haunting questions help me savor this time away, if at least to identify my struggles.

One particular afternoon I find myself in the chapel, tears flowing easily. Forgiveness and generosity touch me. I need both desperately. I don't want to harbor hurts, yet I do. Sharp words and criticisms creep out from my memory, demanding space in my conscious brain. My mother's voice counteracts them with her sage counsel: "Don't take any shingles off your own roof, there are enough other people to do it for you."

I keep remembering the gifts of my life, my family, my friends, the people I have loved and lost. My godmother Ceil Herbein. She had taken me to her home when I was just four years old, just me—a special time for just me, away from the hurly-burly of my siblings. I wished I could have gone to her funeral, but, at twelve years old, I wasn't taken from school to go. I felt her loss keenly, though I had not seen her for over a year. There would be no letters and gifts from the sanitorium all carrying the underlying message "you are special to me." I would no longer have someone who eagerly awaited my childish enthusiasms and confidences. To this day, I continue to pray that she knows how loved she is and how important she was in my life.

I pray that people everywhere will know of the wonder of the world. I look out the chapel windows and see these grounds as a testimony to wonder and splendor. The valley changes in the shifting light; the afternoon sun shimmers over the tree-covered hills. The birds of the air swoop and soar, the breeze moving the trees in a dance.

This is the glory of God.

My friend Cheryl comes to mind, her little sons Jon and Jeff bringing her joy beyond words, her husband, Barry, trying to create successful business ventures. She's living the life I might have. I am pleased not to be jealous or sad. I'm happy for her joy. Her accompanying exhaustion that comes from caring for both boys and dealing with her husband is something I don't envy.

As I dry my tears and say a few closing Hail Marys, I sense a presence on the far side of the chapel. I look around as

I get up to leave and don't see anyone. As I go out into the vestibule, another retreatant approaches me and says, "I saw you praying in chapel just now. You must be very holy." I wonder what she saw that I didn't. I nod to her, unsure how to respond, so I don't. If this weren't a silent retreat I might ask to have coffee with her and ask what evoked that comment. Then I could assure her that I am far from holy, but am in awe of the holy when I meet it.

Our silent days come too swiftly to an end and Sister Maureen arrives for our trip back to Rochester. I sit in back, happy to listen to the light banter back and forth and doze, savoring memories of the silence.

A few days later, Marnie and I meet with Sister Maureen in her office to learn that, ready or not, promises are scheduled for Sunday, July 30. "We'll be using the small chapel at Saint Jerome's convent in East Rochester." She smiles her nervous smile. "It will be more conducive to a small ceremony. You're welcome to invite as many family and friends as you'd like. Within reason of course."

First vows having been the traditional beginning of four years of novitiate training. Promises, the new alternative to first vows, have been enabled by Vatican II and the congregation's recent Chapter, and are yet another modification to the old ways.

The day before our scheduled ceremony, I seek solace along the familiar back road at the college, the farmland, so like that of my forefathers, soothing my anxieties. It helps that walking this road has been integral to intimate conversations over my Motherhouse years with trusted confidantes. I ponder this idea of making promises, a step toward perpetual profession, final vows. I sink my gaze into the landscape; fields of green

and gold and wildflowers accompany me. I watch the birds of
the air, and remember Matthew's gospel:

*They neither sow nor reap nor gather into barns, and
yet your heavenly Father feeds them.*

Making this next step toward final vows, I realize,
means making a step closer to a lasting bond between the
congregation and me. I gaze over the landscape and note
rough spots where plants for some reason didn't thrive.
Like congregations, rough spots are left for those who didn't
thrive, their reasons kept private. I am very aware that scores
of women across the nation who have taken final vows have
abandoned them over this last decade. I'm frightened by the
staggering numbers. I don't want to be a statistic.

I kick a stone ahead of me over and over as I meander
up the road, thinking of the women who have taught me in
the novitiate, some by instruction and others by example. I
understand vows to be sacred promises to live in poverty,
chastity, and obedience. I also realize that any permanent
commitment I make to this papal congregation has to be
approved by Rome. The process isn't trivial.

Promises allow a softer entry into this congregation. There
are no hard and fast words, there are no binding documents.
From what I understand of the process, I feel I can, with full
honesty and integrity, go forward. I can continue to say yes—
until when?

I breathe into the beauty of this landscape and resolve to
hold on tightly for what is yet to be. The stone tumbles into
the hillside and rests next to a boulder.

Father Dorsey invites me to stand, his blue eyes clear and

silver hair gleaming in the afternoon sunlight that seeps through the stained glass windows. He indicates with a small gesture that I should come forward to the podium. I feel safe, his presence a comfort. I take a deep breath. He is a trusted family friend, the man who took my older brother John under his wing when Dad had about given up on him. From what I could deduce, his grades and effort didn't match his ability, his attitude not one that Dad endorsed. Even Manlius Prep School couldn't do what Father Joseph Dorsey was able to do. John became a man after one year at Saint Michael's College School in Toronto, run by the Basilian Fathers. Within a few years of John's success, Father Dorsey, a Syracuse native and friend, was transferred to Rochester's Saint John Fisher College as Dean of Students, his skill in nurturing the talent of young men recognized. In our family, he has been assigned special "savior" status. I'm delighted that he has agreed to officiate our promises ceremony and that he will join us for lunch afterwards at the Maplewood.

July 30, 1972, is thankfully a clear day, with no humidity, and hopefully will make my mother more comfortable since there's no air-conditioning in this tiny chapel. Mom's never done well in heat. She's finally become easier about my decision but I still sense her unspoken disdain for religious life, whatever her reasons. One day perhaps we'll talk. For today I trust in her love.

As I stand, I take a deep breath and look out at those assembled. Dad is good looking in his dark suit and handsome striped tie, his thinning silver hair gleaming, his faith one of the pillars of my commitment. Mom is dressed in her signature navy blue suit and white blouse, cultured pearls draped gracefully, a gift for her thirtieth wedding anniversary.

My brother Tom, just fifteen months older than I am, his Navy crew cut finally grown in, his brown hair styled to include long sideburns, wears his green leisure suit and open collar, very much in current fashion. He's still silent about his Vietnam War experiences. Hopefully one day we can talk about them.

Kathleen, my younger sister the social worker and recent Nazareth College graduate, wears her long ash-brown hair loose with a knee-length green skirt and matching blouse, no longer finding things to lift from my closet. I wonder what she's thinking of my choice, not sure of her support. Even though she's only five years younger, she's of a new generation. While I've been focused on developing a path to serving and addressing social justice issues through a religious life, outside the convent wall, feminism and a new environmentalism have been taking center stage. She's a part of it all. I've listened to her ambitions and adventures, aware that the media has tagged her generation the "Me" generation. The anti-war protests of my era had continued with intensity, the gunshots at Kent State two years earlier changing the level of the game forever. There's lasting anti-authoritarianism marking the era and here I am entering into the service of an institution. With the sexual revolution in progress, the voting age now at eighteen, and women's rights issues on the table, I don't take for granted that Kathleen has any understanding of what I am about.

Mary Jean, John, Jim, and Mark, my other siblings aren't in attendance, partly due to geography and prior scheduled events. Others in attendance include Sister Joellen, a treasured guide throughout so many days of questions and doubts. She has listened well and helped me choose a symbol for the day, something representative of my commitment. We settle on a serving tray, a perfect decision. Sister Elaine is here and brings delicious comfort. Her wise counsel helped me receive with gratitude my mother's gift, a fourteen-karat gold cross, artistic and elegant in its simplicity. Accepting her gift, instead of trying to sell it and give the money to the poor, Elaine explains to me, is another form of poverty, of letting go and being able to receive what is offered. She's agreed to join us at the Maplewood; she and Mom can swap stories about Lima, their shared hometown.

Marnie, who has shared so much of this journey with me, stands next to me, her promises now made. Her stepmother, father, and brother Robert have been with her throughout her journey and continue to be. She smiles at me.

With a fluttery stomach, I step forward. The phrase comes to me, "Be still and know that I am God." I don't have to do much more than that, I determine.

I look at Father Dorsey to calm myself. I breathe in deeply and begin:

I, SISTER ELIZABETH ANNE OSTA, PROMISE TO LIVE THE LIFE OF A RELIGIOUS IN THE SPIRIT OF THE GOSPEL, IN THE CONGREGATION OF THE SISTERS OF SAINT JOSEPH OF ROCHESTER AND ACCORDING TO ITS CONSTITUTIONS.

A shaft of sunlight pierces through the windows as I continue, bracing myself for the next part, pleased with how honest I feel about the words.

I PROMISE TO DEVOTE MYSELF TO THE LOVE AND SERVICE OF GOD AND HIS PEOPLE THROUGH THE PRACTICE OF POVERTY, CHASTITY, AND OBEDIENCE IN PREPARATION FOR PERPETUAL PROFESSION.

There's no timeline, no expiration date on these promises. I feel excited and relieved as I move to the finish line.

I ask our Mother General, Mother Agnes Cecelia, to receive these promises in the name of the Congregation.

Father Dorsey, on cue, says to Sister Rosalma, an administrative council member who is here in Mother Agnes Cecilia's absence:

YOU HAVE HEARD THE PROMISE AND REQUEST OF THESE SISTERS. WILL YOU ACCEPT THEIR PROFESSION OF TEMPORARY COMMITMENT IN THE CONGREGATION?

I step back and note that my knees are not weak, my footing secure. Rosalma steps forward. I smile. She's another of the great women I look up to, inspired by her service in Brazil. She has told me of her admiration for the Irish priests she worked with, a certain radiance accompanying her face when she speaks of them. One sticks in my mind, perhaps because I feel a kinship: "Father Kevin draws little children like a magnet," she once shared. "He's one of twelve children himself so he can relate so easily to them."

Rosalma steps forward and responds:

> YES, REVEREND FATHER, IN THE NAME OF THE CONGREGATION, I ACCEPT THE PROMISES OF THESE SISTERS TO LIVE THE LIFE OF A SISTER OF SAINT JOSEPH OF ROCHESTER, ACCORDING TO OUR CONSTITUTIONS. IN TURN, THE CONGREGATION WILL PROVIDE FOR THE HUMAN AND SPIRITUAL NEEDS OF THESE SISTERS. IT WILL GUIDE THEM IN THEIR DEVELOPMENT AS TOTAL PERSONS IN COMMUNITY AND IT WILL OFFER THEM THE LIVING EXPERIENCE OF ITS OWN LIFE AND WORK.

She reaches over toward me now and I realize I'm to hand her the signed
document. I do. No contracts, no binding terms. Just a promise.

I feel a smile come from within. There is no applause but there could be a celestial choir. Marnie and I follow Sister Rosalma and return to our seats.

It's over, I did it.

I join in singing the Offertory Hymn "Take My Hands." I hear Dad's voice blending with mine and think of the rich faith life I have been raised in, he and Mom never wavering in their commitment to the God they've inherited from their parents and a God they've shared with me.

Once again, Sister Mary Lourdes's refrain from freshman Theology comes to mind, a fitting ending for this momentous event in my life.

"God is good, girls, God is good."

27

HEARTACHES

I TAKE THE PHONE CALL Tuesday night just after we finish the dishes. It's Dad. A call from him is unusual but I'm happy to hear his voice until he starts to speak. "Dear, your mother is doing fine. They're doing everything they can for her."

They're what?

"Dad, what are you saying? What happened?"

"She's at Community Hospital. She's had a heart attack. The doctor says she's doing fine. She should be home in a few days. I wanted you to know."

"Dad, tell me what happened, can you? When was this?"

Dad pauses and says, "Can you come visit this weekend? I'll fill you in on all the details then. I've still got a few more of your brothers and sisters to call. You were my first."

"Okay, Dad, okay," I say, my heart pounding and my mind whirling. "Tell Mom I'll see her this weekend." I put down the receiver and tremble. Mom had a heart attack? Doing everything they can for her? I see her small face and scared eyes. She's always been a source of strength for me and now she's down. Wow.

The weekend can't come soon enough.

I can't believe this. I was just home three weeks ago to celebrate Mom's birthday, her sixty-fifth. We went out to dinner to the Westwood, the local restaurant that had become their favorite. Everything seemed fine.

I'm able to arrange with Clare and Pat to take a car for Friday afternoon through Sunday. As I shoot down the Thruway, I wonder what caused this heart attack? Mom's father died of heart disease at age sixty-five. the age she just turned.

I go right upstairs and find Mom tucked in the converted bedroom that she calls her little nest. It has two couches, two chairs, and a television. Next to her couch is her coffee table that holds anything she might need: coffee cup, Kleenex, ashtray, coasters, and Mentholatum ointment— her proclaimed cure for most anything. She's nestled in on the couch nearest the doorway, her pillow propped up behind her. I lean over and kiss her cheek, a family statute of limitations since forever. No big hugs, just pecks on the cheek. Don't wear your heart on your sleeve. Now maybe don't wear your heart out at all.

I sit as close as I can and study her. Her hazel eyes are puffy underneath. I mention it.

"They've been that way for a long time," Mom says, her red blouse giving her cheeks a glow they need. She looks pale to me. "I'm going to be fine. Dr. Ayers is very pleased with my recovery."

I feel my own racing heart slow down. We sit and watch television, chattering lightly in between during commercials, unless there's an especially good commercial.

One of her favorites, "L'Eggo my Eggo," tickles both our funny bones. I've missed recent episodes of the soap operas, Another World one of her favorites. She fills me in: "Steve and Rachel are going to be married. And Alice isn't doing well at all." Like family gossip, these folks have been part of our conversation since I was in high school. I'm glad for the update.

I can tell Dad is in full command, glad that his bride, as he often refers to Mom, is home. He's busy in the kitchen fixing his specialty, beef stew dinner, and waiting on Mom with caring and compassion. My older sister Mary Jean is coming home the following weekend. I wish I could, too.

I have phone chats with Mom over the next month, convinced she's getting better. She's gone out to get her hair done, had lunch with her friend Katie, and she and Dad have resumed their Friday night dinners at the Westwood, all good signs to me of her recovery.

My Thanksgiving visit confirms my hopes that she's on the mend, as she not only directs the activity for meal preparation but also actually makes the dressing, a signature dish we all love. I'm disappointed that she has started smoking again and investigate lower tar and nicotine cigarettes for her.

I return to Rochester from that weekend more peaceful, confident she is doing okay. I get caught up quickly in the busyness of school. I'm pleased with the progress of my first graders. They've captured the beginning letter sounds and some are actually working on reading. Others play with cars, dolls, beads, and puzzles, their creative dialogue always intriguing.

"You sit here by this girl," says Stephanie to the little girl doll. "And you two boys sit over there and don't bother the girls." She's from a big family and I think I've just heard her mother.

I spot the December 13 *Courier-Journal,* the diocesan newspaper, open on the kitchen table. Dorothy sits with her half-empty coffee cup and glances up as I walk in. I see the headline of the article she's reading: "CICP Survey Nearing End."

"It is to help the Council of Inner City Parishes, CICP, answer Bishop Hogan's challenge made last spring," Sister Grace is quoted in the article as saying. "The bishop challenged them to reconsider their mission to the poor."

I thought the purpose of CICP when it was formed a year ago was to support and protect inner-city parish schools from demise. The diocese committed $200,000 annually to member parishes. A survey now is changing the focus of the dollars? What happened to supporting and keeping schools? And in the space of just a year?

I feel agitated and betrayed. I get a cup of coffee and return to the paper. I read the names of the eleven CICP member parishes being surveyed: Saint Michael's, Saint Bridget's, Mount Carmel, Holy Redeemer, Saint Francis Xavier, Immaculate Conception, Saint Lucy's, Saint Patrick's, Saint Peter and Paul's, and two churches serving distinct nationalities: Saint Teresa's (Polish) and Saint George's (Lithuanian).

School salaries and heating costs use the bulk of the money, dwindling tuition insufficient to cover the costs. Church collections in the city are half what they used to be. Suburban schools are growing. How, the bishop asks, will we continue to serve the poor? Are Catholic schools the most effective service? Should we be getting more parish workers and using the money to provide family support services?

The exodus by many families from the city, a trend across the country, is fueled further here by the 1964 riots that so deeply affected the heart of these neighborhoods. It has left city parishes the challenge of serving families who have great need and little money.

"It seems so silly," Dorothy says. "It's so clear that education is the key to serving the poor." She stands, her spine straight, her gray hair curled in place. "They continue to study and talk and waste time and money on what we already know."

I fold the newspaper and put it in the magazine holder in the living room. I get the duster and polish to do my charge before I go grocery shopping. From the car sign-out book, I note the car will be back by eleven.

Last year, CICP closed the seventh and eighth grades in seven schools and opened a centralized junior high school at Saint Michael's. Four hundred students and fifteen teachers were displaced. I'm grateful that my eighth-grade class, the last one to graduate from Saint Francis Xavier, went out in a blaze of glory with their successful SWING grant and their production of A Christmas Carol.

The recommendations from a diocesan task force chaired by Sister Barbara, a powerhouse of a woman and principal of Immaculate Conception School, will be voted on soon. Her vocal and persistent commitment to education gives this rapid-fire speech advocate credibility that is bound to be tested during the coming days. It's not clear yet if the Human Development survey data will be incorporated into the results.

Sister Aileen, my SWING grant supporter, comes through looking for coffee. She wonders if I've read the *Courier-Journal*. I nod. We both know the survey has some sway with the bishop, his challenge and request for support to the parishes beyond city borders not bringing anticipated dollars or support.

"I just copied this quote," she offers, "from Father Kreckel. I was over at Immaculate for Mass. I thought you'd like it." Bob Kreckel is the associate pastor at Immaculate Conception Parish where Father P. David Finks and he turned the parish into an avante garde diverse and open community. Aileen hands me a slip of paper. I pause from my dusting to read it.

Poverty is not only economic but educational as well. It is the inability to have power in the political workings of society that affect you daily.

"So very true for our people, isn't it?" I ask, as I hand back the quote and clear the buffet of books, candles, and dishes to polish it. "We in the schools have become poor."

The meager responses to the bishop's plea include five thousand dollars from Bishop Kearney High School's project, Help our Poor (HOP), and a fifteen thousand dollar pledge from the North District of Parishes to aid Holy Redeemer School for the 1972–73 school year. It's a start from the surrounding wealthier parishes, but it's clear that the system isn't changing enough.

I think of Egidio, Frankie, Whitey, Ronnie and Johnny, Jeanette, Tracy—children with light or dark brown skin, children who start with languages other than English. Their families work hard to escape the poverty surrounding them. I ache to think of what is to come: parishes pitted against parishes for the dwindling subsidy resources provided by the diocese. As the ax hovers over each location, unspoken suspicions develop about which work is most valued— education or parish ministry. It's clear enough that both are important; the rub is that the price tag for education is higher.

Doris and her husband, Jack, who have served so effectively on the Francis Xavier parish council, have moved to Webster. My whiz kid math student Brian's family is there as well, a new parish benefitting from their skills and service.

Families who stay behind work tirelessly to pay rent, or, if lucky enough, mortgages on houses whose value will never rise as those in the suburbs rise, due to the illegal practice of redlining. The term draws its name from the practice by lenders to draw a red line around a neighborhood on a map, often targeting areas with a high concentration of people of color, and then refusing to lend in those areas because they considered the so-called "risk" too high. Though illegal, it goes on.

Rising tuitions continue to be a concern, as well as the stresses of the streets, drugs and violence the tip of the iceberg. Hopelessness and despair don't linger too far away.

Eleanor, a middle-aged sage raised in this parish, wears her graying brown hair brushed back and is a tireless advocate. She encourages Whitey's Latino parents and Egidio's Italian ones to attend parent conference night. Her six-year-old son Ronnie, one of my students, wins my heart over with his warm smile, his front teeth missing. His sincere ways so resemble those of his mother, the unofficial ombudsman for the neighborhood, able to talk to anyone and better yet, able to listen.

For me, the bleak financial future is brightened daily by the laughter of children— black, white, and brown—as they play together without rancor and walk arm-in-arm when the recess bell rings; children who become friends, opening the possibilities for Martin Luther King's dream for the future.

I put away my dust cloth and polish, satisfied that things are spruced up for the time being. Marlene has been good to her word and the car is back. I've signed it out until two p.m. It will be good to wander and think.

As I go out to do the shopping, I pause as I pull past the eleven-year-old school building, thinking of its future. It was a boon to the neighborhood, meant to give the students a clean, modern environment and lower heating bill: solid red brick fitted with tight windows, each decorated with sleigh bells and Christmas candles, children's images of the coming holiday. I remember drawing similar pictures for the windows of my own parochial school. With every hope, these windows will continue to provide educational visions. I go off with the shopping list, remembering to add another six-pack of beer, a popular item since I first picked one up all those months ago.

The Christmas holiday in Syracuse is buoyed up by Mom's continued recovery. As I sit in the 1950s General Electric Formica kitchen watching her, I'm delighted to see Mom more fully back in charge. I study her small, almost wrinkle-free face, Pond's cold cream her proclaimed secret agent, as she bustles about getting dinner.

She looks good, I decide, both in color and spirit. She's not a complainer or a pill-taker and after sixty-five years and seven children, she seems in relatively good shape. Her own mother lived until age ninety, her father the carrier of the heart disease; his death came at exactly the age Mom was when she had her heart attack. Genetics! Hopefully her crisis is past.

Over drinks and cigarettes, I learn neighborhood news: the Rapsons two doors down are selling their house, the aging Sullivans are doing well, Dad's consulting status at Niagara Mohawk is going smoothly.

I savor telling Dad, a Goldwater conservative, about the election results from my first graders this past November.

With the letters M for McGovern and N for Nixon, the children cast their ballots on election morning. Earlier Ronnie and Whitey had fussed at each other. After I settled them down, we began to tally the results on the blackboard. I was personally delighted to see McGovern win by six votes.

As I circled the M to indicate the winner, I heard a howl in the background. I turned to Ronnie and Whitey. Both were in their seats but Ronnie was sobbing. No one seemed hurt.

I knelt next to his seat and asked, "Did someone hit you?"

He looked over at me, nose runny, brown eyes brimming with tears. "I wanted Nixon to win."

Mom and Dad enjoy the story almost as much as I enjoy telling it. I revel in their undivided attention, something not often possible when others are around.

The arrival of the Chicago grandchildren—Kathleen Mary, a bright, engaging three-year-old, and her new brother, month-old Mark—is thrilling. The pull of children is as strong as ever within me and as I spend time cajoling, coloring, counting, cooing, and carrying, I vow never to lose touch with these gemstones of my life.

Back in Rochester, the *Times-Union* January 11, 1973, headlines lay out the impending situation: "Some Inner-City Catholic Schools May Close." Three plans are to be voted on that Sunday, January 14. Tension is everywhere. My heart droops.

There's much speculation about which way the vote will go. Francis Xavier's 1961 building, with its up-to-date amenities and lower maintenance costs, provides one reason it should survive. Yet Father Beatini has not promoted the school, his focus as a priest of his people on the Italian community.

Father Ray Booth, who chairs the CICP and is co-pastor of Mount Carmel Parish, has voiced his parish's desire to see those in the deeper heart of the city—those in greater poverty—continue to be served. I wince to witness competition over who is the poorest.

The vote is scheduled for seven o'clock and six of us who work at Saint Francis Xavier School—Janice, Ann Marie, Marlene, Ursuline, Dorothy, and me—attend, along with the three others, Betty, Aileen, and Annette, who are parish workers. The meeting is held in the Mount Carmel school hall on Ontario Street, less than two miles away.

At dinner before the vote, we have a frank discussion.

"The end result is out of our hands," Janice says with her usual leadership aplomb. "We need to be cautious not to let this divide us."

We are aware that other Sisters beside us—other Sisters of Saint Joseph, some Sisters of Mercy, and some School Sisters of Notre Dame—are having similar discussions. The fiscal facts don't answer the question that never seems to see the light of day: What will happen in these inner cities if educational alternatives to public education are withdrawn? Poverty prevails and so do the attending realities.

It's a relatively clear night and attendance at the meeting is good. I count over one hundred attendees despite the Super Bowl game between the Miami Dolphins and the Washington Redskins.

Sister Barbara, as chair of the task force, welcomes folks into this sparse school hall with low lighting and drafty windows and promises to get them home to see the end of the game. Chart paper on a rolling blackboard holds the three options. Discussion includes the fact that whatever schools are selected, they must serve children in the poorest section of the city.

I am not ready for the emotional impact I feel when the vote is for the middle plan that closes Saint Francis Xavier. My heart aches. I choke back tears as I look around at families embracing. I hear stifled sobs from the folks from Saint Lucy's, the other school to close. Tears of joy accompany congratulations that fill Mount Carmel's parish hall. I am flabbergasted. Our eleven-year-old school building is being abandoned. I have no doubt that the argument of keeping services for the poorest of the city's poor has won sway over retaining buildings that are in better shape to serve the areas. Father Beatini makes no comment to reporters that evening.

Our trip home is somber, our task clear before us: to accept what many of us believe to be unacceptable.

Several of us gather around the kitchen table. Marlene pulls out the chocolate swirl ice cream and I get the bowls. This isn't a celebration but it does call for something—a consolation. One by one we recount the events of the evening, each of us contributing a perspective. Janice, Dorothy, Marlene, and I have the most invested. Dorothy wonders aloud about the job loss for our janitor. Like unwanted moths that are difficult to capture, details float around our heads.

This plan closes only two schools, Saint Lucy's and Saint Francis Xavier. It keeps Saint Michael's as a junior high and Holy Redeemer, Mount Carmel, Saint Bridget's, and Immaculate.

As I eat my last spoonful of ice cream, I wonder if this cost-saving measure will be enough to help us survive. Time will tell. At least Mom is out of the woods. Meantime, Dorothy, Marlene, and I are out of jobs.

But not for long.

PART THREE

Let life happen to you.
Believe me:
life is in the right,
always.

-Rainer Maria Rilke

28

HOLY REDEEMER

"IS THAT THE BOY who used to be in Maria's class?" I ask as we turn the corner. "The one whose father died?"

It's a cool morning in mid-August 1973. Dorothy, Marlene, and I are on the way to our first visit at our new school. The drive down Clifford Avenue is open, few trees lining the street. Sagging porches are empty, front yards barren of grass. Only litter is abundant, garbage cans overflowing, empty beer and pop bottles and used diapers covering sidewalks.

As we wait at the signal light at Portland to turn onto Clifford, the young boy I asked about crosses on the opposite side of the street.

"I think it is," answers Dorothy. "He looks sad, doesn't he?" I agree, as I see the stoop-shouldered youngster with hungry eyes, wondering where children wandering city streets can get solace. I think he has an older brother in jail.

We arrive at the parking lot beneath the twin domes of Holy Redeemer church. The building itself is in homage to the mixed waves of immigrants it has served: built in an Italian Lombard style overall, but with Eastern European–style onion domes topping the massive square turrets and German stained glass in the windows. The school across the lot is old, dating back to the early part of the century, and sits boldly facing the street, a survivor in the latest rounds of parochial school cuts.

"Here we go," Marlene exclaims as we get out of the car and approach the old doorway. "Let's hope we like them."

"And that they like us," Dorothy adds.

As a result of Saint Francis Xavier's closing, we three Sisters have been invited to teach at the neighboring parochial school just a mile away. We are aware that the salary Sisters garner is far less than that of lay teachers, so we happily are in demand.

The School Sisters of Notre Dame (SSND), whose Motherhouse is in Connecticut, have proudly run Holy Redeemer School for over a century. They also run Holy Family on the west side of the city and, until recently Saint Michael's. When it became a consolidated junior high, Saint Michael's School became a CICP school run by Saint Michael's parish. Here at Holy Redeemer, for the first time in their history, these Sisters are welcoming Sisters from another congregation to work with them.

Sister Mary Smith, a warm, open-faced woman who appears to be in her mid-forties, greets us at the school door. We follow her up a small staircase to a dark narrow landing. Principal Sister Marie Therese joins us, smaller than Sister Mary by a few inches in both height and width. Both Sisters wear their modified habit, a small blue veil reminiscent of Our Lady's blue portrayed in statues and photographs, the veil flowing from a wide hidden band. They take us on a school tour.

As we climb stairs and peek in classrooms still packed up from last June, we hear stories of other staff members whom we'll meet at the faculty meeting to be held just after Labor Day.

"You're all welcome to come set up your classrooms next week after the floors are refinished and the cleaning is complete," Marie Therese says. "Any idea when they'll finish?"

she asks Mary.

Sister Mary giggles and says, "Your guess is as good as mine. You know they work on their own time schedule." We all nod. Years of working with school maintenance men has taught us that their vital assistance is never be taken for granted—nor can it be expected to be delivered in a predictable time frame. "We'll plan on a week from Wednesday, but call and check to be sure," Marie Therese advises.

As participating schools in the Council of Inner City Parishes, we have experienced a myriad of changes since last January's vote to close Saint Francis Xavier School. Hours of meetings have resulted in the reassignment of those of us still interested in serving in schools. Some Sisters have taken this change as an opportunity to go into parish ministry, Sister Elizabeth one of them. She's been hired by Saint Francis Xavier so our connection with her will continue. Holy Redeemer School has offered to accept any displaced Sisters of Saint Joseph as part of their faculty. Dorothy, Marlene, and I qualify, as no miracle has unlocked the doors at Saint Francis.

Newspaper articles in both the *Courier-Journal* and the *Times-Union* continue to follow the story of the schools, watching closely for the fallout from this momentous decision. The work on schools done by the Council of Inner City Parishes has left many of us less than impressed. In the *Courier-Journal*, the task force who worked for two months to create this new system gives as rationale the presupposition that in making these changes, the Church will be able to continue its service to the poorest section of the city in an educational capacity.

We are not seeing the evidence.

Father Beatini's response to the closing last winter, captured in a *Courier-Journal* article a few days after the vote, summed up both the loss and the fiscal reality. He said that when he came to the parish nineteen years earlier, Saint Francis Xavier School, which has existed since 1888, had 650 kids and now there were only 200.

Consolidation has lost further families, whether because they do not want to go beyond their neighborhoods or because they worry that there may not be a full commitment to support the present schools and further shifts may come.

But none of us wants to bring those issues up on this orientation visit. Sister Marie Therese turns to me, her eagerness to move along showing. "Let me show you your classroom, Sister Betty. Mary, will you take Sister Dorothy and Sister Marlene up to their rooms?"

"Wow," I exclaim as Marie Therese opens the door to the first classroom on our left. I look out the six-foot tall windows that line the spacious first-floor corner classroom on both sides, overlooking the parking lot and Hudson Avenue. Light is plentiful and illuminates Sister Marie Therese's pleasant face as I turn toward her.

She smiles when she hears the positive exclamation. "It's an old school but we've tried to keep it up."

"Sister, it's lovely. This is a great classroom," I declare. "I've saved all my materials from Saint Francis. They'll work great in this room," I say as I walk across the creaky floor to the cupboards. "It's like the classrooms when I was in grade school."

I don't tell her how much I'll miss the sink in my Saint Francis Xavier classroom, or the smooth surface of the green boards, the highly polished tile floors, the clean lines of the aluminum-framed windows, or the proximity to the convent and my bedroom that overlooks the school yard. I don't confide my concern about carpooling each day, having to wait on others or keep others waiting. I've determined that none of my fears, anxieties, or disappointments are anything she can do much about. Like the rest of us, she has been subjected to a lot of change, and now she is accepting staff she hasn't personally selected.

Knowing my school days will start an hour earlier and that my sleeping till the last minute has come screeching to a halt by this new assignment to Holy Redeemer alarms me, but the notion of another year with first graders enlivens me. I can do it, I tell myself.

"How many students are typical for the classroom, Sister?" I ask. At Saint Francis Xavier, I had up to twenty-five, which made for a full house.

"We're trying to estimate those numbers now," she replies. "With the registration period we picked up a good number of new students, but not as many as we predicted have come over from Saint Francis Xavier."

She walks toward the desk and picks up a calendar from last school year. "Who'd have thought all this would transpire?" she says thoughtfully. "How are you all doing with these changes?"

I surprise myself by choking up. "We're doing okay," I stammer. "This change is a challenge but it will serve kids. That's what we're interested in." I swallow and continue. "We're so glad to be coming here. You have a good reputation," I say. I'd love to ask her opinion of the whole process but it seems too early to get into political musings. I change the subject and ask, "Does Mr. Collins work here?"

Marie Therese looks surprised. "Bill?" she asks. I nod. "Yes, he's our mainstay. He helps out LeRoy, the head custodian, but Bill is the reliable one. Do you know him?" I share with her that fact that his daughter, Kathy, is a good friend and had been a postulant with me. "This is their parish. I think all five of the Collins kids went here."

"They were before my time. Bill's been here since he retired a few years ago. We started together. It'll be nice for you to see him. Next week, hopefully, if LeRoy finally gets things moving." She smiles.

"If you want to review some student folders, I have some in the office. Meantime, I'll go check on the others. Oh, by the way, your grade partner is going to be Jackie. Her first-grade classroom is right across the hall. I'm confident you'll like her a lot." She flashes a smile and goes out the door.

I go over to the window and look out. From here I can only see the side of the church, no domes in sight. I think about Marie Therese's question: How are you all doing? The decision to close Saint Francis Xavier was not an easy one to accept. I'm still not convinced it is the smartest move. Pressures from within the CICP system by individual school personnel to keep older buildings open—buildings in parishes that are no longer able to sustain the parish, let alone the school—can only spell future disaster.

Last June, as we worked to get children settled in new schools and over the summer, as we cleaned up our years of accumulated books and bulletin boards and bundles of papers, the pain lessened. We polished all we could and left the rest to whatever the parish would decide for the fate of the building. This is what we were asked: to be a part of a new system that would replace the parish school system. As the *Courier-Journal* that reported last January 17 stated: "The new inner city school system is not sponsored by, or affiliated with, any one parish, but belongs to all eight CICP member parishes, to be jointly run by them."

The concept of obedience surfaces. For all of us.

The wrangling over the amount of the diocesan subsidy that should be available continues. Great resistance from the Priests' Council to any increase in diocesan tax is discouraging for those of us in city parishes. The priority to serve their own relatively thriving parishes first casts a pall over any ideas of garnering significant diocesan-wide support. The previous immigrants have left the city for the more prosperous suburbs and abandoned the lovely parishes built by their forefathers, as well as the people who cannot afford, or are not allowed due to racist housing practices, to move to suburbs. Those families who could have afforded to move out but cherished their neighborhoods and welcomed newcomers seem to be battling the tide. An editorial in the *Courier-Journal* by Monsignor Bill Roche criticizes the bishop's leadership, criticizes his own colleagues for fostering what he determines to be the "moral bankruptcy" of the Diocese of Rochester. Voices are heard; criticism, while not always welcome, is printed. Change doesn't always follow.

Hope seems far away. Nonetheless, in a few weeks, six CICP schools, including my newly assigned one of Holy Redeemer, will reopen for another year. This much we can provide.

Holy Redeemer's pastor, Monsignor Joseph Vogt, is a small man who has a brother named George, also a priest. He is determined and devoted and oversees a parish that has boasted a school since 1867. Like Father Beatini, he watches from a distance, caring, but with tasks of his own to attend to.

The Hudson–Clifford neighborhood is more commercial than the area on Bay Street where Saint Francis is located.

Out this new classroom window I can see the corner grocery, Collaco's. On the right is Wandke's Restaurant and across from it, Yalowich Drug Store, all immigrant-founded anchors for the neighborhood; for me, new lands to explore.

I'm curious about how many Francis Xavier families will come to Holy Redeemer. I think about the recent Italian immigrant families from Francis Xavier, the Carteris and Novellis. Both mothers are skilled seamstresses who work at Hickey Freeman. Their husbands work at Bausch & Lomb and they, too, have steady jobs, fluent English not necessary for their gainful employment. Their children bring home the language; they bring home the bacon. Will they want to come this far north, from the familiarity of their own neighborhood within this unfamiliar land, for the sake of a Catholic education? For some it may be only a mile away, but for others it is a mile too long.

29

SAINT MICHAEL'S

VANESSA, WITH CHUBBY BROWN CHEEKS and pink plastic barrettes, and her dainty cousin Debrine, expertly handling her brown hearing aids, are among the six-year-olds I teach. They bring joy of discovery and excitement to school every day. Tiny Patrick, even tempered with brown eyes and hair the color of the earth, carries with him a hunger to read that fuels me to prepare lessons that feed him. I learn that his auto mechanic father was crushed to death under a car when Patrick was just three.

I am surprisingly happy at Holy Redeemer. The short commute with Dorothy and Marlene turns out to be pleasant and provides the assurance that I arrive on time. I find myself smiling each day as I walk into the big, airy Hudson and Clifford corner classroom. Though I doubt I'll ever find another principal as understanding and supportive as Janice, I enjoy Sister Marie Therese very much. Her gracious, gentle manner and smiling countenance do a lot to make her approachable. A real key to my esteem of her is noting how children cling to her, always a good sign in my book. They can spot a phony a mile away.

I continue to learn skills for teaching and am happy to apply techniques learned from my graduate course work at the University of Rochester. I read into the night the works of educational hero Sylvia Ashton-Warner who, in her book Teacher, has taught me how to introduce students to the written form for key vocabulary words—not words demanded by a prescribed text, but the words the children themselves identify as the ones they want to learn—a process she developed while teaching Maori children on the North Island of New Zealand.

Tag board, the wonderfully bendable and resilient paper, is the essential ingredient for word cards, the simple and almost magical system I'm experimenting with. Ashton-Warner advises that children need something they care about to spark their interest in words. A parade of pupils line up at the table where I sit with marker, tag board cards, and a listening ear. They are specific in their requests: *ambulance, airplane, policeman, fireman, helicopter, minister, church, house, school, mouse, sidewalk, attic, ladder, television, animal, giraffe, gorilla, giant, monster, money, grandmother, bicycle.* Each day, I learn a new array of interests as children come to request their words. I carefully print the word and before the marker has dried, the children snatch up the tag board and skip off. I'm astounded and as happy as they are.

Fire engine, zoo, building, skyscraper, tower, tree, playground, street, store, cartoon, check, family, cousin—words from their lives, words that become the hot topics of their tales when they bring their word boxes to story time.

They draw pictures on construction paper from their lives: double houses with two front doors, apartment buildings with five stories. They dictate stories based on their pictures that I write for them about little brothers, big sisters, aunts and uncles, cousins and mothers, but, not as often, fathers. They count everything they can and spell words from their boxes and from their world. They sing and play triangles and musical blocks.

They watch, with full attention, the movie that is a staple in my educational toolbox, The Red Balloon.

"How come that boy took the balloon?" Patrick asks.

"'Cause it wasn't anybody else's," Vanessa answers.

They are innocent, unaware and oblivious that the dollars that fund their school are shrinking. They learn their letters but don't know about the letters "CICP." They do know of hard-working mothers and sometimes fathers who pay tuition for them. They know to behave, for this is serious business, this money spent on their behalf. *They'd better behave.* And they do.

The school year goes well, new relationships formed, more children served. Then on June 11, CICP discloses an $80,000 deficit. Teacher pay is being held up.

As school closes for this year, more bad news is delivered.

On June 23, the CICP executive board votes on yet another proposal. Two more schools are to be closed, this time Saint Bridget's and Mount Carmel, the ones that Father Booth was so pleased to keep in the mix.

Saint Michael's is being converted back to an elementary school to absorb the students from Saint Bridget's and Mount Carmel. The displaced seventh and eighth graders find their way into the neighboring public schools.

My heart sinks as I think of the frustration and anger all these closings have caused. While Dorothy, Marlene, and I are safe at Holy Redeemer, others are not. Clare has been teaching at the junior high. What next for her?

An article in the June 26 *Times-Union* tells the tale with this headline:

PRINCIPAL CRITICIZES CHURCH'S PRIORITIES

> The church's verbal commitment
> to the poor in the inner city
> is just that—verbal .... We
> had hired a fund-raiser and the
> priests' senate approved it," the
> principal of one of the closed
> schools stated "then the Bishop
> stopped it, overriding the advice
> of the priests."

Angela Reyes, parent of two brown-faced, curly-haired boys who attend Mount Carmel, is also quoted: "The administrators of the diocese have stabbed us in the back." Hearts are broken, families are bereft, and emotions run rampant.

The following day, the story continues to unfold in an article in which Bishop Hogan confirms that he has vetoed a fund-raising campaign.

> "We have poured $1.2 million into
> the six inner-city parishes since
> about 1967. That's 20 per cent of
> our total diocesan funds for six
> parishes.... We are asking whether
> there are other ways to serve the
> people of the inner city."

It's been disillusioning. I've stopped listening to gossip and just struggle to find hope for the future. These children deserve better.

After dinner, I'm called to the phone.

"Is this Sister Betty Osta?" I hear the male voice on the other end of the line say.

"Yes, this is Sister Betty."

"Sister Betty, this is Father Dan Brent, Superintendent of the Diocesan Schools."

"Yes, Father Brent, how are you?"

"Well, I'm guessing you are aware of the most recent decision of the CICP," he says.

Since Holy Redeemer has remained untouched, I am curious to learn why he is touching base with me. "I am," I reply.

"Well, Father Booth is here with me now and we'd like to ask you to consider becoming the principal of the new K–6 Saint Michael's School."

I gulp.

He goes on. "We've talked with several of your colleagues and your past and present principals. We think you have the right spirit to provide leadership in this new school community."

I am floored. My jaw drops open and my heart begins to pound. Holy smokes! In the midst of this heartbreaking melee, I am being approached to step in deeper.

"What about the principals being displaced?" I ask. "Doesn't either of them want to do this?"

"No."

I ask for time to mull over the question. "When do you need to know?" I ask.

"As soon as possible," Dan says. "And we'd ask you to keep this request confidential. There's a lot going on right now. Call me at this number as soon as you can." I take down the number and tell him I'll get back to him. My hand is shaking as I put the black handset back in the cradle. I sigh and go to my room. I sit on the edge of my bed. I'm shivering. Dan Brent calling me. Ray Booth too.

I lay down and put my hands behind my head and stare up at the ceiling.

Whew.

I've had a cordial relationship with both Dan and Ray. They have been running the CICP meetings together and are devoted to consensus. They have listened far longer than many might have been able. The wrangling and backbiting about who is the poorest of the poor, and who needs the money more, has been impossible to contain or respond to. It's difficult to tell how this newest proposal that closes two more schools and converts Saint Michael's to a K–6 school can make a difference.

In every phase of this journey, the numbers are staggering. Debates have gone on in the Priest's Council for months and have yielded no solutions. No collective will has emerged to do anything radical to change the way things are done. No one is willing to give up his or her portion. The diocesan tax on each parish doesn't begin to reach the amounts needed.

I feel the breeze coming in from my open bedroom window and prop myself up on my pillow. I remember on the night of the vote Father Ray Booth, the soft-spoken and soft-hearted chairman of the group, saying to his parishioners, "No decision in my entire priesthood has upset me more, especially the means used to reach the decision." Ray had been distressed, even though his school made it through that cut. He must be even more distressed now. Yet he's asking me to step up. I realize dismay is to be found everywhere, at every level, and feel compassion for these men forced to make no-win decisions.

I am twenty-eight years old, have been an educator for eight years, and have been an aspiring member of the Sisters of Saint Joseph for seven. I'm being asked to be the principal of a school not yet fully configured. I'm being asked to go into the frying pan of politics. Is this really happening? Yet isn't this what I've been chomping at the bit to do, to make a difference?

I sit up on the edge of the bed. I see my copy of Bonhoeffer's *Letters and Papers from Prison*. I flip it open, hoping for guidance.

Trust will always be one of the greatest, rarest, and happiest blessings of our life in community . . .

I have no idea why I'm so calm all of a sudden. I think I'm going to say yes. Someone has to do it. Why not me? I trust these men who are asking and I trust the women I live with to support me. Let's see what happens.

I guess I have a phone call to make.

30

DIANE

"I'll get her," I say over my shoulder to Joanne, the newly hired kindergarten teacher. "You go back to your classroom."

"Her name is Diane," she shouts as I take off like a shot out the door, keeping the little brown head in sight, my heart pumping fast. I see her approach the intersection of Clinton and Clifford.

"Oh no, darlin', don't try to cross," I say aloud, the traffic swallowing my words. She turns right onto Clinton and I keep pace as she crosses tiny Evergreen Street, her five-year-old legs running as fast as they can. My twenty-nine-year-old legs are keeping up, and just past the convent, I catch her in my arms. Frightened and determined eyes meet mine. Her pink shirt wrinkles under my grasp. "No," she shouts, "no!" I feel a sudden pain and look down to see blood on my arm where she's bitten me. The pain in my arm doesn't rival the pain in my heart at what must be a series of struggles already encountered in this young life.

It's the first day of school at Saint Michael's. It's my first day as principal of this school—of any school.

I hadn't imagined the scenario of a runaway kindergartner as my first challenge, but here I am. It's a clear day in early September, a warm breeze pushing past us as we huddle on the sidewalk, cars whizzing by. I have no idea what event triggered this escape. I just know I am glad to have this little one safe in my grasp, away from cars and other dangers inherent in this neighborhood that is the unspoken territory of the Clinton Avenue Boys, a gang of youth noted for drugs, larceny, and nasty behaviors.

I continue to hold her, my chin resting on her head, pink barrettes holding cornrows tightly in place. This is a child who is loved.

Since I said yes to the job of principal, I've received letters and calls of support from all facets of my life: Sisters with whom I live, friends in the congregation, and friends from without. My father, whose position is vice-president of employee relations at Niagara Mohawk Power Corporation, weighed in with his vote of confidence and support. "Liz," he said, in my visit with him over July 4 weekend, his big brown eyes sparkling, "don't let them see you quiver. It's okay to be scared, just don't tell them you are." Whatever management skills I've inherited are thanks to my parents—Dad with his corporate know-how and Mom with her dazzling domestic skills, managing seven children that arrived within ten years. Her system for making lunches still puts me in awe.

As this little one fidgets in my arms, I hold tight and slow my breathing, hoping hers will follow. I realize that not quivering is not just intended to support my authority, but also to reassure anyone under my leadership that the skipper has a firm hand on the tiller. Best to communicate calm.

Even as our academic year starts, I'm filled with anxiety about the future of these schools. I wonder if Diane and her family have any notion about the disillusionment and despair that have been chronicled daily by the diocesan weekly *Courier-Journal*, the afternoon *Times-Union*, and the morning *Democrat and Chronicle*.

Over the summer, articles report details that seem impossible to comprehend. A June 23 vote began with the decision to close the junior high program at Saint Michael's and the K–6 programs at Saint Bridget's and Mount Carmel. Saint Michael's reopens as a K–6 school with the hope that children from Saint Bridget's and Mount Carmel would be able to find a new school home.

Most of the representatives see no way out and vote yes: Immaculate Conception, Saint Lucy's, Saint Michael's, Saint Francis Xavier, Holy Redeemer, and the Spanish Apostolate. Not surprisingly, abstentions came from Saint Bridget's and Mount Carmel, the schools slated to close. The only no vote was cast by the Black Caucus, with Saint Patrick's Parish absent. Backroom deals and a developing distrust darken the days.

Reports continued. The July 3 protest meeting held at the Mount Carmel school auditorium rang with cries of, "We can do it," as parents from the two closed schools told their stories in English and Spanish and clamored to be given a chance to raise money to keep their schools open.

Sadie Macluska, whose son has attended three different schools in three years because of closings, said, "We're being used as a pawn on a chess board. They said the plan would be in operation for five years and now they've sold us." Macluska's husband, maintenance man at Mount Carmel, will lose his job unless the building can be rented out. Stories of disappointment and loss fill the newspaper pages.

I kneel down and hold Diane closer, soothing her with calming words. "It's okay," I say softly. "You're safe now, it's okay." Her eyes are full of curiosity. My arm throbs.

"You know what?" I ask. "Just like you, this is my first day of school. I'll tell you a secret. I'm scared, too." She listens and looks at me with wonder. I think of Dad's admonition not to let them see you quiver and wonder if it applies to five-year-olds. Somehow I sense that this is the right move to reassure Diane: yes, I'm scared, it's okay to be scared, but I'm not running away.

This past summer has been so full of drama that this small runaway seems a minor incident—except, of course, to Diane.

In the midst of July's chaotic clamoring, a light emerged. A July 19 article in the Democrat and Chronicle announced that Mount Carmel would not be closing. A Wilson Foundation gift of $135,000 is saving it. CICP votes to reopen Mount Carmel, a school staffed by the Sisters of Mercy.

Saint Bridget's, a Sisters of Saint Joseph School, gets no reprieve. Father Joseph Vogt, pastor of the parish, says, when interviewed by the Times-Union, "We're not down and out ...We hope to set up some center to serve the poor. Despite numerous problems, Saint Bridget's future may be brightening. Urban Renewal offered to buy some of the buildings ... to establish a day care center." It is clear that the school will not reopen.

I look down Clinton Avenue as I stroke Diane's back, her body calming, tension lessening.

So much is riding on the backs of these little ones. We are stopped in front of Saint Michael's convent, a red brick building that no longer houses the School Sisters of Notre Dame, who have taught at Saint Michael's for over one hundred years. The building is now a part of the Catholic Workers Movement, run by the Sisters of Mercy as Bethany House, a home for pregnant teenagers.

How many more transformations will be in the works as

the insufficient education dollars that remain are converted into funding for alternative mission services? And how effective will the alternative services be in these stressed neighborhoods in comparison with the anchor that a school can be?

I loosen my grip on Diane and stand, reaching down to take her hand. Her feet are planted firmly, so I pick her up. She doesn't resist. I pass the rectory, remembering words from the recently retired pastor of Saint Michael's, Father Benedict Ehmann, Clare's uncle. He issued sentiments of "great disappointment," lamenting that schools have to close, acknowledging that "necessity demands it." He posited a final question: "Why did the problem surface so late?" A question never fully answered to any satisfaction.

Both lack of trust and the absence of full disclosure of finances have haunted the CICP since its inception. Hiring an outside facilitator by using funds from a shrinking treasury didn't sit well with the parishes. Bob Molinari, the executive director, was to work miracles, fundraise, organize, and soothe. Over the past years, it didn't happen.

I put Diane down as we enter the building and we walk up the few entryway stairs hand in hand.

"Shall I stay with you a while longer?" I ask. She nods, her eyes sleepy.

I take her to my office and sit her up in the padded black rocker, one of the first pieces of furniture I borrowed from the Saint Francis Xavier convent attic. I wind the small wooden music box from my cousin's wedding. Strains of "Till the End of Time" fill the quiet space. Diane's eyes widen.

As she slowly rocks, I write a note and check for phone messages, nodding to the secretary in the adjoining office.

I slip her the paper, asking for Diane's address and phone number. I rewind the music box, wipe the now dried blood from my arm, and see that she is settled.

"Do you want me to take you to your class now? I think it's snack time."

Her dark eyes light up a bit, the wariness subsiding.

I lift her from the rocker and take her hand. "Here we go," I say as I lead her from the office, her pink shirt and pink barrettes all neatly in place.

I look down the hall to the left and note how quiet the classes are. The first-grade class on the right is staffed by one of the Saint Bridget's teachers, a top-notch teacher I was happy to get. The anxious days I spent throughout August in my small cheaply paneled office with a high window that lets in bits of light on gray days seem worth it now. I have a good handle on the student population, staff, policies, and procedures. I make a mental note to add procedures for runaway kindergartners to my files.

We approach the classroom and I knock. Diane's hand tenses in mine. Joanne opens the door. Tables and chairs are located in a square in the center of the room, juice and cookies are on a side table, a play corner across from us is filled with stuffed animals, picture books, puzzles, trucks, and cars. I nod to Joanne and take Diane to the stuffed animals. I hand her a small pink teddy bear.

"This bear," I say as I kneel next to her, "needs you to help her. She's a little scared in this new classroom. Will you hold her and see if we can find a place for her to sit near you?" Her eyes look into mine and then at the bear.

Joanne follows us as we move toward the tables. "Diane, look what we found for you." She extends her hand and Diane takes it and follows her to a place with her nametag. "Shall we make a tag for your bear?" Joanne asks. I smile and follow, kneel for a minute to stroke Diane's head. Then I slip out slowly, waving goodbye. Diane's eyes shine.

I am glad already for the decision to bring the rocker and music box to my office.

The view from the only office window when I stand on tiptoe is of the parking lot and the original combined church-school building from the late 1800s. As I look out, I'm aware that a new piece of history is unfolding during these days.

Over muggy August days, with the help of silver-haired Grace Conway, diocesan director of personnel, I interviewed each teacher she recommended to me, teachers she had interviewed first to determine their willingness to work in this new school. Grace was clear and I was in agreement that old angers and alliances have no place in this new school.

I was familiar with several of these candidates from group meetings and conference days. I was pleased they'd chosen to come on board. Their youth and eagerness gave me confidence that they would be here for children.

"Are you ready to work with a new faculty and bring one hundred percent commitment to this school?" I asked. Without even blinking, each candidate agreed. That's the assurance I needed to get off to a smooth start.

We need to leave the past behind and move to the future.

The two newly assigned co-pastors of Saint Michael's parish are Father Tony, olive-skinned and gentle, and Father Paul, hefty and loud and genuine. Like me, they don't quite know what they're getting into. The idea of co-pastors is becoming more popular, two men sharing the responsibilities equally for saying Masses, hearing Confessions, and attending endless meetings.

Both of them have been on hand on several occasions with other volunteers from Saint Francis, Holy Redeemer, and even Mount Carmel and Saint Bridget's to move in the smaller desks and carry furniture from the second floor to the first-floor classrooms. Their spirit and joviality helps to establish a fresh spirit.

I am blessed and grateful for Sister Clare, the only other Sister on the school faculty, vigorous and vivacious, who by all outward appearances enjoyed her work at the junior high and has agreed to stay and teach sixth grade. Over summer vacation, she and I worked daily readying the building for a new population. Laughter became our hallmark as we did our own share of moving desks, chairs, and bookshelves up and down stairs to create new classrooms.

At one point, as we lugged a huge metal cabinet up the stairway to a second-floor classroom, listening to the shelves rattling within, we got into a fit of laughter and couldn't go forward or backward.

"Kind of like CICP," Clare quipped.

I stop back at lunchtime to check in on Diane. She doesn't see me. She's feeding her bear. I wink at Joanne and leave to continue a tour of the rest of the building, tiptoeing down the hallways in wonder, looking in at the sights and listening to the sounds of what is the new school year: new sneakers, spellers, uniforms, and notebooks; summer vacation stories told, students chattering, desk chairs scraping as children stand and recite.

As I return to the office, calm seems to prevail. I settle

down at my desk to try once again to contact Diane's family to let them know about her day.

Before I know it, dismissal has arrived. I stand at the stairway and wave to the students marching in orderly lines out the doors. I spot Diane, smiling and waving. I wave back.

Despite the odds against us, we have both made it through our first day. The only decision left for the rest of my day, is if, when, and where I should get a tetanus shot.

31

THUNDERSTORMS

I STAND ON TIPTOES at the tiny window in my office looking out at the lightning of the thunderstorm, one of my joys since childhood.

Last month while visiting my mother, an August storm loomed as we chatted on the front porch. I looked around at the shimmering elm trees that lined our street, aware of how much I had grown to love storms. My senses felt fully alive as the earth vibrated with the energy that the skies were about to release.

"I think I'll take my shower now," I said, as I stood next to Mom who was sitting in her sentinel spot, ashtray and drink nearby, a Taylor Caldwell novel, *The Sound of Thunder,* in her lap. She'd taken to porch sitting once the seven of us were off and on our own. Over the years, younger couples moved onto the street and Mom befriended them all. They'd stop for a chat, watching their children's kickball games from the porch that graced our 1920s colonial home.

"Do you have to go right now?" she asked. "Can you stay for the storm?" Something in her voice caught my attention.

"Well, I could stay but ... Mom, are you afraid?" I asked tentatively.

Her eyes looked apologetic.

"I've hated thunderstorms since I was little. Just sit for a bit, will you?"

I was incredulous. I remembered hurricanes where she'd gathered us onto Dad's bed, lit the room with candles, and told us stories. I treasured memories of snowstorms and thunderstorms huddling on one of the two living room couches, seven of us tucked under blankets, Mom presiding with humor and grace, telling tall tales.

Our favorite story, the Crooked Mouth Family, was one we'd beg for again and again. My mother's mouth would contort as she imitated each of the imaginary family's idiosyncratic facial motions, twisting her mouth first to the right and then to the left, then up and then down. The fun part was when it came time to blow the candle out. Pa tried and couldn't do it because he blew right past the flame. As each successive character was asked, "Will you blow the candle out?" they answered, "Well, I'll try." With that Mom would imitate each of their unsuccessful attempts. Finally, the youngest son was asked: "Will you blow the candle out?" He said, "Well, I'll try," and wetting his two fingers, he pinched the flame out. Never did we tire of Mom's imitations and her glee in telling it.

"But Mom, you made storms such fun for us. I love storms."

"I know and I'm glad. So will you stay?" she asked, her hazel eyes hopeful, her lightly frosted brown hair moving gently with the escalating breeze.

I can still see her face as the sky lit up that afternoon, a twitch with each crack of lightning. It wasn't too long before we retreated indoors, a doozy of a storm splashing rain up the steps and onto us.

The autumn storm I'm watching from my small office window doesn't punch as big of a wallop, but still there is lightning. I see it flash past the end of the building.

Lightning. Oh my God, Clare! Suddenly I remember

how terrified Clare is of storms. I race to her second-floor classroom, taking the steps two at a time.

In the year and a half I've lived with Clare, I've learned of her intense fear of storms, far beyond my mother's. Her sixth-grade classroom is the first on the right at the top of the stairs. I approach breathlessly. The desks all face front, away from the doorway, and there isn't a peep. I poke my head in to see how Clare is. She isn't there. An assignment on the board reads, "For bonus points, complete page 87 in your English book." Unbelievably and thankfully, these experienced Catholic school students are all industriously at work. Even Rosella.

I step quietly back into the hall. I know from previous storms that the first thing Clare does is plug her ears and the next thing she does is find a spot with no windows. At the convent, it's the chapel. In Wegmans on West Avenue, it's the ladies room.

My curiosity about this fear of Clare's was satisfied over dinner at Clare's mother's house during the summer. A silver-haired sage with twinkling brown eyes, Laurette had worked for years in the rectory at Saint Monica's. She knew her way around church jargon and politics and kept current through frequent visits from her brother-in-law, Father Ben.

"Well, Betty," Laurette explained in response to my question about Clare's fear of storms, "it's my fault! When I was a young teen we all went to watch the circus train when it was coming to town. Right down on Railroad Street, not far from where you all live now."

I imagined a group of children being fascinated by carloads of tigers and lions and elephants and bears, lining the tracks that ran from Goodman Street along Railroad Street.

"We jumped and waved and hollered and hooted," Laurette

said, a smile of memory painting her face. "And then a storm came up out of nowhere. A freak streak of lightning crashed right into us. It sliced right into our friend Marion. She was struck dead, Betty. It was the worst thing I'd ever seen in my life."

I drew in my breath just imagining this horror.

Laurette continued, her voice shaky. "When I had children, I vowed no such thing would ever happen to them." Her jaw was firmly set as she continued.

"I made sure whenever there was a storm, they'd be safe with me. I took them to the old glider in the basement. That's where we'd go."

I have a lasting image of the mother and children huddled together on the bench of an old porch glider in the dark basement, rocking it back and forth as stormy noises raged outside.

I remember the story and begin to look around for the safest place Clare might find. I peek into the broom closet next to Clare's classroom. Crouched in a tiny ball, ears plugged, she looks up.

"Is it over?"

"No," I say. "I'll stay with the class. They're doing fine. Stay put."

I feel more secure in this post as principal than I would have thought possible. The faculty is top-notch, starting with Clare, a seasoned pro. We are a K–6 school now and have one class per grade level. The enrollment is adequate for our first year, many families holding on to this beacon of light amidst dwindling resources. Maureen is the fifth-grade teacher. She has dark hair that's almost black, fair skin, and height that lends her an air of authority. She runs a tight ship, providing exciting science experiments that keep students engaged. Marie, with her warm smile, soft features, and a Long Island accent, holds fourth graders captive with her skill for storytelling, with some of the best tales coming from her students as she coaches them in writing skills. The first, second, and third grades are staffed by young teachers who want to work with city children. Their dedication and enthusiasm, along with their creative activities, make the classes work. Teachers share responsibility for music, art, and physical education classes on our shoestring budget. It works well because of the willingness of these teachers to go the extra mile. Guitar playing brings freshness to some lessons; museum tours and special visitors from the fire department, police department, and art gallery supplement and enhance the reading, writing, and arithmetic skills being taught. A rich curriculum is developing from the meat and potatoes of people who care.

Discipline issues are ever present even with those well-disciplined sixth graders during the thunderstorm. Thankfully federal legislation provides Title I services to parochial schools, including social workers and psychologists. We happily rely on them.

Joanne, the kindergarten teacher, has already won stripes for her handling of Diane who has joyfully settled in, her bear still her companion.

Additionally, Clare continues to be a master in her ability to bring out the best in all students. She has a knack for getting students to work together. The presence of both Puerto Rican and black students in addition to the few neighborhood children who are descendants of Irish and German immigrants gives us all—staff and students—a chance to become familiar with other cultures. While the school offers a Catholic curriculum, other religions are welcome. Parents are eager for this unity for their children despite cultural differences. The families choose this smaller school where they feel discipline is stronger and civility is stressed. They don't come from a single parish or a single neighborhood anymore. They come from many places to find safety and community for their youngsters. Together we work to provide such an environment.

Amazing artwork decorates the hallways. Self-portraits hang outside the primary grades. Each child shows himself or herself amidst their family, with houses and apartment buildings crayoned in place, bunnies, puppies, and kittens adding to the warmth of their notion of home and family. In the upper grades, nameplates with elaborate designs decorate each desk and pictures of detailed cars only dreamt of fill the walls, wheels almost spinning.

Many children remember Roberto Clemente's tragic death in 1972 in a plane crash while taking supplies to earthquake victims in Nicaragua. A lasting pride in this talented icon opens the way for discussions and creative artwork. One student paints a baseball with Clemente's signature, another draws the plane after it crashed, the detail astounding.

Portraits of Martin Luther King Jr. accompanied by each artist's essay about this national hero make for fascinating reading. "He was like my father," one essay reads. "My father was killed, too."

It is a Tuesday when I hear the knock on my office door and look up to see short, serious, pre-pubescent Victor from Clare's classroom. I gulp. Clare rarely, if ever, sends for anything from the office. She had reluctantly agreed to serve as vice-principal, to step in only in case of my absence, declining any further opportunity that attempted to take her away from her first love: teaching.

I nod to Victor, who presents me with a note. "Sister Clare said to give you this," he says dutifully. In Clare's neatly written script, I read, "Can you come up? RG is on a tear." I stand from behind my desk, nod to Victor to go ahead back to his classroom. "Tell her I'll be right there." My stomach churns as I stop by the secretary's office and say, "I'll be in Sister Clare's room."

As I ascend the stairs, two at a time, I glance out the two-story landing windows at a blue sky, the golden leaves on the towering oaks gleaming in the sunshine. How bad can it be, I wonder. As I reach the top stair, I see Clare, standing sentinel at the door.

Clare had first alerted me to Rosella's defiance after we'd had our first fire drill. Instead of returning to the classroom, Rosella went on home. Her lack of steady attendance was an alert to our social worker, Art, whose phone calls had gone unanswered. His attempts to visit in person ended with no one answering the door, though he heard voices within.

My first and only encounter with this tall, regal looking pre-pubescent teen had been disastrous. She was in the downstairs hallway after the bell had rung. I knew her name, her reputation for noncompliance preceding her. I approached her.

"Rosella, can I help you?" I asked.

She was standing looking out the hallway door. Dreaming of going out it perhaps.

Her lack of response brought me round to the next question.

"Did something happen in your classroom? Are you okay?"

She spun around, her eyes ablaze.

"What you people always asking 'bout? Something happen? You okay? I ain't 'bout to tell you nuttin'. You all can mind your own business."

She stormed off in the direction of her classroom. I stood transfixed, watching her ascend the stairway, hoping she was headed for her classroom. I waited a few minutes and crept up the far stairway and wandered down by her classroom. I didn't get close enough for her to see me. I wasn't certain she was in there, but I hoped.

Art—our wise pipe-smoking, bearded gem of a social worker whose own peaceful demeanor helps us all—shakes his head when the subject is Rosella.

"We may be on our own with this one," he concluded at one of our team meetings about Rosella, earlier this fall. "She's one of those youngsters who's growing up alone despite a house full of people."

Her abilities tested in the average range according to Andy, our young long-haired psychologist. "She has capacity to excel if she is motivated," he told us at our last meeting.

Neither Art nor Andy is in the building today.

As I approach the doorway, Clare comes over and speaks softly, not taking her eyes from the classroom. "I sensed it coming." It's like one of the thunderstorms Clare feared so much—rumblings before the lightning strike. As she reports it, the class has been working on an art project. "She's called the other girls bitches, has refused to pick up a desk that she tipped, and is taunting them and won't join in the assignment."

Clare sounds scared. "I feel like she's about to blow. I've asked them all to do seatwork. I can't keep her in here anymore. It's not fair to the others."

She turns her eyes to mine and says, "They're afraid of her and frankly so am I."

I remember my previous encounter with Rosella. I don't have a clue how to handle this one, breathing deeply in an attempt to keep my own fear at bay.

"Did something trigger it?" I ask.

"I don't know. They're not talking. She just needs to leave."

"Do you think she'll come? " I ask warily.

"Well, it's worth a try."

With that, Clare moves down to aisle, past girls with white dickey blouses under their plaid uniforms and boys with dark slacks, white shirts, and ties, to Rosella, whose uniform looks bedraggled. She leans over and speaks to her. Amazingly, Rosella looks up at me and picks up her book, starts down the aisle toward me.

"Sister Clare says you need my help," she mumbles.

"I do, Rosella, I do," I say, thankful Clare has engaged her to come with me with this strategy. I tell her I absolutely do need her help, in the worst way. "Thanks for being willing to come with me."

I turn to lead the way to the door when I hear a crash. I spin around in time to see the already tipped desk pushed yet again, the books, papers, and pens spilling out onto the wooden floor.

I look at Rosella, who looks away, and then to Clare. I keep moving. Whatever this stormy child is up to, it's clear we need to remove her.

Once outside the classroom, I point down the stairway. "We'll go to my office. I have a project that needs your help."

I follow her, not certain she will follow me. The level of

anger in this child is frightening. Without home support, I have no notion what we can do.

When we arrive at the office, I invite her to sit in the rocker. I remove the music box, which I treasure, not certain Rosella has the capacity to hold it gently. She accepts the offer to sit in the rocker. I tell her I'll be right back and watch from the secretary's door as she pushes herself back and forth in the chair.

I write a note to the secretary asking her try to reach Rosella's family again. Maybe this attempt will work. I go back in the office and pull a chair up by Rosella who is rocking with a fast, regular rhythm.

"Rosella," I say casually, "you sit for a while. I have some work to do and then we'll talk about the help I need." She shrugs, her rocking rhythm never slowing.

I feel the weight of this child and this job. What possible intervention that hasn't already been tried can undo the hurt of what I surmise has been many years? Her record indicates little cooperation from her family despite repeated attempts. I wish I had a reference directory of strategies for helping hurt children.

I fuss with papers on my desk and see Sue Pinero's name. She's the principal at Number 20 School down the street. We've been talking about doing some joint activities. Rosella's rocking rhythm helps slow my heart beat a little. I twist a pen in my hand, straighten some papers, and step into the office to see if there's been any contact with Rosella's family. No luck.

I come back and sit near Rosella again on a chair that doesn't rock.

"Rosella," I say, "I've been thinking. And now I need some help. You know anything about Number 20 School?"

Her rocking slows a bit.

"Yeah," she says reluctantly, "My li'l brother go there. He in the first grade. He couldn't come here 'cause his Daddy say he wouldn't pay."

I am stunned to hear this many words in one string from this child. I dare the next sentence.

"I'm supposed to call the principal of Number 20 School. We want to start a program for our two schools to cooperate together."

I pause and watch for a reaction. Rosella's eyes follow mine. I remember the tipped desk and the angry child who sits before me. The impulse to punish her diminishes as I see a light in her eyes for the first time.

I go for it.

"What would you think if some of our sixth graders went on Friday afternoons to help some of their first graders?"

I hold my breath, wondering if this might be a key to some softening. I smile as interest colors a face that has been suspicious and angry since I've first seen it.

"That might could work," she says, her eyes tentative.

I want to hug her but don't.

"How about if you and I write a note to Sister Clare to see if she would like the idea? Then you and I can talk some more about who should get to go."

"That all right as long as that nasty white girl don't come. She's a bitch."

I'm grateful for this truth and this opening.

"Well, you and I can decide who should come, once we get Sister Clare's okay."

Rosella nods and rocks some more.

I breath deeply, grateful that, for the moment, the thunderstorm has abated.

32

NUMBER 20 SCHOOL

I PULL MY JACKET TIGHTER around me against the brisk November air as I pass the tiny convenience store with the heavy metal grating over the doorway. I keep moving and turn down Oakman Street toward Henry Lomb School Number 20. The name Lomb is big in Rochester, Bausch & Lomb optical company one of its lucrative manufacturers since the early 1900s. Lomb also served as a captain in the Civil War, led efforts to organize and finance the Rochester Public Health Association, and cofounded the Mechanics Institute, which ultimately became the Rochester Institute of Technology. It's impressive, though Rochester schools tend to go by their numbers rather than their names, one of many factors that could make them seem less personal than a small school like Saint Michael's.

My six-minute walk to this neighboring public school three blocks away takes me down a cracked concrete sidewalk with the grass patch next to it filled with detritus of the neighborhood: empty cigarette packs, broken beer and whiskey bottles, beer cans, used disposable baby diapers, lottery ticket stubs, candy and snack wrappers.

The building is bigger than Saint Michael's but looks to be almost as old. I notice that it appears better maintained as I ascend the first few steps up to the first floor. I think of the cockroaches I spot occasionally in our basement hallways, in spite of often reminding our part-time maintenance man, who we share with the church, to remember to set up traps.

Mrs. Sue Pinero, the principal at Number 20 School, a Puerto Rican woman with a petite figure and warm smile, welcomes me graciously. Her Catholic training showed when we first met at the Title I Principals Meeting. "Sister this and Sister that" was peppered throughout her early conversation, though I encouraged her to call me Betty. Today she does. She offers coffee and introduces me as Sister Betty to her office staff, her secretary pool of four women twice as big as ours, her school population three times as big. She stands aside as we enter doorways, allowing me to go first. Since I've become a Sister, I find I am uncomfortable with the deference so many afford me. Still, my most gracious response is to accept it with a thank you.

Our plan to collaborate comes together easily, both of us eager. We settle on the first Friday afternoon of each month. Six Saint Michael's sixth graders will visit and read to six Number 20 School first graders. We'll have parent volunteers escort them. I'll plan to be in attendance when possible.

Sue then treats me to a brief and enjoyable tour of the school. I don't see even one cockroach. I am especially attracted to the first-grade classroom; the children eye me intently as they fill in their worksheets on beginning alphabet sounds, very similar to ones I had used as a first-grade teacher at Francis Xavier and Holy Redeemer. The classroom with more than twenty-five students is orderly and calm, the teacher on alert, her principal and a visitor observing.

"The children are just finishing up their folder work for the morning. Jose, can you tell our visitors what work we are doing?"

A surprised and proud Jose stands near his desk and lifts his paper so we could see it.

"We're using our listening ears to tell what sound we hear at the beginning of each word. Like 'B' for boat," he says as he points. I grin, charmed by his composure, wondering if our first graders are at a comparable level. I promise myself I'll go back and check.

Our class size for primary grades seems similar, though I suspect this school, because of double grades, qualifies for Title I reading specialist assistance. Both Francis Xavier and Holy Redeemer had such services. At Saint Michael's our numbers don't justify it.

Once back in her office, Sue speaks in a confidential tone. "Frankly," she says, "I'm delighted to get a chance to know you. We were heartsick when your K–6 building became a junior high. It seems it's been a rocky time for the Catholic schools. What is it called, CCIP?"

I explain the name, surprised at her reference to the initials of the plagued organization. I agree the times have been tumultuous. Media coverage of school closings and openings and changes in the configuration of the schools are more widely noted than I'd imagined.

At twenty-nine years old, I find myself an advocate of public education, where my own teaching career first started. I have heard others in the parochial schools denigrate the public schools and find myself defensive. Children from poverty often don't have the luxury of a tuition-based school. Also, I've been trained and certified for public education, never considering it inferior. The fact that parochial schools enroll the students who can afford to attend is an advantage for families. Educators in the city schools are as dedicated as those anywhere, perhaps more so for their challenge is often greater.

The place parochial schools hold in the educational arena is a unique one. Both smaller class size and parents who are buying in provide a more cooperative base than is possible to obtain in public schools. The freedom to have a religious foundation can provide a value-laden environment, something many public educators provide but not as a group.

The other key factor, I have learned through my graduate work, is the factor of choice. When families can choose which school to attend, the investment is already greater. I'm learning that choice is a powerful factor in so many aspects of life.

"It's a tough neighborhood," Sue says, "and we need all the supports we can get for these children."

I heartily agree, finding myself in admiration of this new colleague.

Her reference to a "tough neighborhood" without saying the name Clinton Avenue Boys confirms the experiences we are having. Police officers often shoo these unemployed young men off the corners at dismissal time. We are encouraged to post staff outside to make sure children who are walkers get across the neighborhood streets toward home. Clare is familiar with "the Boys," some of them siblings of her junior high school students from the previous two years. There's not much opportunity for interaction, nor is it desired by the Boys, or Sister Clare.

Somehow, Sue's acknowledgment eases my feeling of isolation. As a new principal, I feel awkward about so many things, not certain what I should view as a real threat or as an imagined one. I am glad to have this particular fear confirmed as real.

As Sue is interrupted by a phone call, I remember an unsettling call I received on a muggy afternoon over the summer.

"Sister Betty," Reverend Mother's voice said in her saccharine way, "This is Reverend Mother Agnes Cecelia."

I'd been a bit aghast and wondered what this was about as she continued.

"I understand you've been asked by the diocesan office to be principal of Saint Michael's. Am I correct in assuming you've said yes?"

I had been amazed and puzzled. I could see her in my mind's eye, her newly permed gray hair pulled back by her headdress, her cheeks pink, her lips pursed tightly as she spoke. Before I could respond, she continued.

"Dear, I need to explain so you can understand the protocol for appointment of one of our Sisters to the position of principal."

I gasped. I'd never for a moment considered asking the Motherhouse or getting permission to say yes to Father Brent. He was the boss, wasn't he?

"I learned from one of the Sisters that you were offered and accepted the position. That's not our usual way of handling these matters."

"Mother Agnes," I began, "I was called by the superintendent of schools. I thought he was the right one to respond to. I didn't realize about the lines of authority."

"Yes, dear, you were put in an unfortunate position. It's all right."

I breathed again and smiled. I realized I was in the middle of a classic pissing contest. I listened for what was next.

"What I'd like you to do, dear, is send a letter to me asking my permission."

Permission? I smirked.

"Of course I'll grant it, but then we'll have something in writing. Can you do that for me?"

Before I was able to stammer an answer, she asked, "Did you sign a contract with Father Brent?"

"Not yet, Reverend Mother," I said, grasping the phone tighter in my hand, "the appointment to sign one has been delayed because Father Brent is on vacation."

"Well, that's fine, dear," she said, "but do get back to me promptly, won't you? And you needn't date your letter to me. We'll see to that detail."

As I recall the conversation now, I remember thinking of the intrigue behind the call. I realize I don't know the half of it, nor do I want to.

I wonder who Sue has to answer to. I could loan her Mother Agnes.

As she finishes her call and comes back, I decide my comfort with her is strong enough to risk going a bit further.

"Sue," I begin, "I have a sixth-grade student who's pretty troubled. I think her brother is in the first grade here. Her name is Rosella Green."

Sue smiles. "She was here in school the last two years until your school reopened as an elementary school. Troubled is a good description. Have you been to her home?"

Had I been? Well, no, that was the social worker's job, wasn't it? I was caught up short with the notion that I might, like this public school contemporary, visit homes of our students.

"I think we share the services of Art Connor, the social worker. He's tried on several occasions to arrange a visit without much success."

Sue smiles again. "A gray-haired, bearded white male isn't going to have much luck with this family. The grandfather rules the roost. The first time I visited, I was greeted with a shotgun."

I hold my breath.

"He never used it, but he had it nearby, just in case he didn't like what I was telling him, he told me. We were concerned about Rosella's attendance and attitude. I try to accompany classroom teachers on what may be difficult home visits."

She pauses and offers me a piece of candy from a jar on her desk. I filch one out. She goes on.

"Rosella is a tough one. Her mother is pretty volatile and strung out on drugs most of the time. There are a couple of older kids, too. Not good influences, I wouldn't imagine. I think Rosella's been on the losing end of getting any attention or support. We never reached her. She's got such a tough exterior."

I sigh and nod. "That matches the little we know. I've been hoping if I can give her some responsibility for our tutoring program, she might come around. But since we first talked together, she's been absent," I say.

Sue nods as a knock on the door interrupts her. I stand as she replies she'll be right there. We agree to meet again in a few weeks and set our program. I leave satisfied with what feels like some solid support and important inroads.

33

THE BEGINNING OF THE END

I'M SITTING IN THE UNADORNED AUDITORIUM at Saint Michael's original school hall, torn window shades pulled down in haphazard fashion, in a meeting with more than sixty other concerned, committed women and men as the executive committee of the Council of Inner City Parishes gathers. Diocesan officials, pastors, principals, Sisters, priests, teachers, parents, leaders, and representatives from each of the congregations are here.

It's the end of January 1975. The last word on the CICP schools hasn't been said. More newspaper articles and more mayhem are afoot.

A little more than one hundred years ago, in June 1872, members of Saint Joseph and Holy Redeemer parishes held a similar meeting for the purpose of prudent planning. Theirs was one of dreaming, of considering the advisability of building a church and forming a parish nearer their homes in the northeastern section of the city. By May, the committee sought a pastor and chose Saint Michael as a patron saint. Before the meeting was closed, plans were drawn up for a combination church and school. The work of architect O. Knebel, mason Michael Henricus, and carpenter Dominic Nura totaled $16,000. In fear that work might come to a standstill because of lack of funds, seven members of the new parish mortgaged their homes and gave promissory notes in the amount of

$8,000. The results were stunning: what some still consider to be the most beautiful church in Rochester, gorgeous inside and out. The organ and acoustics are fabulous. The tall gothic revival church, with its bell tower and five-building campus, dominates the neighborhood. Over the front door, a statue of the Archangel Michael keeps the forces of evil—represented as a dragon—underfoot and in check.

A century later our passion to have lasting influence on the life of Rochester is similar, our chances of a well-funded vision not nearly as optimistic.

Clare, Dorothy, Barbara, and I all sit together. Folks from both Mount Carmel, salvaged for this year at least, and from the now-closed Saint Bridget's sit together. Two teachers from Holy Redeemer, Jackie and Mary, are side by side, both doggedly determined to carry on. Eleanor from Saint Francis Xavier Parish and her youngest son, Ronnie, who now goes to Holy Redeemer, are also in attendance.

I look around and see, with gratitude, that Sister Rosalma, one of the councilors from the motherhouse, is here. Her presence consoles me.

Youthful Sister James, SSJ, education director for the diocese, is in attendance along with her colleague, ruddy-faced Sister Roberta Tierney, assistant superintendent for the diocesan education office. The folding chairs are old, the hardwood floor creaking. The atmosphere has a restrained buzz.

All of us gather with heavy hearts, some with angry hearts. The meeting is to determine the future of education for the inner-city parishes of Rochester. Co-pastor of Saint Michael's, Father Tony Valente, says the opening prayer.

"Oh God, open our hearts so we can hear one another. Lead

us to do your will in helping those in need. Teach us your ways, lead us with your wisdom. This we ask through Christ our Lord."

A collective "Amen" is heard as correspondence is distributed to all in attendance. The first is from Sister Marie Louise Blaakman, RSM (Religious Sisters of Mercy), titled "A Stand Taken on the Inner-City Issue from Our Lady of Mount Carmel Staff." Sister Marie Louise, who wears contemporary clothes, is asked to read the statement. She stands forward and speaks clearly, her eyes determined. Other sounds fade into the background.

> *As involved members of this inner-city community, we can no longer remain silent to what we believe the Catholic Diocese of Rochester, the Council of Inner-City Parishes, and the Department of Catholic Education is failing to respond to in a positive manner. Rather their response is asking to be relieved of the responsibility of offering the alternative of a quality Catholic school education for those unable to finance it for themselves.*

The words continue to challenge the three groups for their inability to stand up to this overwhelming problem. Within a few minutes, she returns to her seat to a murmuring crowd. There is no applause.

The second letter, the purple dye of the dittoed copy blurred, is distributed by several of us from Saint Francis Xavier Convent. It affirms our support of education in the inner city. As it is distributed, Tony calls me forward to read it; a formal statement stating we are in full support of continuing the educational mission of providing Catholic schools in the inner city. I finish by adding a closing sentence to indicate that while we support similar educational goals as the staff of Mount Carmel, we do not support the critical sentiments presented in their recent statement. Our team had been vehement that negativity would not add to the conversation. We'd been of one mind to keep our statement supportive.

As I return to my seat, I get a thumbs up from Eleanor. I slide in next to Clare, who nods support. Father Valente quickly resumes leadership of the meeting, thanking both groups for their statements.

Tony looks tired to me. His thinning dark hair hangs down on his forehead as he reads a letter from Bishop Hogan that has been sent in reply to the formal CICP request for diocesan monies that have been accrued from the recent Diocesanwide Joint Appeals Collection.

The response letter states that the designated $200,000 commitment to the inner city is the diocese's limit in giving financial assistance to the inner-city schools. There are more murmurs and chairs shifted.

Tony looks up and gives a half smile, begging for perseverance.

Father Brent, superintendent of the diocesan schools, clears his throat and steps forward. He wears his clerical collar and black suit coat. His small stature doesn't match the giant he is in his work. His supervision of the schools and organizational skills have been praised, his meetings with staff crisp and clear. He pushes at his brown hair and shifts his weight to get his footing. He is the bishop's representative.

He reports that the diocese has completed its study regarding the viability of the CICP school system and reads out the seven findings of the study.

Hands wave to be recognized for comments. Father Valente reminds the audience that the time for discussion, questions, or debate has not yet arrived.

Father Charlie Mulligan, in his role as member of the new three-person diocesan committee, points out that the financial savings this year for the schools has been significant. Yet, he further notes, the income is still insufficient, with a debt of $41,844 at present.

Diocesan treasurer Jack Ritzenthaler notes that it appears this level of yearly deficit will remain constant with the current fiscal structure.

There are whispers and glances exchanged among audience members.

Father Brent then outlines the potential areas of income: diocesan support, tuition, candy drive, parish support, Partners' Club, donations, Wilson Foundation.

More murmurs. Once again he clears his throat then reads the final recommendation from the report:

It is the recommendation of the diocesan office that the CICP commit itself for the coming 1975–76 school year to one Catholic school of approximately three hundred students. An admissions committee will be set up to select students and a site committee will work to determine the location.

Heads shake in incredulity. One school? Really? Clare nudges me and Barbara Jean says in a stage whisper, "Are they crazy?" Over three years we have gone from seven K–8 schools to four K–6 and one junior high, then to four K–6 and no junior high, to this proposal for a single school. The tension is palpable, the murmurs audible, but still no comments are solicited.

My thoughts stray to Sue Pinero and the launch of our successful collaboration this very afternoon. Five students from Clare's class (unfortunately Rosella was absent), along with sixth grader Stephanie Cook's mom, went to School Number 20 and took five first graders to their school library where they read favorite stories together. I was able to stay for the first twenty minutes and saw the start of what promised to be a great collaboration. Damn, I think.

Father Charlie reports that three parishes—Holy Redeemer, Saint Francis Xavier, and Saint Bridget's—have responded to the appeals request saying they will be able to give nothing to school support from their parishes. Not even Holy Redeemer, while they still have a school? I think of my happy days teaching there. I think of how the gracious Sister Marie Therese and my friends among the Sisters of Notre Dame must feel this slight. I think of Father Vogt and the responsibility of the cost of maintaining their magnificent but aging buildings on such scant Sunday attendance.

Saint Michael's parish council has sent a letter stating that if a vote is taken, they go on record as not being in support of a one-school system. If such a system is voted in, they will instead direct their monies to a religious education program. I look at Clare. Neither of us has been privy to the parish council meetings at Saint Michael's. Co-pastors Tony and Paul have alerted us that ever since the original elementary school and convent closed, the council has been less enthusiastic about the use of the school building. Heating costs alone are exorbitant, with oil prices skyrocketing during this energy crisis. They've supported the CICP system so far, but there was no guarantee for how long they would continue. Tonight we know.

I watch as handsome middle-aged Father Charlie stands again to clarify the budget. He has a rough and ready look with his unruly salt and pepper hair, his clerical collar not as well fitted as Father Brent's. His posture is casual as he states that the budget payments that have been distributed don't yet include the salary for the CICP executive director or the bookkeeper. He also points out that the last page of the report shows what the consequence will be if the Wilson Foundation monies are not available. The implication from a quick review shows that the projected single school would then be able to accommodate only two hundred students rather than three hundred.

I feel close to tears. It is evident that we are sitting at a meeting that is signaling the death of the inner-city Catholic schools. There is little left to say. All the questions, all the "what ifs," all the possibilities have been explored. All the fingers have been pointed.

Father Valente opens the floor to questions. The first one regards the Wilson Foundation money. Will it be forthcoming if there are to be only one or two schools? Tony defers the question to Patricia Walker, executive director of CICP. An elegant-looking African American woman attired in a crisp beige suit with black piping, she reads an excerpt from a recently received letter:

> *The Wilson Foundation made a significant pledge of support to the education of inner-city children through the funding of CICP. If that system of education is to be changed as to the number of*

*schools and/or the number of students educated, we
consider the original grant to be cancelled . . .*

SIGNED: *Richard Wilson and Katherine Kling for the
board of managers*

The next question, "Why is a two-school plan not being considered?" is posed by a tall, stately African American parent from Holy Redeemer Parish and is quickly dispatched by Father Brent. "There is not enough money."

Ron Keller serves as chairman of the Partners' Club, an independent group that has been supporting CICP for several years, and takes the floor. "I am delivering this letter tonight to Father Mulligan. It reads: 'On the supposition that CICP does provide an acceptable educational system ... I do hereby offer my services as a chairman for fundraising through the Partners' Club and elsewhere as requested by the diocese for the year 1975–1976.'"

He steps out into the aisle and moves up to the front where Father Charlie is sitting and hands him the letter. Hearty applause follows.

Father Ray, a pensive, gentle spirit, is on his feet, recognized by Tony. He tells Ron that any additional fundraising efforts have been stopped by the diocesan office until completion of their diocesanwide fundraising appeal.

There is general rumbling throughout the auditorium. Tony calls for order, then announces the date of the next meeting, Sunday, February 9 at Saint Michael's. The meeting is adjourned. We move quickly to the car, Clare announcing she's up past her bedtime.

As the five of us pile into the silver station wagon and Clare starts toward home, Barbara Jean sputters, "They know what they want to do. They're just going through the motions."

I wait to hear Dorothy's reaction. As our oldest member, a stalwart teacher and spiritual soul, her words carry weight.

"I hope these children can get a lot from this semester. It looks like it will be their last."

I bite my lip and leave the car first. What will this mean for Rosella, I wonder? And for me?

34

AND THEN THERE WAS NONE

FROM THE BACK OF THE CAVERNOUS Saint Francis Xavier Church, I can see its historic marble altar, which had formerly graced the sanctuaries of Saint Patrick and Sacred Heart cathedrals, and the chalice and altar cloth in place for Mass. Here in the back, before the flock gathers, I have time to reflect on what is happening.

The church was founded in 1888 by German immigrants. The list of its former pastors read like a German roll call: Father Joseph Wetzel, Father John Baier, Father Michael Krischel, Father Francis Kunz, and Father George Weinmann. More recently an Irishman left his mark, making his way into the people's hearts: Monsignor Patrick Moffatt.

All their faith and care have been inherited by the current Italian congregation, led by Father Beatini, who, with his fluent Italian, provides a link from their homeland to the present wave of immigrants.

I watch as women wearing black mantillas put quarters in the metal box and light candles for their intentions. Sons in jail, husbands who drink, daughters gone astray, babies yet unborn, children lost. I'm learning their stories. They are the faithful, many still conversing with each other in Italian. Father Beatini, his huge heart matching his stature, has been good to them, hearing their confessions, saying their novenas, offering them solace. He nurtures them well and the people worship him almost as much as their God.

The school that they have scraped up money to support is now lost to them. Still they don't stop coming to Mass. They put their meager donations in the collection basket. "La vita continua," they say. "Life goes on."

I marvel at their faith. It's innocent and trusting. It doesn't hold grudges, bitter tastes steamed away by the feasts they are on the way home to prepare. *Pasta e fagioli*, pasta and meatballs, ziti, gnocchi, regional sauces, Parmesan cheese, finished off with cannoli and *dolci*, sweets of all kinds.

As the Mass ends, they genuflect and process down the aisle that is bordered on either side with Stations of the Cross. They nod to each other and bless themselves with the holy water from the gold fonts at the doorways. Laughter from the parking lot spills back into the now quiet church where I remain in my back pew, listening to the lightness of the banter coming in from the front steps as the faithful file out the massive doors of this nearly century-old church.

Today the current pastor, robust and slightly balding Father Joseph Beatini, a man with a ready smile, stands on the steps at the back of the church and greets the faithful as they exit the Mass.

"Hey, Father," one says, "how come you no come to dinner with us today, eh?"

Before he can answer, the question is answered for him. "You gotta girlfriend you gotta visit, right?"

Laughter erupts. They all smile, the jovial, rotund Father Beatini cheering them on.

"Next week, you invite me and I'll bring the girlfriend, okay?" he responds, his robust joy so appreciated.

As I hear their voices fade, my heart sinks. I bury my head in my hands. These, I think, are the people of God. These women and men who go forth, day in and day out, carrying their sorrows like potato sacks, putting them down long enough to greet one another with love and camaraderie. Their joys show in their kindnesses, the love of family and the pride so evident.

"My Joey, he's an altar boy soon, right, Father? He's a good boy. He likes it here. His sister not so much."

The tears well up in me as I listen, wishing I could roll back the clock, the calendar, the years and be with these people in their day, when their Church was growing and their spirits soared with confidence in the goodness of their God.

Now it seems that many live in fear of people different from themselves as Puerto Rican and black families populate the neighborhood. Those who can afford to have packed up and left. The others stay, struggling to hold on to the faith they have nurtured with their pocketbooks, their vows of marriage, their children's lives.

Many in this parish have come from their native Italy, a sizable number directly from Caltanissetta, a Sicilian town that lies in an area of rolling hills with small villages, crossed by the River Salso. They have left behind the terrible smell of the sulfur mines that employed them. In a 1911 report on child labor, Booker T. Washington stated, "I am not prepared just now to say to what extent I believe in a physical hell in the next world, but a sulfur mine in Sicily is about the nearest thing to a hell as is conceivable." To this new land they brought instead their memories of the taste of Amaro Averna, the bittersweet, thick liqueur their city produced, and the smooth sweet taste of Caltanissetta's award winning *torrone* nougat candy. They also bring their hopes of leaving behind their poverty.

They have come here to their Sister City of Rochester, on the Genesee from their smaller city on the Salso. Caltanissetta became one of Rochester's first Sister Cities in 1965, joining an international Sister Cities program begun in 1956 to promote world peace. The public market, only a few blocks away, fills with the sound of them on Saturday mornings.

"*Ehi, quanto per le arance?*" can be heard as they barter for oranges.

"*Un dollaro per una dozzina,*" comes the reply.

"*Pensi che sia stupido. Questo è troppo,*" can be heard as they walk away. "You think I'm stupid. That's too much."

A relaxed rapport exists among these people, a love that is almost tangible in certain moments, despite some of their words.

I wish so much that I'd been older when my Italian-born Grandpa Osta lived with us. I wish I had asked him all the questions that now fill me as I listen out the open door to these people of God with their priest.

My grandfather's wife, Marietta, whom he met in the lumber camps of Pennsylvania and who had lived in a neighboring town in Italy, would have had stories to tell had she lived longer. Her death from diabetes at a young age left all the stories with Grandpa, Aunt Emma, Uncle Louie, and Dad. Where did he go to school? Was the priest in his parish nice? Did he like his classes? What was his favorite thing to do? Who were his friends?

From Aunt Emma I know he loved spaghetti, a special Sunday dinner whenever we all gathered. I also knew he treasured America, praising his adopted country whenever he could.

As the people drift from the parking lot and the

conversations outside the door quiet, I am again left with my own reflections.

What am I to do? How am I to continue service to the Church? As a novice in the Sisters of Saint Joseph, I am serving as principal at the bequest of the Bishop, Reverend Mother giving her okay. It has been my dream to be of service, and the inner city now has part of my soul.

"Is there a divine plan in all this?" I ask aloud in the empty church, feeling the frustration of watching schools close and seeing the families who can least afford it scramble for sanctuary in suburban Catholic schools, tuition costs often prohibitive. No urban parochial school option remains in these neighborhoods. Public schools, while no horror, can't provide what many savored: the option to choose the intimacy of these small neighborhood value-based schools. They want something a bit more for their children. For that there is no shame.

The Prayer of Saint Francis comes to me in this church bearing his name. To go forward in grace, I need help. I say the familiar prayer, seeking guidance for what lies ahead:

Lord, make me an instrument of your peace...

I continue until the last line and wipe away my tears.

Where there is sadness, joy.

I stand and straighten myself, glad for this time alone. I note the sanctuary lamp, the red glow signifying the presence of the Eucharist.

I breathe deeply, genuflect, and leave, ready or not.

The *Courier-Journal* reporter Carmen Viglucci's February 12 headline strikes to the core: "And Then There Were None ..."

The reference, whether from the British rhyme or the Agatha Christie novel, resounds ominously. The article that follows leaves no room for doubt.

Plagued by financial difficulties, The Council of Inner City Parishes Sunday night, February 9, threw in the sponge on the increasingly uphill efforts to maintain an inner-city school system.

The image stays with me from the Saint Michael's meeting at the end of January of Father Brent, his blue eyes pleading, as he explained the option of continuing one school. Sister James Lynch, coordinator of educational services for the diocese, echoed his plea, outlining the advantage of continuing a Catholic school presence in the heart of the city. Father Charles Mulligan joined in the team presentation with numbers and statistics to promote the viability of maintaining one school.

Their beleaguered appearance, their weary and wary spirits, showed in this final effort to promote their plan to fellow colleagues who, it turned out, had already made up their minds.

> The end came in dramatic fashion when the CICP executive committee … voted to "terminate the CICP School System effective June 30, 1975." The meeting took place at Saint Michael's.

The CICP school system, begun in 1971 to pool monies with the purpose of supporting and keeping inner-city parish schools, started out with seven schools and 1,481 pupils. The diocesan subsidy, like welfare, was never enough. Now the whole project has lasted less than five years, a failed experiment. The last four Catholic schools in the inner city, serving 750 students, would now close their doors.

The newspaper article goes on:

> It signaled the end of a Catholic school presence in the Rochester inner city and came after various diocesan officials made strong pleas to continue one school.
>
> The historic end came in dramatic, though calm fashion. Sister John Bosco called the roll.

I sit alone in the dining room. The others have gone upstairs. I'm not ready yet. I'm not ready to say it's over though I know it is. I'm mad. There is so much more than a sponge thrown in.

Hours, days, weeks, months, and years of heartache and hard work by so many have been scrubbed, made moot, and the Church, its credibility dampened, has started on a trajectory that won't easily be reversed.

Talk of new ways to continue the inner-city ministry, and a promise that the $200,000 subsidy is still a commitment, both ring hollow.

I push at the papers on the table, remembering. I think of the little ones: Patrick and Debrine, Egidio and Frankie, Ronnie and Dominic, Whitey and Stephanie. All children whose educational choices rest solely with peers in overcrowded public schools where staff is often overwhelmed by endless demands.

It's been a good ride helping these families and I am resolved that we will not quit these children now. We will spend our time wiping tears, finding new schools, packing boxes, and preparing for whatever is next.

I stand up from the table, fold the paper, and return it to the basket, nestled in with other accounts of this historic closing. I pause for a moment at the bottom of the stairs before tiptoeing up. I wonder if I've been tiptoeing too long around the people with power. Could there have been another ending that might have given more choices? I wonder how the ending of this alternative educational choice will affect our future as a city. I don't have to wait long to find out.

35

DAVID AND GOLIATH

I spot Sister David Mary in the congregation's dark green Impala just where she said she'd be. I pull the blue Saint Francis Chevy Bel Air up next to it. We are in the Corpus Christi Church parking lot on Main Street, a solid yet cozy church built of red Medina sandstone in the Romanesque style and boasting neither bells nor steeple. It's the week of Easter recess, and I am meeting up with Sister David Mary, our regional coordinator and one of my favorites in the current administration of the Sisters of Saint Joseph.

The congregation's leasing arrangement with Hallman's car dealership allows more and more Sisters involved in ministries other than teaching to have the use of cars. Whether visiting parishioners, running storefront centers, or becoming physicians, religious life is opening up to a myriad of possibilities, many of which require dedicated personal transportation.

As I walk around my car to David Mary's, I wave. She opens the passenger side and says, "Step into my office." We both chuckle as I adjust myself in the seat.

"The reason I wanted to meet with you before we go in to meet Monsignor is to let you know the whole story behind your appointment and why the Sisters walked out of the school. It's important that you understand both sides."

I rest back in the seat, feeling the warmth of the April sun through the windshield.

David Mary turns to face me as much as the steering wheel will allow.

"You might remember late last fall when it was announced that the Corpus Christi Convent had been sold," she says. The *Courier-Journal* carried the article telling of Monsignor Maney's move to sell the convent as a way of helping get revenue for the church.

I nod, remembering the scuttlebutt about this. From what I'd heard, Monsignor Maney hadn't shared his decision to sell the convent with any of the Sisters living there.

David Mary goes on. "The Sisters learned about the sale of the convent when they read that article. Monsignor had talked with no one, not even the parish council."

"Wow." I gasp at hearing the official confirmation of the rumor. I could only imagine how that settled with Reverend Mother, her authority ignored once again.

"At any rate," David Mary continues, her brown eyes alive, dark hair framing her round face, "lots of meetings have helped us to come to a bit of an understanding."

With that she smiled—or was it more of a grimace I saw?

"The Sisters, all six of them teaching here, have resolved that they are not willing to serve in a parish school where they have been so poorly treated."

I take a deep breath. As I watch birds skittering in maple tree branches near the rectory side porch, I wonder what I'm getting into this time.

"Because I was principal here several years ago and know Monsignor quite well, I met with the Sisters to see if there was any room for reconciliation. Each of them feel it important that they take this stand."

She raises her eyebrows and nods her head, not giving me any clear clue as to her feelings about their action. "As I told you on the phone, when the council met, we were unanimous in our recommendation of you as the new principal here. Mother Agnes Cecilia thinks you're a perfect choice."

I take another deep breath.

"Your work at Saint Michael's and with the CICP has kept our Sisters in good stead in the heart of the city, a place we want to be."

"I'm glad to hear that," I interject. "Especially after the mix-up when I said yes to Father Brent for the Saint Michael's job."

David Mary smiles. "That situation was unfortunate. As you know we serve in the schools at the behest of the bishop. Father Brent was asking you on the bishop's behalf. Because CICP schools were not associated with a specific parish, the lines of communication got muddied. You handled it the best way you could."

She looks out the window toward the three-story wooden rectory and says, "The service of the Sisters is quite valued throughout the diocese as the economic times become more stressful."

I roll down the car window, the breeze welcome.

"Now, the situation here at Corpus is this," David Mary continues. "Monsignor Maney doesn't know anything of the other Sisters leaving yet. He knows that Ellen Dorothy is stepping down as principal, but that's all," she says.

Oh my, I think.

David Mary goes on, "I'll introduce you to him today as the new principal. Staffing isn't his domain. We can work that out later on. Once we get past this part, the rest will unfold. We'll see about an appointment for you to meet with him again after July first." She pauses. "You all set? Any questions?"

"Do any of the Corpus Sisters know about me taking this job?" I ask.

"I met with them last night," she says. I see the wear and tear on this handsome woman, her eyes lined, as I listen to the underbelly of this, my new assignment. "They're glad that it's you. They knew the congregation wasn't willing to leave the school in the lurch. So here we are. Shall we go in?"

I put my hand on the door handle and inwardly wince.

Is all this intrigue necessary as a part of working in the Church, I wonder?

The housekeeper greets Sister David Mary warmly. From their conversation, I can tell they've had a good relationship in the past. "How's that handsome husband of yours?" David Mary asks.

"Oh, he's as ornery as ever. I don't know why I put up with him." The woman shakes her head as she leads us into the modestly appointed parlor where an upholstered sofa that shows wear and two small matching chairs are positioned around a wooden coffee table with a glass top.

David Mary and I sit next to one another on the sofa. After the woman leaves, David Mary says, sotto voce, "I intentionally didn't introduce you to Mrs. V. One word from her and the whole parish would know there's a new principal. We've enough rumors to control for now."

When Monsignor John E. Maney enters the room, both David Mary and I stand. He's average height, with a slim build, thinning dark hair that's graying at the temples, and horn-rimmed glasses that cover his small middle-aged face. He wears a black suit with no hint of the red of his office, a color reserved for more formal occasions.

"How good to see you, Monsignor," David Mary says, her engaging smile hard to resist. "I'm so glad you could meet with us today."

My stomach churns as I watch this strong woman, a real David standing up to Goliath. I imagine her name is after her parents, David and Mary, parents' names being the origin of so many religious women's names.

She uses her charm, never referencing the recent articles or the anger that has ensued. This is the man who had sold the convent out from the nuns who have served the parish since the early 1900s. I watch her closely, taking mental notes, another lesson in Church politics.

36

COMMUNITY LIFE

"WORRY," MY AUNT VERONICA ONCE TOLD ME, "not only doesn't help; it robs you of the present moment."

Despite her advice, I had worried over the past year that my appointment as principal might bring jealousy from others. Even with the newest assignment of principal at Corpus Christi, I find Aunt Veronica is right. Not only do I not experience jealousy, I receive sympathy and understanding for the task at hand, and offers of support.

I've lived in community for seven years, five of them here at Saint Francis. Unlike my childhood family where I often got stuck peeling the potatoes or doing the dishes while my older sister scooted out at chore time, the culture here doesn't allow unfair burdens or special privileges. Decisions and division of labor are democratic and egalitarian. Charges are shared, mine so simple I feel like I'm cheating—cleaning the dining room and entry hallway weekly and grocery shopping once a month. Cleaning bathrooms, mopping the kitchen floor, upstairs hallways, and living room, and all the other sundry assignments are divvied up with few if any complaints. We are on our own for breakfast, and rotate cooking and meal cleanup for dinners. During the school year Barbara comes in and sees to a substantial lunch for us, freeing us to be on duty as needed during the noon hour. It's a system that seems to work.

The greatest challenge for me in living with a group of women is gossip. I hate it. I grew up with an admonition from my mother that helped me through grade school and high school: "Don't say anything you wouldn't want to see in print in the newspaper."

"You should hear what the fifth-grade teacher said about that little Santiago boy. If he had a brain in his head, it'd be lonesome." Tongues clucked, eyes rolled.

Often Dorothy speaks up in her soft and kind way. "Maybe I should see if there's a way to help the Santiago boy. I already have one that I'm tutoring. He might fit in."

"Did you notice Mrs. Neri at Mass? She looks like she might be pregnant again. Doesn't that man know when to stop?"

"There's a baby clothes sale at Genesee Settlement House this weekend," Betty says, her parish ministry skills aiding us all. "I'll bet she'd be glad of any help at this point."

I do all I can to sidestep the gossip and backbiting, my disdain perhaps stemming from being the girl in the middle of seven children with an older sister who often distorted the truth to fit her advantage. I've heard the phrase "the spirit of Joseph" used to describe non-judgmental love. I hold onto the idea of this man who without question married a woman already pregnant. It's something to contemplate.

I'm grateful for generosity when I receive it: offers to swap dates for the car sign-out or to do shopping errands, help with class projects or sign-up to cover extra chores that other Sisters know my work as a principal keeps me from.

"Oh, Betty, if you need the car that night, take it. I can rearrange my errands."

"I have to run right by the grocery store tomorrow. Can I pick up anything and save you that time?"

With no coaxing at all, Clare volunteers to serve as treasurer once Dorothy decides she's had enough. She likes to make the numbers come out right, Clare says. She sees to it that we each receive our monthly allowance of fifty dollars, the amount doled out for toiletries, clothing, and entertainment. It's quite an increase from the five dollars received monthly when I first entered. Food and gas for the car are paid by the common fund. Clare assesses how we're doing financially each month and gives a full and fair report.

I often look to Dorothy for counsel about house matters big and small. Her rock-solid character, enhanced by her silver-hair status, almost never fails. I trust her. Maybe, at times, too much.

When it's my turn to prepare the Sunday meal, which is usually well-attended by the majority of Sisters, I seek her guidance on the time and temperature for the roast beef. I'd cooked hamburgers and hot dogs for my brothers and sisters, but roasts and big dinners were my mother's purview. I remember the succulent medium-rare pieces of mouthwatering beef accompanied by mashed potato, canned peas, and one of Dad's specialty salads with just the right mix of iceberg lettuce, diced celery, onion, olive oil, and vinegar. I want to replicate it and show off a bit. This particular Sunday morning after Mass, I'm thinking of calling Mom to ask for help when Dorothy comes into the kitchen.

"Dorothy, what temperature would you suggest I use to cook the roast for today's dinner?"

Dorothy goes to the stove and turns on the gas burner under the kettle for what I expect will be a cup of tea.

"Oh, for roast beef, you always want to be sure to cook it thoroughly. Three seventy-five should do it for about an hour and a half or two."

I watch as she takes a teacup from the cupboard.

"Do you need any help? I'll be back from my visit with Anne Elizabeth by three."

I smile at her generous offer. Her goodness continues to attract me. I watch her put her teabag in the mug.

"I should be fine," I say and go on to ask, "So if we're eating at five o'clock, I should probably put the roast in at three-thirty, right?"

"Well," she says thoughtfully as she brings her tea over to the table where I'm sitting, "you might want to start at three so there's time for the meat to rest, before you carve it."

Wow, I think, *meat resting before it gets carved. She really knows her stuff.*

At four forty-five that afternoon, I almost scream when I peek in to check the roast, the brown, crusty outer layer sizzling, so obvious to me that it's overcooked.

At that moment, Dorothy comes into the kitchen. I am sure I've misunderstood and done something terribly wrong.

"Dorothy, look," I say, reopening the oven door, "I wrecked it. What did I do wrong?"

Dorothy turns her head at an angle and looks at the roast.

"There's nothing wrong, honey," she says, placatingly. "It looks perfect to me. It's

beautifully well done. That's how I love it."

I am glad at least one person will enjoy the meal.

The others recognize Dorothy's hand in the meat preparation. Several wink as I serve the meat. "Dorothy helped me prepare the meat. We even rested it," I announce, sharing the responsibility. She beams with pride.

Each night as I ascend the stairs, I see the poster on Clare's bedroom door that says, "People, like kites, are made to be lifted up," and smile. The Sisters who are parish workers bring home tales of helping families find ways to make ends meet: standing with them in lines that seem endless to get food stamps; making prison visits with mothers whose sons have made bad choices; directing young women away from the streets and into schools. It's hard not to be in awe of this kind of service.

Daily prayers are said on our own. Attendance at daily Mass is another personal decision. The one commitment we make to each other, besides sharing expenses and cars, is a weekly community time together where we pray and share a meal. It's an expected attendance, essential in these days of increasing distractions. We often end with song of some kind—"The Sabbath Prayer" from *Fiddler on the Roof* and harmonizing of Te Joseph—a practice that continues to thrill me and fill me.

The outgoing principal at Corpus, Ellen Dorothy, meets with me in late August. She's a vibrant woman, neatly attired in gray that highlights her similarly colored hair. Besides overwhelming me with the overview of the job, she counsels me to personally contact Sister Francis Marie Kehoe, an eighty-seven-year-old who still tutors in the school.

"I'm not sure she'll continue, but it's important that she feel welcome to, if she'd like," Ellen Dorothy advises me.

Before I get a chance to call Sister Francis Marie, she spots me in the cloakroom at the motherhouse, after a congregational Mass and celebration.

"Say," she says, "aren't you the one that's going to be the new principal at Corpus Christi?"

I look at this tiny nun, with a forelock of white hair peeking out from her headdress. She's shorter than my five feet two inches by at least an inch. She has pink cheeks and watery blue eyes and wears a modest, well-worn suit with the traditional profession cross. She studies me as she waits for a reply.

I nod. "Yes, Sister, I am." I'm hoping for a chance to ask her to rejoin the faculty.

"You're pretty young to be a principal, aren't you?" she says directly.

I'm momentarily speechless. I wait a moment then retort lightly: "You're pretty old to still be teaching, aren't you?" She giggles a wonderful giggle and a friendship that is to span a decade begins.

Sister Francis Marie, known by her family as Sadie, was born toward the end of the nineteenth century, November 30, 1888. She was christened Sarah Esther Kehoe, the youngest of eleven children. She loves to tell that she was raised between Jordan and Elbridge outside Auburn, New York. She shares that she was quite young when her mother died, leaving her father to manage the brood. Tales of working in the button factory and the heroics of her older siblings, who all worked hard to keep the household running smoothly, contained no trace of self-pity, but rather pride. She actually made you wish you were there with her. She was tiny but mighty and reveled in retelling the tale of her fall from the toboggan sled and no one discovering she was missing until they all reached the bottom.

Arrangements are made for her to move into Saint Francis Xavier Convent, where she will be able to ride in each morning with us to her ongoing tutoring mission at Corpus Christi. Francis Marie, whom we often call Sadie or Francis, was one of the Sisters displaced when Monsignor Maney sold the convent out from under the Sisters. She doesn't dwell on his error, simply saying, "He could have talked it over."

She manages the stairs with little effort, assistance not required. A few of the Sisters she lived with accompany her on the day of her move, bringing the few possessions she carries with her. We don't snoop. We don't need to wait long to find out what she has brought with her: infectious laughter, admirable accomplishments, and an indomitable spirit.

She entered the Sisters of Saint Joseph in what she calls "olden times," sometime in the early part of the twentieth century. One of her assignments was to help open the congregation's mission for the "darkies," as she called them then, in Selma, Alabama. She developed a deep love for these people of color who she said taught her about faith of a different magnitude.

She served at Saint Patrick's Home for Girls in downtown Rochester in the early '20s. She is proud to say that the first time she was ever in a high school classroom was as a teacher. Her quick wit helped her navigate around the tallest of students, and still does.

She makes friends for life, many of whom she receives as guests in the parlor on Sunday afternoons. Some are former students but more often visits are with her favorite grandnephew.

"Johnny came and we had a lovely intercourse this afternoon," she once announced, her innocence beguiling.

Sadie insists on taking a spot in the schedule for preparing meals, salmon loaf her specialty. Her conversation is current, peppered with opinions she's proud to express.

"President Ford did the right thing," she proclaims in

regards to the recent pardoning of Richard Nixon.

She is silent when we might expect a traditionalist view, such as when issues are raised about how often we should pray together. She goes along with what she can and tells us she's willing to adjust with the times. She delights, as I do, in our mini-concerts during dishes, joining in the harmony. She teaches us not to fear too many soapsuds left behind on dishes. "It'll clean out your innards," she tells us. And often it does. Her presence brings a solid dimension that helps keep us grounded.

A great fortune for me is that Clare is coming to Corpus, teaching junior high, her specialty. Eileen, Christine, and Marcy from our convent also have signed on, providing a strong continuation of Sisters of Saint Joseph at Corpus Christi, despite Monsignor Maney's poor judgment.

Even with so much change surrounding us, we find a gentle pattern to each day and an underlying effort on each of our parts to make this life work. Our personal prayer time blends with the community time we spend together.

We pledge to bring our best to the table and trust it will be received.

37

CORPUS CHRISTI

"HERE'S THE MORNING MAIL," Marge says as she puts two folders on my desk, her freckled face smiling in satisfaction.

"I've sorted it into parish, pupil, and personal," she says. "I've also prepared some replies for things requiring an answer. I'll send them out once you've approved them. They're in this folder."

I breathe deeply and count my blessings as longtime secretary Marge teaches me about school policies, procedures, and protocols. Without her, I realize I'd be sunk. Her no-nonsense manner, sharp sense of humor, and clerical skills all combine to make her an invaluable asset. She's short like I am, with a head full of dark wavy hair and blue eyes that sparkle as she scans the office. Her voice has a clear quality much like a shipmaster could use, this school her ship. She knows routines and I walk carefully as she guides me around things I have no idea about. My job, I decide, is to keep this secretary happy. I do my best with occasional flowers, making time to chat, and hoping at some point to manage a lunch out.

It's both a help and hindrance that Marge has children in the school, bright ones at that. She knows the scuttlebutt and shares it, even when I don't want to know it. She helps me navigate rectory routines, which are different from the procedures we used at CICP-run Saint Michael's. Corpus Christi is still a parish school, the pastor very much the boss and bingo the primary funding source.

The rectory housekeeper/secretary Mrs. V. (whom I'd seen but had not really met on the first visit with David Mary) rules the roost, I learn. Best not to cross her, Marge advises.

"Her bark is worse than her bite, but neither is very pleasant."

Nothing seems to get past Mrs. V. so I don't even try. The weekly report for the church bulletin on school activities needs to be in promptly with no typos, I'm told, Thursday morning by ten on the dot. I do my best to comply, finding a few flowers and compliments go a little way to calming the waters when they roil.

My monthly meetings with Monsignor Maney are held in the dated parlor of the rectory, where David Mary and I sat, the oriental rugs faded, the Victorian upholstered sofa sadly sagging.

In mid-July I'd shown up uncharacteristically early for my first solo meeting with Monsignor Maney since my initial introduction by Sister David Mary. It was a hot, sunny day, the temperatures soaring into the mid-eighties. As I sat waiting, I realized the good Monsignor might think me daft, on a day this warm, if I came in wearing the red and white plaid jacket I had on. As I slipped it off and folded it on the front seat, I realized I had on an equally too warm for the weather white sleeveless turtleneck that could add to the daft assessment. My sandaled feet and dark blue skirt wouldn't bring question, I mused. When the appointed time came, I rang the doorbell, confident I was more suitably attired.

In the parlor where we held our meetings, I was grateful to see that windows were open, a soft breeze moving the curtains. Halfway through our conversation about curriculum and the monthly Mass for the children, I noted Monsignor's eyes roaming up and down my arms. At first I thought a bra strap had slipped or a bug was crawling on me. I shifted in my chair.

As I made a note to add the monthly Mass schedule to the teacher bulletin, which I would publish in their opening-day packets, Monsignor cleared his throat and leaned forward.

"Sister, I must ask you, is this how you will dress as the school year opens?"

I stammered, "Well, yes, Monsignor, a skirt and blouse ..."

"But with naked arms, Sister?"

Incredulous, I choked back a guffaw. I looked down at my arms that until now had seemed innocent appendages to my torso. I had never thought of them as naked or sensuous in the least. I took a deep breath, realizing now was no time to equivocate.

"If it's this warm out, Monsignor, possibly," I said cheerily. I held his gaze until he looked away.

Since that conversation, we've had no more discussion about my attire; of course I've remained cognizant on meeting days to have at least a short-sleeved blouse on. No sense in making him anymore uncomfortable than he already is.

Our meeting agendas generally consist of updates on school and parish events. I learn quickly that Monsignor's concerns are primarily financial. He barely pays attention as I tell him of student achievements that show the skills of the teachers: sixth-grade teacher Gene's science lessons that include making active volcanoes as if they lived in Hawaii; fifth-grade teacher Mary's strong readers writing a play we hope to perform for the parish. I'm quick to praise the staff and highlight notable activities, inviting his participation.

"Sister, are you aware how much the electricity bill is? When you write your next weekly teacher bulletin, will you please advise the teachers to turn lights out whenever possible. The west side of the building gets plenty of light in the afternoons."

I don't mention that by the time the sunlight comes to that spot, the school day is over. Instead I smile and make a note.

Catholic schools like the one I attended in the 1950s—with two full classrooms per grade fully staffed by nuns and nominal tuition—are long gone. The urgency to promulgate Catholicism through education has declined, Protestantism no longer the threat I was once taught it was. Heaven has become open to more than just Catholics.

John F. Kennedy's election as the first Catholic president has helped promote better relations among different faiths, and Vatican II opened us up to a new world vision that includes all religions.

Today's Catholic schools serve predominantly as a choice for families. Some Catholic families who can continue to support the parish school, if there is one. The perception of stricter discipline and smaller classes has been one of the strongest reasons for recent enrollments by children of color.

Monsignor Maney sits next to the mahogany table by the Prince Street window, backlit by the cloudy day. I'm unable to see his eyes behind his dark horn-rimmed glasses. There are no lights on in the room. There is no coffee offered, no ceremony. Just business.

He continues his agenda.

"Sister, just after the Christmas holiday, we will be moving into the celebration of the country's bicentennial. The parish council has expressed an expectation that the school lead our activities."

I gulp and then smile. Local observances have already have begun in earnest, folks painting mailboxes and fire hydrants red, white, and blue, the wave of patriotism and nostalgia sweeping a nation exhausted by the Vietnam War and Watergate.

I think about my seventy-two-year-old uncle, a retired carpenter, who is building a new fence in front of the century-old farmhouse in Lima, a rural town outside of Rochester. He wants something he can paint that's bigger than a mailbox, his patriotism and pride in his country flagging his status as an Army veteran. But I doubt a patriotic paint job is what the parish council is hoping for.

I'm confident that the skilled teachers of Corpus Christi school can handle this celebration. It's one more thing on the long list of school curriculum, testing, parent conferences, and student counseling, but it is a staff that is up to the challenge.

As I learn more about the finances, I discover a surprisingly high percentage of families in this school pay the escalating tuition, bingo providing another large part of the teacher salaries and utility bills. Twenty-five percent of our student population is either Puerto Rican or black. Our faculty and staff includes service providers funded through federal Title I funds that help us to boast a strong program. Math lab, reading lab, speech therapy, social work, and psychologist services along with physical education and library services support our comprehensive curriculum. A school nurse is provided by county funds, and Sister Frances Marie and Sister Frances Cecilia serve as tutors, Francis in reading and math, Frances Cecelia in French. It's evident the school has been well run and, up till now, has held a place of pride in the parish. I only hope that can continue. Yet the fact that Monsignor sold the convent out from under the nuns does not bode well.

As the snows begin to melt and crocuses line the walkways outside the doors, signs of hope are intermingled with more change. Dear Father Brent is stepping down as superintendent of the diocesan schools. I feel a pang since he was the one who got me involved in administration to begin with. When I learn more about his plans, I can do nothing but celebrate. He's leaving to be married, his colleague and assistant Sister James the lucky bride.

What may become joy for many priests and nuns, once they've reached a decision to leave, is heartache for the Church, losing so many bright, articulate, and caring women and men. Still, I feel that new pathways to God are being forged.

The replacement for Father Brent is a well-regarded woman who can hopefully smooth some of the waters left murky from the CICP days. Sister Robertina, a School Sister of Notre Dame and former principal of Saint Philip Neri, brings years of dedicated service and smiling eyes, the most prominent thing I remember about her from past encounters. She has a reputation for being open and competent. I'm eager to meet with her.

Sunday nights I create the weekly teacher bulletin for delivery in mailboxes by Monday afternoon. I usually open it with an inspirational quote:

> *Darkness cannot drive out darkness; only light can do that. Hate cannot drive out hate; only love can do that. —Martin Luther King, Jr.*

The bulletin details upcoming events within the school and parish. I'm pleased that within the week of announcing the request from the parish council about a bicentennial celebration, a small group that includes the art teacher, music teacher, and two other staff members have volunteered to plan it. Talk of an essay contest has begun along with plans for dramatic readings taken from significant historical events. Excerpts from Martin Luther King Jr.'s "I Have A Dream" speech are included.

Meetings, phone calls, paperwork, and, when I can schedule them, classroom observations fill my days, along with occasional visits from classes of children, which I savor.

Twenty or more kindergarteners sit attentively in the spacious office, a converted classroom, as I tell them, as part of their lesson on community helpers, what a school principal does. After letting them see the PA system and where the school bell is kept, I sit behind my desk and pick up the papers in my in-basket.

"When I come to school, I, like you, have papers. After I read them, I put them in this box for Mrs. Malone. Then she comes and brings me more papers. We shuffle them all day long."

I wink at the teacher and giggle at the sad truth of my description. As I finish, a brown-haired, brown-skinned youngster raises his hand.

"Do you ever make paper airplanes with your papers? My teacher showed us how to make them and we can show you, too."

I smile inwardly.

I am awed to see that when misbehaving children, who seem few in number, respond to any scoldings I give, their fear and trembling of "The Principal" is firmly instilled. I find it a weighty responsibility.

The school's proximity to the Memorial Art Gallery a

block away provides an engine for the creative arts to the teachers who staff the school. Field trips, experiments, and performance are all a part of this interactive and innovative school.

When I can, I save visits to Clare's class for last, the artwork and quotes uplifting and inspiring. After one particularly difficult morning visit with a parent whose seven-year-old daughter has been defiant and rude to the teacher and to me, I gleaned an understanding of where the child had learned such behavior. On this day, I copy an Anne Frank quote from Clare's bulletin board filled with quotes. It becomes a daily reading for me, one that no belligerence, of child or parent, can overrule: "I still believe, in spite of everything, that people are truly good at heart."

38

CYNTHIA

SHE IS ONE OF THE BRIGHT ONES, serious and studious when she needs to be, sincere and sweet when that is called for. Her silky mocha skin shows her youth, no lines or creases interrupting smooth, rounded cheeks, the curve that accompanies her nervous smile flawless.

She wears her blue plaid uniform jumper and white blouse as sophisticatedly as anyone can, the skirt length within guidelines.

Her eyes dart around the former classroom that serves as the office and she sits on the edge of the cushioned armchair nearest the door, ready for flight.

She's here because the school nurse hopes I will counsel her not to carry her child to full term.

Of course what we hope for thirteen-year-olds who are babies themselves is time. Time for them to grow and mature and become all they are meant to be before they re-create themselves in their likenesses.

But not this one, whose perfectly shaped lips are set straight in determination. Her hips and stomach don't yet reveal the results of the pregnancy test, denial still possible.

Cynthia: a nickname for the Greek moon goddess Artemis, the virgin huntress, untamable, romantic, and regal, protector of young girls ... and, in a strange twist, also the goddess of childbirth. Cynthia tells of her own mother, dreams melted, hope gone. She tells of two other abortions, encouraged in the past by the nurse and the principal. But not this time. This child vows to be a better mother, one who will spend time with and love her baby, one who will be different, just you wait and see. Her vows carry her back to those other times they made her end her dream. This time she will bring this new baby to life; this time she will hold tight and this baby will be born and will be loved. There is no talk of a father, no reality that sharp. She is full of hope and innocence that has its own beauty, that place in time where one can dwell in possibility.

I listen, suspending judgment, hoping to learn from this gift, a chance to understand about something I may choose to vow away.

Hail Mary, full of grace, blessed art thou amongst women and blessed is the fruit of thy womb ...

An angel of love has appeared to Cynthia and she conceived of love. Her hope and her dream.

Her wish at age thirteen to walk with her classmates to receive her eighth grade diploma will not be granted. By the end of June her protruding belly will tell the tale of her active adolescent adventure into the adult sexual world. It's not for promulgation or display.

The time is past when pregnancy outside marriage would be shamed and punished. I have a youthful remembrance of Annalee and a few unwed mothers who came from the South to become live-in nannies in our predominantly Catholic neighborhood while they awaited the birth of their children.

It was a very real reminder to us young girls of consequences. Chances were their children would be adopted after their births, their reason for being away from home hidden from "polite" society.

Today's society, even the Catholic Church, offers more compassion and realism about innocent and precious new life. From Cynthia's perspective, lack of permission to participate in graduation may seem like punishment, dashing hopes again.

Abortion, for some, may be a choice to resolve the "problem," but not for this young teen. Neither shame nor difficulty will trump her desire, her love, for this child. I think of the irony that if she had chosen an abortion, she could have crossed the stage. With a few phone calls, a high school placement is promised. When I tell her, her eyes shine. But are they full of future hope? Or present sorrow?

39

TO KILL A MOCKINGBIRD

A THREAT OF SNOW is in the forecast though it's almost the end of April. The sun makes occasional appearances to warm this day that otherwise threatens to hit only forty degrees.

SISTER MEL AND I ARE SCHEDULEd for one of our afternoon visits to see her sister, Margaret, whose brain injury, sustained in a bicycle accident as a young child, has necessitated significant care. Since her parents' deaths, Margaret has lived at Newark Developmental Center in Newark, New York. Her nephew Mikey, with development delays due to Down Syndrome, is also a resident. Both are innocents, both overjoyed with visits from Mel. I'm happy to ride along.

Mel peeks her head in the school office door just as the private line phone rings. I wave her in and answer it.

It's a "fan-out," a process used to get messages to all the members of the congregation. Once I take the message, I'm to call it on to four other convents.

As I write down the message, I find my hand shaking.

"It is with deep sorrow that we share the news that earlier today, Tuesday, April 27, 1976, Sister Maureen Murphy has been arrested and accused of the murder of her infant son. Further information will be forthcoming. Sisters are asked to refrain from making any comment to the media."

My mind races ahead. *How can this be? How did ...? Who? Where?* My heart is pounding as I pass the paper to Mel. I watch her expression darken. Storm clouds appear from out of nowhere, making the steel gray sky more ominous.

I call the message forward to the four convents on my list. Each time I repeat the words, "accused of the murder of her infant son," I shiver and close my eyes to the images that flash before me. I hold back tears. I deliver the message verbatim, reiterating that questions will be answered tonight.

When I finish the last phone call, I look over at Mel. We sit in silence. What is there to do? I whisper a Hail Mary, choking back tears at the words "blessed is the fruit of thy womb."

Maureen, sweet, petite Maureen. Principal of the Montessori school, a place that nurtures young children. Maureen, whose spirit of innocence is a characteristic many take note of.

We finally depart, a suspended reality surrounding us. Neither of us knows Maureen that well. She lives at Our Lady of Lourdes Convent and is known as a shining star for her love of children.

A news bulletin is already on the radio: "Brighton nun arrested in death of infant son."

We drive the forty minutes to visit Margaret and Mikey in stunned disbelief, saying little.

Margaret, now grown beyond childhood, claps with joy at the Donald Duck dot-to-dot book; Mikey, a pre-adolescent boy, rubs the shiny cover of the car book. As we visit in the day room, where a television is suspended from the ceiling and florescent lights provide illumination, we see couches and tables filled with residents of varying abilities, some rocking, some staring, some drooling, others doing puzzles. I think about Maureen, a Montessori educator. Maria Montessori's early work was with children with special needs. She emphasized independence, freedom within limits, and respect for the natural development of children.

It's impossibly sad to put Maureen's vocation and devotion to children together with her alleged action of taking the life of an infant.

While the forecast for snow never materializes, our spirits are chilled. We drive the forty minutes home and Mel drops me at Bay Street, both of us glad of the trip. I am not looking forward to the awaiting weather from within.

At the house meeting, facts are scant. We are told a trial is pending. Details are sparse, the newspapers filling in gaps. Maureen told the house coordinator she was staying home from work with stomach cramps. That afternoon a Sister found her bleeding and unconscious. Two Sisters took her to the hospital where it was determined that she had given birth. The Sisters went back to her room and found an infant boy in the wastebasket, wrapped in plastic with panties stuffed in his mouth.

I wince and force myself to stay for the prayer service, a biblical quote creeping into me:

> *And she brought forth her firstborn son, and wrapped him in swaddling clothes, and laid him in a manger; because there was no room for them in the inn.*

Together we sing, gentle words needed, faith faltering.

> *Lord, make me an instrument of Your peace.*
> *Where there is hatred, let me sow love;*
> *Where there is injury, pardon;*
> *Where there is doubt, faith;*
> *Where there is despair, hope;*

Where there is darkness, light;
Where there is sadness, joy.

How could such a thing happen? How could it even be imagined?

I'm thirty-one years old. This could be me. I dreamt once I had a baby girl and left her with Mother Agnes Cecelia as her babysitter. I had awakened from the dream joyful.

Oh my God, poor Maureen.

The poor Sisters at Lourdes. Eleven others who lived with Maureen. Eleven whose lives are changed forever.

Two weeks earlier I sat across from Maureen at a conference. A friend had called my attention to her swollen ankles. "I hope she doesn't have heart trouble," she said.

She surely does now. We all do.

Mockingbirds don't do one thing
but make music for us to enjoy.

-Harper Lee, To Kill A Mockingbird

40

THE DAYS AFTER

I STARE OUT MY BEDROOM WINDOW, across the school building roof to the trees beyond, leaves just coming in, the bright lime-green color so emblematic of this season of rebirth. Just ten days ago we were celebrating Easter, singing Alleluias and songs of Resurrection.

Over Easter recess, I'd visited home, pleased that my mother's health remains stable. I'd taken time to catch up on schoolwork. School's been back in session just two days. It feels like eternity.

I breathe tentatively, afraid of loosening the floodwaters that lurk within me. I have to get to school.

Images of Maureen and the baby keep flashing in my mind, her situation so impossible. The depth of what must have been her anguish fills me. Every fiber of me understands her shame, her desperation. Tears fill my eyes and I shake myself.

The morning newspaper has more detail: Maureen's loss of blood after the birth causing loss of consciousness, intimations that she temporarily lost her mind. That's all it can be, I tell myself. Can desperation and shame cause one to take a child's life?

At our Wednesday faculty meeting, Marie, faculty leader for the day, leads the prayer for Maureen and all the Sisters that healing may begin. Somehow we carry on, little said, drying our tears and wondering. The next morning after the faculty meeting I find a bouquet of flowers from the faculty with a simple note: "Our prayers are with all the Sisters."

This, I think, is what community means. Caring and compassion when it is so needed.

Next to the flowers is another note from little Mary, the student who had been so rude some weeks ago. An apology, I hope. When I open the card, I burst out laughing. Instead of an apology, a crayon-drawn portrait is enclosed, of me I imagine, with a note that says, "You are a big fat dope. My mother told me." I tuck the card into the edge of my blotter next to the Anne Frank quote. A perfect combination.

The phone rings and I take the call. "This is Mrs. Isquerardo, Diane's mother." I listen as sixth grader Diane's mother tells her tale of frustration about the teacher who is tutoring her daughter. She's making her do homework. That doesn't seem fair. I suggest a meeting as I listen to the barrage of injustices that are lining up. "The tutor is Sister Francis Marie. She's here on Monday, Wednesday, and Thursday mornings. What day would you be able to meet with her?" I ask politely.

As we settle the date, I thank Mrs. Isquerardo for her concern. "We'll be able to settle things next week when you come in. Thank you so much for your call," I say.

I jot a note to Francis Marie, aware that she will be brilliant in this meeting. I can hardly wait.

The water's swift movements calm me. I look out over the blue-black expanse and am reminded of things eternal, things that go on with or without me. I move toward the water's edge, the chilly liquid lapping onto the stony beach. I lean down and pick up skipping stones, round flat ones that can glide over the surface. With each one I send skimming across, slight ripples move toward the shore and disappear. I skip another and watch it sink. It leaves no void, the waters undisturbed. I stand still and watch the waves as if in a trance, hearing their soft lapping on the shore.

I'm thirty-one years old. I've careened through my career with luck and grace. Memories of my years at the Foreman Center fill me with joy, friendships formed, children tucked in my heart. Round-faced six-year-old Christopher Brown's exclamation when I tie his shoe, "That was bery good, Miss Osta."

I smile when I think of Francis Xavier, the SWING grant I was awarded my first year at the school. I still see the eighth-grade boys cleaning up the yard, leaves sticking to the tines of their rakes, pride gleaming on their faces.

The innocence of the first graders at Francis Xavier and Holy Redeemer, the shiny-faced children who line up as we instruct and who bring joy because they can't help it. Diane's pink barrettes, Rosella's light peeking out briefly from under the bushel of fear and hurts she has hidden it under, Cynthia's glow; so many others for whom my hopes and fears are visceral, whose ultimate fates I may never know.

Soft air pushes past my cheek. I need to get back to the convent for dinner, then to a board meeting tonight to discuss the latest financial bad news for Corpus.

I'm glad I've taken this detour on the way back from my dentist appointment. A favorite spot, this rocky outcropping on Lake Ontario across the street from the popular Don and Bob's Diner and ice cream stand brings me closer to calm than I have been in weeks. The spring sun slants toward the water, creating a glistening pathway I wish I could walk on.

Was it just last year I was at Saint Michael's? Did we really open and close it the same year? I shake my head, disbelieving. I won't soon forget the Clinton Avenue Boys, the reality of gangs in the city. Nor will I forget the goodness of the co-pastors Tony and Paul, their support warm and personal right up to the end when they gave Clare and me two classroom mementos, intricately hand-carved German crucifixes.

I walk down the shoreline beyond some driftwood and let my mind drift to other things. Speculation is that the trial date for Maureen will be set for the first part of next year. The Sisters at Lourdes are holding up with admirable nobility—and are fragile. Maureen's location isn't disclosed except to a very few. I don't ask. The Leadership Team, the new governing group of six women elected at the last General Chapter, are remarkable in their compassion and competence under the masterful direction of the new president, Sister Jamesine.

The question of Maureen's continuing membership in the congregation has been resolved by consensus, affirmation of the decision resonating in each separate congregational community. She stays.

At Francis Xavier, support for Maureen is unanimous. The reality is still too difficult to absorb. There is no quarrel; the congregation will pay for her bail. We number six hundred and seventy-seven, counting Maureen. A new solidarity has arisen.

I look down the shoreline to realize I've come quite a distance. Cottages that seem too close to the edge, erosion a continuing issue, loom above me. Time to turn back, I decide.

With the west sun behind me, I think about tonight's parish board meeting. I had recently arranged for Monsignor to meet with Sister Barbara, a respected colleague and friend who after the CICP days went to work for the urban vicar's office.

She did her best to prepare him for what was happening financially at the diocesan level. The looming bottom line indicates dwindling funds and less subsidy money for the schools.

Monsignor Maney was the proud pastor of Corpus Christi parish for just over twenty years. The church and school have the distinction of having been started by the Most Reverend Bernard J. McQuaid, DD, first Bishop of Rochester. His design included a school, an idea that was to be replicated throughout the diocese. Built in 1888 of the distinctive, durable, reddish-colored Medina stone quarried nearby, the church with no bells or steeple has long stood the test of time. Yet more tests are to come.

Sister Barbara, her neat ash-blonde hair and business-like demeanor a suitable match, her arms appropriately covered, did her best to be clear with Monsignor that securing school funds for the future was an issue, the diocese no longer able to provide assistance.

"Parishes I've met with so far seem up to the challenge," Barbara said, maintaining eye contact with Monsignor. "Some are considering raising tuition. Others may hold an extra bingo night. Some are looking into other fundraisers."

As if she hadn't yet spoken, Monsignor Maney spoke. "Sister, I have spoken directly to the bishop several times."

It was clear he was agitated, his voice rising to a higher pitch. "I'm very concerned about getting my organ repaired. It's a priority. I understand about fiscal constraints but this organ is very historic and can't be let go."

Barbara and I exchanged glances, glad that Monsignor's reassignment to another parish had been already been announced for the fall. It will be a change for the parish but clearly it is time.

His twenty-year tenure, first as administrator and then as pastor, has been noteworthy on many accounts, but his last act of selling the convent without communicating with the Sisters seriously eroded his leadership. Prior to that, in his day, he'd received great accolades serving at one time as secretary to Bishop James E. Kearney. Popes Pius XII and John XXIII had also honored him. He was well traveled and at one time served as vicar general of the diocese, but resigned within a year upon his physician's recommendation. He did keep his role as chaplain of the Newman Club of the Eastman School of Music, which may have helped fuel his vehemence about the organ repair. Whatever his reasons, I sense that once he understands the dreary financial situation, these coming days will be rough.

My gaze across the lake, which seems like an ocean with no northern shoreline visible, thrills me. Then like a breaking wave, I'm suddenly aware of how weary I am.

I recall the fan-out from early this morning. I flashed back momentarily to the one about Maureen. This new announcement wasn't as shocking but it was certainly daunting. Sister David Mary is going on leave from the congregation. David Mary, whose visits to Francis Xavier always buoyed me up. David Mary who gave me hope, her style of leadership sensible and sensitive. Well regarded and beloved by so many, David Mary, who introduced me to Monsignor Maney. A meeting to discuss it is being held tomorrow. Until then, we're asked to say nothing. I wish some word of why could be shared. She's a vital, talented, and attractive woman. I hope it's love that is taking her from us.

We've said nothing about so many things of late. The

looming presence of unwanted reporters and television journalists has not entirely subsided. Ms. magazine's Catherine Breslin has met enough "no comment" answers that she stopped pursuing those of us in the congregation and those who taught with Maureen. Yet her evident persistence is disturbing, talk of a book to be published difficult to accept.

I try to take deep breaths but they don't come. I pick up a few more stones. I skid one across into the stream of sunlight, its run splattering softly. It seems to dance along the water forever.

Questions start to push their way in. What will happen next? How do I keep going? I toss my last stone and let it plunk into the depths of the waters. Eternal waves capture it and it is gone.

It's time I climb the hill to the car that will carry me back to home, my sanctuary that seems to have serious cracks in the walls.

41

THE FALL OF 1976

I SIT ON MOM'S FRONT PORCH as I sip my coffee. The tree-lined street with 1920s homes is charming and calming. The neighbor's red, purple, and yellow mums are vibrant. Mom's hanging geranium basket is still flourishing.

I awoke this morning looking forward to returning to Rochester for a dinner meeting with Sister Robertina, the new diocesan superintendent. She's asked if I could meet with her Monday night.

I'm glad for the weekend home with Mom and Dad, glad to find them both in good condition. Their list of medicines grows while their pace slows, yet their spirits continue to lift me up. They listen to my school tales and are eager to learn what the dinner with Robertina is about. I am too.

While music plays from the kitchen radio, Dad sits in his chair at the Formica kitchen table, the Sunday crossword almost solved. After Mom fusses in the galley part of the kitchen, she retires to the second-floor den where she tunes in to a Sunday movie, the old ones her favorites.

I leave early enough Sunday night to have a leisurely drive back to Rochester. I smile as I think of my latest exchange with Dad. Once we returned from Mass at the cathedral in downtown Syracuse, Father Champlain more pleasing to Mom and Dad's aging theology, I set about cleaning a bit, because I could.

After I cleaned out the refrigerator, I rearranged it to accommodate the new big bottle of cranberry juice that both Mom and Dad have recently learned is good for health. I'm glad they care enough to try whatever will prolong their lives.

After a few minutes of poking and prodding, I proudly swung the door open so Dad could approve the new arrangement.

"Look Dad," I proclaimed as I pointed to the top shelf, "I've fixed the fridge so you can reach the cranberry juice easier. I put the milk on the side and slid the condiments back."

Dad looked up from his paper and surveyed my handiwork from a distance. "Why, that's lovely, dear," he said. "Once you've gone back, it shouldn't take us too long to put things back the way we like them."

I smiled, learning a new lesson in effective helping.

On my Thruway drive, one I've become so accustomed to over these thirteen years in Rochester, I listen to classical music and think about the upcoming dinner meeting on Monday night.

Robertina seems a good fit in her role as the new diocesan superintendent. She's fair, open, and has an easy chuckle. Her brown eyes and reddish hair remind me of my Irish relatives. At the opening fall diocesan education orientation meeting, she received a standing ovation from the principals and teachers after her remarks.

She spoke with empathy, acknowledging the difficult times we are all facing, her own first year on the job not excluded. "Beside declining enrollments, and increasing heating and utility costs that are driving our tuition costs higher, we have to contend with fewer parishioners contributing fewer dollars."

She charmed the audience of mostly women, fewer in religious orders than in past years, as she told of her own years in the classroom, her time as a principal. "Often," she recalled, "my favorite time was the weekend." Laughter filled the room as she continued.

"This is a call," she said, "a call to serve. It brings us together and will keep us together."

Her simple smile and peaceful presence brought calm to us all. She ended with a a statement of gratitude for all assembled assuring them that Thoreau was a good guide for our schools that excelled because of love.

> *Do not hire a man who does your work for money,*
> *but him who does it for love of it.*

As I pull into 314 Bay Street, I feel refreshed, remembering the weekend that has just ended as I look forward to learning more from Robertina.

Monday night I drive over to Guiseppe's, a little Italian neighborhood restaurant across from Bausch & Lomb on Goodman Street. We're not far from Francis Xavier or Saint Philip Neri Convent where Robertina lives. Saint Philip Neri is the next parish over. Like Francis Xavier, it's an Italian parish, but it's not as poor as Francis Xavier. Everything east of Goodman Street is a bit brighter and better kept up, increasingly so as one moves further from the center of the city.

Once seated across from this woman of position and purpose, I scan the room for parishioners, something that is becoming a habit even though I don't wear a habit. Both

Robertina and I wear contemporary dress: conservative dark skirts, blouses, jackets, sensible shoes. Many religious of the day wear some kind of outward religious symbol—a cross or crucifix—as jewelry. We don't stand out in a crowd as religious women, but we are recognizable. Tonight Robertina wears a silver chain and simple silver crucifix around her neck. I have my pewter pin crucifix on the lapel of my jacket.

I've taken up smoking again, saving money from my monthly fifty dollars to buy my Lark cigarettes, though I'm careful not to smoke in public places where I might create a scandal, something I'm sensitive about. It's important, I think, to let people, and especially children, keep their illusions of Sisters.

My own illusions are jarred a little bit when Robertina orders a Manhattan. I know nuns drink. I drink too, and was responsible for bringing one of the first six-packs of beer to Francis Xavier. Beer has since settled in as a regular item on the grocery list. I know others like myself who smoke. So why am I so stunned when this prominent figure in the diocesan structure orders a Manhattan? I guess it's okay to order my Johnny Walker Red on the rocks, and I do. No scandal given or taken from the waiter's nonchalance at our orders.

Robertina, a School Sister of Notre Dame, their Motherhouse in Wilton, Connecticut, had been principal at Philip Neri until she began her role as assistant superintendent for curriculum and then deputy superintendent. She's the first woman superintendent for the Rochester diocese and the first woman to be in attendance at the otherwise all-male statewide superintendents' conference in New York City. It's about time, she says.

Maybe even too late, I think, as our crisis in funding and other challenges continue to unfold.

As we chat over our cocktails, I learn that her congregation, the SSNDs, a predominantly education-oriented congregation, have missions around the world, some as far away as Guam. We swap stories of travel, family, and mutual friends as we sip and order our meals.

Our conversation shifts to the local stories and I recount tales from the farewell dinner held last spring for Monsignor Maney, a homespun event filled with laughter, those in attendance aware that the good Monsignor was relieved to no longer be responsible for overseeing the decline of the parish he helped build.

His work was lauded for stabilizing the budget in his early administrative days and later opening the way, as Vatican II decreed, for a strong parish council.

I told her one of the great quotes of the evening. "Monsignor knew when to hold 'em and when to fold 'em," school board president Phil said in his remarks.

Lucia, the most veteran teacher on the faculty, presented a book of poetry made by students along with her own remarks. "Monsignor, you've brought us music, a lasting gift," she said, her reference to the organ that Monsignor Maney secured for the parish many years ago, the same one for which he was still seeking repairs before leaving.

Robertina's eager to learn more of the nitty-gritty of parish life that affects the schools. "You and I both know, Betty, that these schools are often the center of parish life." The schools bring in families who are the backbones of church volunteer work. The schools hold events that pull the community together. Even bingo is a community builder. Will the parishes be able to pull together without the financial "burden" of contribution to the schools? Or will they just decline faster, having lost their reason for participating?

Robertina wants to know about Monsignor Maney's replacement, Father Delaney, a weary, balding middle-aged man. She's also interested in learning more about the assistant pastor, Father Jim Cullen, assigned to Corpus late last year after he rejected an assignment at the wealthier Saint Aloysius parish.

She asks about him first. "Do you know anything more than the newspapers say about why he wouldn't take the assignment at Saint Aloysius?"

"He found the opulence offensive," I say, "the rectory was too nice." I remember Sister Elaine's lesson on poverty, the cost incurred when one doesn't use the housing already provided by the parish, ultimately more expensive in the long run. I recall Sister Elaine's lesson on poverty of spirit about what seemed to me to be an opulent gift of the gold cross, given with love and good will by my mother; I learned to receive it with good will and a thank you. To make a show of spurning such a gift can be ego-driven self-righteousness, I learned, and hurtful to the giver. Even Jesus did not spurn the expensive oils that Mary Magdalene lavished on him, Elaine shared, but instead was grateful.

Robertina raises her eyebrows and takes another sip of her Manhattan. I watch as she starts her salad and wait before I speak again, trusting her with what I am about to tell her.

"Robertina," I say directly, "it hasn't taken long to discover Father Cullen's aversion toward Catholic education. He can barely sustain a conversation with me, often scurrying away whenever talk turns to the school."

I poke at the lettuce leaves as I consider how much to tell of all I know. I see she's listening and go on. "Sister Marcy, one of the junior high teachers from our convent, has become good friends with him. She tells us he doesn't believe maintaining schools with such small populations is the best use of church resources."

We both eat a few more bites, digesting this information.

"He's also," I say evenly as I finish my salad, "opposed to bingo." Though I have only been in the parochial school leadership for two years and teaching within the system for three, I know without a doubt that suggesting bingo be messed with is about as heretical as saying one doesn't believe in the pope. Bingo is Catholic education's cash cow.

"Father Cullen believes that people already struggling with gambling addictions are being invited weekly to spend what little money they have gambling." I slide my salad plate away and wait for Robertina's reaction.

"Though his point is well taken," she says as she finishes her salad, "I doubt he'll be able to unseat it. It's become a time-honored tradition in Catholic churches and we are known for running fair games in safe environments. The people who come are faithful." I sip my scotch and remember the time last spring when I took a turn calling the numbers for bingo. Amidst cries of, "Call my number, Sister!" that accompanied each draw from the metal caged drum, I observed laughter among families who played this game of chance with hope and faith and pure communal enjoyment. On the other hand, there were clearly a few people who were obsessing, truly gambling. Some folks can't take the wine at Communion due to alcohol addiction. It is hard to weigh the costs and benefits.

I'm grateful that Robertina and I are seated in a booth that provides privacy for our conversation as we mention names and discuss personality issues. She slides her empty Manhattan glass aside, an indication she won't have another. I take a last swallow of my scotch with a piece of warm Italian bread. As our entrees arrive, I'm glad for my choice of eggplant parmesan, its crisp breading and chunky marinara sauce inviting. Robertina's rare prime rib, garnished with greens and potato, also looks delicious.

Robertina doesn't ask again about Father Delaney and I'm relieved. I'm happy to keep what I know about him to myself for now. I don't tell her of the recent staff meeting when I was left alone with Father Delaney, of his slurred speech, his groping hands, and my hasty exit. She wants to know more about Father Cullen.

"Actually, neither priest seems very invested in the school," I conclude.

Robertina slides away her plate and shifts in her chair.

"I wanted to meet in person," she says, "because these coming days may prove to be a bit more difficult. I know you and your congregation have already had your share of difficulties."

This unspoken reference to Maureen is gentle, and enough.

She continues on to talk about the diocesan subsidy, the monies set aside for education. I know before she says it that the amount for Corpus Christi is being reduced. I gulp when I hear how significantly reduced.

"We went over the numbers several times and several different ways. Even with the support from the parish, what we can offer as the diocesan subsidy isn't enough to keep your school open."

I wish I had that last sip of scotch left and wince. "Can you tell me more?"

I hadn't expected this so soon, hoping for more time. When Sister Barbara met with Monsignor Maney last spring, he didn't seem worried. His focus, I realize now, wasn't on the school. Shortly after that meeting his new assignment was announced.

We order coffee and I ask, "Who else knows about this?"

She looks at me evenly, her auburn eyebrows raising as she speaks. "Betty, that's just the reason I wanted to meet with you privately. The press will be all over this and we want to spare families as much anguish as we can. Your school board is good, right?" she asks hopefully.

"Yes, very good," I say confidently, Paul's face coming into focus. He's the secretary's husband, father of three children, their oldest having graduated last year from Corpus. "We have a very active school board," I say feeling some hope. Paul has been a hero of sorts throughout my year and a half here, keeping the school board responsive and open. He's been a lead player in making sure bingo stays in place. He's the only reason the board meetings are worth attending, keeping the politics and in-fighting to a minimum.

"You leave the financial worries to us," he tells me time and again. "Your job is to keep good education happening."

It has also been a relief to have the rectory parish administrator collect the tuition money and write the payroll checks, arrangements Paul made for us.

I tell Robertina about a new faculty member who's joined us at Saint Francis Xavier, Sister Eileen. "She's been a welcome addition and appears to be a masterful teacher," I say of the dark-haired Irish woman who has become an easy part of our convent life. She makes friends easily and reads a situation with skill before barging in. And she adores Sister Francis

Marie.

Robertina twirls her coffee cup around on the saucer. "I'm glad to hear there's an active board. And your strong faculty will be a help. We'll be setting up a meeting soon. I'll want you there as well as your faculty. We'll need to work together on this one."

I've been through the closing of Francis Xavier, Saint Michael's, and the CICP schools. Am I ready for more?

I look up at Robertina, nod, and sip my coffee. Her soft brown eyes warm me. As we go out into the night, I sigh, grateful for the opportunity to work with this woman of such skill and sensitivity.

42

LAST FRIDAY

THE DAYS DARKEN as December turns into January. No definitive word about the future of the school has been given. From my office, I can see the rectory, yet the distance between the church staff and the school seems to be widening. Communication from the rectory office secretary is terse and infrequent, the light banter of previous phone calls missing.

A favorite line of Mrs. V.'s that I jotted down is: "The Lord fits the back to the burden." I certainly hope so. From what she doesn't say, I suspect things are changing at the rectory as well; new alliances are being formed, the school no longer in her favor. When I ask to speak to Jim, she says in a measured voice, "Father Cullen is unavailable." To whom, I wonder.

I say little about anything. I feel I am walking on eggshells. I had shared with Robertina the gossip both from the school staff and the nuns in the convent that Father Cullen is actively advocating to end bingo as a church-sponsored activity. He is mute on how else we will raise the money.

I watch as Father Delaney slips deeper into the morass of the drink. His eyes are runny, his black suit jacket often stained, his thin hair uncombed. His decline leaves Father Cullen the de facto pastor. I feel the weight of so many things tumbling down around me. Thank goodness for Paul, the school board president. His optimism and skill in negotiating are talents I treasure. A major meeting will be scheduled soon, I suspect.

Meantime I listen and wonder.

Our first week back to classes in the New Year brings a change for our First Friday Mass celebrations. Father Cullen will now be the celebrant, replacing Father Delaney. I can only guess at the reason. I receive an informal note from the rectory, with no signature, welcoming all the children grades three through eight to attend. This will be a distinct change from Father Cullen's previous non-participation with the school. His friendship with one of our teachers, Sister Marcie, may be of help, I hope.

First Friday Mass, a time-honored devotion in the Church, is rooted in a seventeenth-century apparition to a young French nun, Margaret Mary Alacoque. Attendance at nine First Friday Masses with special prayers offered to the Sacred Heart of Jesus, it is said, will result in the fulfillment of twelve special promises, the last of which is that you will not die without receiving the sacraments, the Sacred Heart a safe refuge in the last moment.

As a teenager, I knew nothing of the promises of the Sacred Heart but I did have a keen appreciation of First Fridays and attended faithfully, especially during my senior year at Most Holy Rosary High School in Syracuse. We were given a delayed start to our classes so that after Mass we could break our overnight fast, a requirement before Communion in those days. Cars and freedom coupled with a free hour found us meeting up at different restaurant each month, laughter and strengthening friendships unintended benefits. My favorite was the Syracuse Hotel and eggs Benedict.

On this First Friday, as I shepherd the children and teachers into the church, I'm not quite sure what to expect with Father Cullen as celebrant for the school children. I've attended several Thursday night Masses, which are drawing more and more people, some from outside the parish boundaries. Many find him to be a charismatic preacher. Father Delaney's gentle and passive style worked well to include all the children. His services were brief and respectful of the children's point of view.

I silently have questioned if we should be insisting that our school children of other Christian traditions attend the Catholic rituals. I don't pose the question publicly and am pleased when Sister Clare affirms the same line of thought by including a teaching unit about other religious faiths into her eighth-grade curriculum.

"They should know about each other's rituals and traditions," she said. She is well regarded by her students and the faculty; her opinion matters.

Jimmy, a slick-haired, dark-eyed Puerto Rican boy from her class, has spent numerous hours with me in the office when his chatterbox behavior has become too much. He was proud to tell me of his new role in this ecumenical adventure.

"Sister Clare says we're going to learn about each other's churches. I'm gonna play the drums to tell about mine."

An Evangelical church on Goodman Street close to Norton has become a popular place of worship for some of the Latino families. The popularity of guitars and drums has spread to many churches, the "Folk Mass" now popular in the Catholic Church as a result of Vatican II's liturgical reforms.

The shift to modern folk music for the Mass instead of organ and Gregorian chant has not been without its naysayers. Many, myself included, have been schooled in Gregorian chant, its majestic splendor, punctums and all, unparalleled. Yet I find a new energy and aliveness in the lyrics of new songs, their tunes staying with me long after the Mass, especially, Ray Repp's "Allelu":

Allelu, allelu, everybody sing allelu,
for the Lord has risen, it is true.
Everybody sing allelu.

The fact that so many young people are composing songs of praise and adoration pays off. Popular songs from Joe Wise, Ray Repp, and even Joan Baez and Peter, Paul and Mary make their way into Catholic Folk Masses, spurring a much-needed resurgence in church attendance, especially among the young. Father Peter Scholtes's song,"They'll Know We Are Christians By Our Love," and his "Missa Bossa Nova Folk Mass" have made waves throughout the Catholic community and have brought a whole new world of sound to the ears and hearts of the faithful.

As this First Friday Mass gets underway, I hum "They'll Know We Are Christians" to myself as I watch students filing in their usual orderly fashion into the pews and kneeling with appropriate reverence. It is Christianity, after all, that we celebrate, and I relieve any misgivings with the knowledge that most of these children share a Christian background. Watching their quiet wonder in church, I feel joy, and feel more justified for their required presence here. I sit in the back, a watchful eye as the usual fidgeting and fussing erupt here and there, as always happens whenever groups of children are herded into confined spaces. Teachers give their sternest looks and the children settle down.

Father Cullen, generally well groomed, wears his straight brown hair in a bowl cut, bangs coming down around his striking baby blue eyes and pockmarked face. Today there is a small bandage on his left cheek, a shaving mishap, I suspect. As he comes out onto the altar, he steps down in front of it, not a usual place. The children don't notice the difference but we adults do. We wait for what is next. Sounding like Mr. Rogers, Father invites the children to come to Jesus's Mass and be a part of his remembrance table. I take a deep breath.

I've attended a few Thursday night Masses where he invites those in attendance to stand with him in the sanctuary during the consecration, the space around the altar ordinarily reserved for those ordained to celebrate the Mass. I gulp, hoping he knows better than to invite these fidgety youngsters to stand with him.

I needn't have worried about where the children would stand. Instead of inviting the children forward, he steps down one more step closer to the pews and begins to tell them the tale of the Crucifixion in his own words.

"Boys and girls," he says, as he raises his arms, "you know that Jesus has died for our sins. Every time we do something that we know is not right, we know we can be forgiven because Jesus has died for us."

He moves back up a step and centers himself under the crucifix that is above the altar.

"Can you imagine him as he is nailed to the cross, blood dripping from his arms?" He raises his eyes and arms higher.

I cringe. I want to stop him. He goes on.

"Look up at me, boys and girls. See my arms," he says as he stretches his arms out, the alb flowing downward. "See the wounds where the nails are going through them?"

My stomach is churning. I watch as this young man, who is close to my own age at just under thirty years old, creates a scene of horror for innocent children, many of whom may have no one at home to help soften the tale he tells. I catch my breath and feel my heart pound.

I've studied the Crucifixion intensely during my novitiate years, even drawing diagrams in my notebooks of the crucified Christ. But I have done this as an adult religious woman. I take another deep breath as he continues.

"Watch here, children, watch here." His eyes roll up toward the ceiling, his arms extended as if on a cross. He draws the attention to himself and when he seems satisfied that the children are all looking forward he says:

"Do you see Jesus? I am being nailed to the cross."

His baby blue eyes are looking out at the back of the church, not focused. They seem glassy. He doesn't put down his arms for what seems a very long time. He stands squarely in the center of the steps, his medium height and slight build planted solidly. The children watch and so do I. What is he trying to do? I wonder if he is rational. He seems unearthly in his story telling, his voice raspy. It's not clear to me if he is aware of his surroundings, if he realizes these are young, impressionable children in front of him. I wonder if he knows there is anyone in front of him. It feels as if something very wrong is happening. What on earth is he trying to prove?

This priest, who has caused dismay in the diocese, who is the center in the parish of rumors of change, is now going overboard with little children, acting as if he is Jesus. This shouldn't be.

The children don't fidget but the adults shift uncomfortably. I feel my own concern turn to anger as I watch this "show" continue.

"I am dying to forgive your sins. To forgive everyone's sins.

I am Jesus."

Oh my. Now he's actually said it. Does he believe it? My anxiety escalates, my breathing erratic. How can I stop him? His eyes remain raised above those of us in the congregation. He trembles a bit. I am afraid he will faint.

He finally puts his arms down and turns up the steps and goes back up to the altar. He quietly prepares the chalice and blesses the hosts. Then with the same unearthly dramatic voice, as he elevates the round wafer, he proclaims:

Take this, all of you, and eat of it:
for this is my body which will be given up for you.

He genuflects and continues, his eyes rolled upwards:

Take this, all of you, and drink from it:
for this is the chalice of my blood,
the blood of the new and eternal covenant,
which will be poured out for you and for many
for the forgiveness of sins.
Do this in memory of me.

There is a pause and a prayer, then a rustling of pages, and he begins to lead the Our Father, his voice sounding more normal. The church fills with the sound of children's voices.

Thankfully, he does not invite the children up around the altar at Communion time, but rather comes down the steps with the chalice full of hosts. The teachers monitor the Communion line as it goes forward, inviting only those children who've received their First Communion, one way to tell whether or not the children are Catholic. We are stepping ever so slowly towards ecumenism, but the Eucharist is still reserved only for Catholics

I am in the back and can't hear what Father Cullen says to each child as he distributes the host. I can only hope the passion play has ended.

As I join in the line to receive the host, I look closely to see if his eyes are focused. They seem to be.

I feel great relief when I hear the words, "The Mass is ended, go in peace."

I go to the doorway and guide the children out, their orderly conduct a comfort compared to the dramatic orchestration of this Mass. I trust the teachers to nurture and comfort the little ones as needed.

I follow along behind, glancing at the altar as I leave. Father Cullen has genuflected and left. I wonder as I walk across the parking lot if this should be the last First Friday.

43

I AM . . . I SAID . . .

ONCE AGAIN I SEEK SOLACE in the back pew of Saint Francis Xavier, watching the flicker of the vigil lights as they cast dancing spirits on the ceiling in front. All is silent but for two older women bent over the pew in prayer, their rosary beads softly clicking through their fingers. I imagine the comfort they find in this time-honored repetitive prayer.

I think about my own pale blue rosary beads, the silver crucifix with the tiny image of Christ, a gift from my godmother Ceil. I still see her silver hair, dark eyes, and gentle smile. I remember times with her at our table on Ruskin Avenue in Syracuse, me nestled next to her—my special place, my special person.

I wonder about the beads. Does the feel of them provide comfort as they are touched briefly, each Hail Mary lifted to heaven?

I have long since stopped saying the rosary, a family tradition begun in my childhood. How do I pray now? My mind wanders at Mass, the pages of my breviary bringing less comfort, the Biblical references to slaying enemies frustrating me. Yet I carry the belief in the goodness of God, the goodness of life. I cling tenaciously to a feeling from deep within that brings me to tears of joy. Is it God within me? The same God who has led me to this call of religious life? The same God who now is hearing my questions? I bury my head in my hands to block out distractions. I feel the familiar tears. For now it is enough.

Tonight, there is only Sadie and me, she sound asleep after her first full day home from a weeks' long stay at the infirmary, recovered almost completely from her bout with pneumonia. I noted earlier as I brought her tea that her blue eyes are still a bit runny, her tiny frame more frail. The familiar wisp of white hair peeks out from her nightcap. She is ready for sleep, she says.

"Once I say my prayers, I'll sleep in the arms of Morpheus."

She is a delight to live with, her joy and lack of complaint inspiring. We are glad for her return, glad to be recipients of her wisdom and peace. She is glad, too, to be back.

"It was all right out there at the infirmary," she says, "but it's better to be here."

And it's better to have you here, I think.

I tiptoe away and slip down the stairs, warmed by her presence, knowing our days with her are sliding on.

It is a great comfort that eighty-eight-year-old Sister Francis Marie Kehoe, whom we call Sadie, has returned. When she became ill with pneumonia, we collectively determined it was best to find her professional care. Where better than the congregation's infirmary, a brick building behind the motherhouse, where full-time staff would see her back to health? We were of one mind that this was to be only a short-term arrangement; that Sadie would return. Sadie was in full agreement.

"Oh, it's good you brought Sister Francis Marie here to us," the receiving Sister at the infirmary said as we wheeled Sadie into the building. "To you folks, pneumonia is a huge thing. To us out here, it's no big deal." Our doubts about letting her out of our sight redoubled with that statement; we wanted a big deal made over our dear Sadie. Luckily Sadie had stamina to overcome it all and return to her "mission."

It will also be good to have her back at school soon, I think, recalling the meeting that Sadie and I had with Mrs. Isquerardo, Diane's mother, who came with a list of grievances about this tutor working with her daughter who dared to assign homework.

After I took Mrs. Isquerardo's plaid wool coat and hung it next to mine on the back of my door, I offered her coffee, noting her head of soft brown curls and her pretty bow lips highlighted in pink lipstick. *Diane has her mother's looks and will look like this eventually*, I thought. After I got the coffee, I went to the small room behind the office where Sister Francis Marie did her tutoring.

Pens and pencils neatly placed on the table, clean paper in a stack, she looked pert in her black dress, the veil pressed and falling neatly on her shoulders. She stood when I entered, picking up a manila folder. "Is she here?"

I nodded, certain that the complaints could be addressed one by one without incident.

When we entered the office, Mrs. Isquerardo who had been polite to me, stood when she saw Sister Francis Marie.

"Oh Sister, I didn't realize ... I didn't mean to ..."

I invited her to sit down, indicated a chair for Francis Marie, and made a formal introduction.

"Mrs. Isquerardo, I know you called with concerns about Diane's tutoring program," I said, "I'm sure Sister can help sort them out."

Mrs. Isquerardo's eyes were glowing as she looked at Francis Marie's habit. "I didn't realize you were a real Sister," she said apologetically.

Francis smiled and said, "Your Diane is a bright girl. If she put a little more effort into her work, she wouldn't need tutoring. She's learning her times tables." She opened the folder she'd brought with her. "Here's something I've been helping her with. Maybe you could too," she said, as she handed a paper to Mrs. Isquerardo.

Mrs. Isquerardo looked briefly at the paper and then at Sister Francis Marie, and nodded. "Sister, I called about the homework but now that you say she can do better, I will see to it that she does. Sister, I'm very happy with all you are doing for her. Thank you so very much."

I sat back and exhaled.

"De nada," Francis Marie replied.

Mrs. Isquerardo practically fell off her chair.

"Please call if you have any other concerns," I said as I stood and walked toward the door, laughter billowing inside me.

Sadie stood, picked up her folder, and moved to the door. Mrs. Isquerardo waited to shake her hand.

"Thank you again, Sister, very much."

I stifled a giggle as I watched Mrs. Isquerardo go down the hall.

Francis came to the doorway, a twinkle in her blue eyes. "Guess we took care of that one. She sure liked this oldster in her habit, didn't she?"

I nodded, "Not bad for an eighty-eight-year-old."

Tonight I thrill to be home alone, Sadie tucked safely in bed. In the silence of the quiet house, I play Neil Diamond's *Soolaimon* album, which belongs to Sister Elizabeth whom we call Betty, even after I was dubbed Betty to keep from confusion.

I listen to the album, which often fills the house with African drumbeats, its lyrical greeting soothing. I am thinking about silence, community, caring, compassion. I nestle in near the stereo, the volume low, and listen for the song "I Am ... I Said," whose words resonate within so deep within me.

Neil Diamond's gravely voice fills me. I sit quietly and let the words seep in. I do sometimes feel that no one hears at all, not even the chair.

I have seen many of the best and brightest leave this congregation. Leave this church. Women and men who have inspired me, who have asked the questions before me, questions with no answers. They are gone; I persist, uncertain. I've almost memorized the Rilke quote on my dresser:

> *The point is to live everything.*
> *Live the questions now.*
> *Perhaps then, someday far in the future, you will*
> *gradually, without even noticing it,*
> *live your way into the answer.*

I turn up the volume just a bit. Could I become old in this community? I think about Sadie, satisfied, secure, serene Sadie. She's become old and is none the worse for the wear. Could I cast my lot with others, be moved from mission to mission at the whim of the hierarchy, no ongoing family to speak of?

A coldness shrouds me.
The music plays on.

44

LOSING FAITH

I FINGER THE TINY SILVER MEDAL that sits in a small cedar jewelry box on my dresser. An image of Saint Francis Xavier is intricately embossed on it, along with words around the oval portrait that read, "Saint Francis Xavier, pray for us."

IN THE SEVEN YEARS AT THIS PArish, I have learned about this man who helped Ignatius of Loyola found the Jesuits in Montmarte, France. Our own Jesuit high school, named after Bishop McQuaid, helps make a connection, as the Jesuits are well regarded.

Ferdinand of Spain invaded the much-contested Navarre, a Basque stronghold in 1512, when the noble-born Francis was six; his father died when he was nine. He left his native land to study in Paris and, after skepticism, was persuaded by Loyola, his college roommate, that he should join the priesthood. He was a tireless evangelizer whose travels led him to Italy, Portugal, India, and Japan, where his missionary work brought thousands to the faith. In his forty-six years, his miracles included raising to life those thought dead, praying over shrouded corpses commanding them to rise in the name of the living God. His deeds assured him a spot of remembrance and reverence in the Church.

Here I am in a church named in his honor, pondering his miracles and hoping for present-day miracles.

On one occasion during my time in the novitiate, as part

of an ecumenical experience, Sister Maureen arranged an evening of attending a Pentecostal prayer service for those who wished to participate. The idea of such radical belief in a living God who gave the "gift of tongues" and spontaneous healing was becoming part of an international charismatic movement of historically mainstream congregations adopting beliefs and practices similar to Pentecostals.

So, in a small church tucked into a city neighborhood, where others Sisters and friends reported healing miracles, a small group of us knelt and listened and sang. Songs of praise were sung: "How Great Thou Art," "Just A Closer Walk with Thee," and "The Old Rugged Cross." Prayers asking to feel the Holy Spirit's power rang out through the sanctuary filled with people of every shape and complexion, part of this international reawakening. "Hear us, Lord Jesus, hear us." "Heal us, Lord Jesus, heal us."

Soon enough people began to go forward, some walking with difficulty, others holding infants, some with bandages. I looked around at the women I'd come with. Their attention was forward. I was restless. Those of us still in our seats sang "Amazing Grace" as people moved forward, bringing their faith and their need, trusting, allowing themselves to be prayed over in tongues. Then they were slain; at the signal from the preacher, they physically fell into the arms of those prepared to catch them, believers, certain of the healing power of the Lord. I watched for visible signs of change as each person fell, was caught and lifted upright, and prayed over again. I couldn't see any. Prayers by the leaders continued; so did the singing. "Thank you, Lord Jesus, we thank you for this sign of your presence in our sister, in our brother." "I once was lost but now am found, was blind but now I see."

Some people who had been slain trembled and shook and shouted "Alleluia" as they returned to their seats. One Sister in our group went forward and asked for prayers for her injured leg. She claimed it was healed. Our return car ride was filled with oohs and ahs about the "miracle healing." I sat silently in the backseat. I listened and remained unmoved, curiosity holding me more firmly in place than faith.

As we neared home that night I thought, *Am I not being asked to commit myself to a faith that can transform? Shouldn't I be open to speaking in tongues? Being slain in the Lord? Shouldn't I be joyous in prayer, moved by the Spirit to do good works and follow Christ into the depths of human need, ready to be used as a servant for the good, for the God?* I found myself miserably unready for such a challenge.

Since my early days in the congregation, I have tried to achieve some sort of peaceful state. Yet day after day I fail again and again to achieve anything close to what I determine could be a sanctified state.

I find myself escaping after dinner to avoid conversation that might annoy me: gossip about parishioners, talking about the petty annoyances of who washes dishes "wrong," who doesn't do this or that right. I am impatient, yet I am no better than those who I judge, my own inner charity lacking.

Thankfully, the joy of private prayer time, as in my novitiate days when I knelt in the tribunal in silence above the fray of the humanness below me, has not faded. Yet somehow in communal prayer, kneeling here in the convent's small chapel at evening's end, I remain impatient, wanting more and believing less. These prayers of the community, recitation of Vespers, singing songs before retiring for the evening, quiet after ten at night, are efforts to stoke the flame of faith. The flicker I have is dimming.

Tonight I sit in the dark in the chapel, the light of the sanctuary lamp casting red shadows over the walls. I try to pray. I continue to find myself moved to tears by goodness, the people of the parish filling me with joy. I am touched by their simplicity, people whose lives are lived quietly, with no flamboyance or pious proclamations of faith. I watch them fumble with change purses as they put what they can in the collection basket. They work for meager wages, cook suppers for their children, come to open houses and special liturgical events. They celebrate birthdays and holidays and somewhere find joy.

They are not seeking religious life, nor are they pretending they are holy. Their faults are not covered with the veil of religion; their work is holy in its steadfastness. If they drink in excess, they apologize. If they gamble and lose, they seek assistance when funds run dry. If they win, they share what they can.

My own faith in a living God, who is not slaying people, is not running dry, but I find my belief in the "One True Church" waning. These faithful people pray to a God, their God, on their own terms. The support they seek through us, the flawed workers in the Church, puts a spotlight on the question of my own authenticity. How could I pretend to lead? My faith is drawing strength from them, women like Eleanor, whose crooked-toothed smile never fails to brighten a day. Mrs. Carteri, whose work as one of Hickey Freeman's seventeen hundred workers brings her quiet pride, her skills learned as a child in Italy. These women trust in what comes with each day. They don't ask for more.

I find so little I can offer. I find so little the Church can offer.

ELIZABETH OSTA

A month before I entered, in July 1968, Pope Paul VI's encyclical *Humanae Vitae* proved to be a crushing blow to those who had so many hopes for the reforms accompanying Vatican II. Couched in lyrical language that seemed antiquated and insensitive to the needs of the many, birth control was banned. Pete Seeger's rendition of the satirical song "The Pill" tells of a twenty-two-year-old Catholic woman whose hope for approval of the Pill is desperate. Written by Scottish songwriter Matt McGinn, the lyrics spoke the truth of many beleaguered women "pining for the Pill." Those voices were lost as the ban against contraception was reaffirmed.

Rome-ordained Father Charles Curran, a Rochester native teaching at Catholic University, sent out glimmers of light as he and six hundred others made a statement challenging the encyclical by asserting that Catholics could dissent from "authoritative non-infallible teachings when there were sufficient reasons." Individual response to the encyclical could be up to the individual conscience.

When I entered there was upheaval in society. The political parties had just confirmed Nixon and Humphrey as presidential candidates, anti-war protests continued, and race riots plagued the nation. And seven million American women were on the Pill, many of them Catholic.

In view of the Vatican's lack of adequate response, the divisions that erupted were long overdue. This dialogue was needed. This international Church of ours was in big trouble and brilliant holy men and women were on board to help save it. In 1964, Austrian-born theologian Bernhard Häring, a priest of the Redemptorist order, told his Catholic University seminarians in 1964, "All of us dislike a fellow who always speaks to us and never listens. If the Church doesn't listen to the world, then the world will never listen to the Church."

I discovered that not only were the efforts of people to be heard falling on deaf ears, the theologians were being punished with letters of discipline, warning, and reprimand from the Vatican.

During these years inside the Church, I find the Vatican with all its gold, glitter, and gall tarnishing the Church I have grown up in, the Church whose incense and Gregorian chant had furrowed deep inside me. Just as the curtain falls away from the Wizard of Oz, for me the curtain surrounding these fallible robed men in Rome has fallen away.

On a Saturday night, a few of us settle in for a made-for-television film on the Public Broadcasting System titled *Catholics*.

I thrill as the helicopter lands on the island off the coast of Ireland, the modern-day priest played by Martin Sheen making his way up the wind- and rain-swept hillside to the safety of the stone monastery where Trevor Howard as Father Abbott receives him with caution.

While this tale deals with a fictional conflict in a fictional time when the Vatican has decided that Catholics must give up their unique traditions in favor of ecumenism, the story resonates.

Martin Sheen as a Vatican representative brings word from the Holy Father that the Latin Mass can no longer be said at this monastery; the hierarchy feels that the international notoriety the monastery has attained, with crowds coming from around the world, is causing confusion.

The Latin Mass—where the priest said the Mass with his back to the people, where the words were not translated, where faith was called upon without reason—is the ritual that stirs the monks, and the English Mass seems empty—even sacrilegious—to them.

Father Abbott holds the anger of his monks at bay, encouraging calm and prayer. The renegade group that disobeys holds a prayer vigil all night to change the course of the Vatican decision.

Father Abbott's personal struggle with prayer comes to light, his story as powerful as the waves that threaten the shoreline.

The struggle, shown in the film so exquisitely, is mine: faith elusive; change unsettling.

I climb the stairs to my room, knowing something important is shifting within me. I reach for Bonhoeffer, whose familiar words from his poem "Who Am I?" resound deeply.

45

THE QUESTION

MARY STANDS TO GREET ME, her office as meticulous as her attire. Her brown hair and black suit are in place, her efforts at welcome feeling a bit mechanical. She's relatively new to this position, a bit nervous, recently retired from classroom teaching. She is cordial and characteristically distant, my relationship with her not a personal one. Her job as director of vocations is to update my commitment letter to the congregation and to assess when I will take final vows. I miss Sister Mary Anne.

The few times I have been here, in this relocated and much smaller office on the fourth floor, I have never been entirely comfortable. I escape by looking out the window, watching the tops of the majestic evergreens that mark the division between the college and Motherhouse as they wave in the light winds that caress the earth this spring day—mid-spring on the calendar, early spring in our city near the Canadian border. Daffodils aren't out yet, but spring is in the air, its scent rising from the moist soil. I know birdsongs are just beyond the closed window, little chirps and longer serenades.

I recall the February retreat with Father Broadbent, a tall, lean, monkish-looking man who was helpful in his counsel to me, encouraging me to look deeper and trust more as I pray. Good advice.

My days throughout the winter were filled with the

busyness that accompanies the lives of children and by the politics that accompany adults. My job as principal has become complicated not only by funding, but also by who will shape the future of Corpus Christi School, the rectory not first on the cheerleading team.

By this point, after so many meetings with vicars and priests, I find I can no longer sit silently. I have begun to document the whirling forces that impinge upon our future.

I include letters and surveys sent to families who are being asked to fundraise for their future.

I often sit up late into the night at the dining room table, pulling together the facts, as I know them, for Sister Mary Ellen, the congregational representative, giving her details of what is in place so far. Speculations from many sources are plentiful. I keep in touch with Robertina, the amount of the diocesan support still up in the air. Bingo is still in place for the time being, though a conversation to stop it has begun. The school board is united in their support of bingo and in their own efforts to find resources, strong allegiances and friendships for lifetimes being formed as they struggle to keep the school alive.

As a result of a meeting that included Monsignor George Cocuzzi and Bishop Lloyd Joseph Hogan, a proposal is being explored to reopen Saint Francis Xavier as a K–6 school. I was dumbfounded to hear talk of opening a school. Many of us who have gone through the closing of the CICP schools could not believe our ears or eyes. My writing goes on into the night with explanations and data to help encourage responsible decision-making. The children and families who are being served by these schools need a voice and need to be involved in what is to come next.

Paul, the board president, and Mike McFadden have become solid companions for me on the journey through balancing budgets and trimming expenses. New volunteers have stepped forward, saying with their time and energy that this school matters to them. I spend time finding ways to put them to work, whether as helpers in classrooms, tutors for little ones, or teaching an art class. We are rich in this kind of support.

Our goal to save Catholic education in the city is daunting. Still, hope springs eternal. I ended my most recent missive to Sister Mary Ellen with a Robert Kennedy quote: "The future is not a gift but an achievement."

Now, as I watch the tall pines trees sway out Mary's window, I think of the Sisters I currently live with, each of them engaged in a ministry of her choosing as much as possible. Betty's work in parish ministry at Saint Francis Xavier is thriving, her stories and relationships expanding, her friend Jenny a frequent visitor. Clare, my soul mate in so many ways, keeps the graduation rates high with her mastery of bringing out the best in students and teaching them despite their frustrating behaviors. Eileen, in her first year at Corpus and at Saint Francis Xavier convent, has fit in like a glove, smoothing the way at the convent with generosity, doing more than her share of chores, including laundry, her specialty, to assure harmony, all the while making certain her fifth graders are happy classmates as well as good readers.

They are sensible and secure women who've become fine companions. My days have become more predictable, my work appreciated and respected. In this third year as a principal and second year in the same school, I am developing systems to make the process more efficient. I am also becoming clear that the job of principal would be far more effective if it were separated into two parts: an education leader who does teacher supervision, curriculum development, and parent partnering, and an equally important role for a building manager, collecting funds and seeing to maintenance and repairs.

This afternoon appointment with Mary has provided me a chance to go off on my own. I left just after dismissal and arrived by our agreed time of 4:00 p.m. She offered coffee. I declined.

So here we are.

After a few pleasantries are exchanged, she asks, "So when do you think you'd like to make your final vows?"

It's a question that has never been asked so directly, a question that loomed off in the distance. Now here it is, my promises without a timeline about to expire.

I am startled by the question.

But more startled by my response.

I look out at the trees, the depth of the blue sky beyond them bringing the deep evergreen color inside me now. I pause for a moment and then blurt out, "I won't be making final vows."

I floor myself. Tears flow from somewhere deep inside that has been dammed up for years. I feel a release, an endless supply of tears all rushing forward. Mary looks surprised and passes the tissue box to me.

I can't speak. I can only sob. Mary leans forward tentatively and says some words, her attempt at comfort I imagine. Where this unrehearsed answer has come from is beyond me. Yet as I shake with the release of it, I know it is right.

I sob into the tissues, trying to gain some composure. Finally I eke out, "I'm surprised as you are that I've come to this."

I blow my nose and straighten a bit. "But it's the right thing, the right thing." I sob again.

"Would you like to talk with someone? Anyone?" Mary offers, her discomfort evident.

I think of Rosalma, the visionary congregational counselor whose time in Brazil opened her heart, soul, and mind to life beyond these walls and even this city.

"Is Rosalma here?" I blubber.

I stare out now at the evergreens, my entire being overwhelmed. The sobs subside enough for me to stand and let Mary lead me down the stairs to Rosalma's office.

Time seems suspended. I nod to Mary as she leaves, and once seated in Rosalma's office, the soft mauve colors relaxing me, I sob all the harder.

She is kind and quiet. Finally she says, "You've given your all to this, dear Betty, all you could."

I'm not sure the tears will ever stop. Rosalma talks of timing and sharing this with others.

"I'm as surprised as anyone," I stammer, still trying to believe the sentence I have said. I won't be making final vows.

The relief is still washing over me, now coupled with grief at the loss of some of these women, giants in their faith, dedication, and devotion.

I think of Barbara, Robertina, Clare, Sadie. Already I miss them. Already I know the depth of my feeling for these heroic women, like Rosalma, who have given up so much to be a part of this congregation. A sacrifice I now know isn't for me.

I need to "live everything" and I can't do it within the

confines of the Sisters of Saint Joseph. I wish I could. Oh how I wish I could.

Rosalma has said it for me. I've given my all.

46

THE LAST DAYS

I MOVE INTO THE TURMOIL of the last days at Corpus with a new peace. The myriad problems that seem insurmountable at times are no longer mine alone. I have surrendered.

I continue to believe in the benefits of parochial schools, not because they are better than public schools but because they offer families the blessing of choice. They provide alternatives that give hope to those who need it. One size doesn't fit all. We work side by side with public education in neighborhoods where all hands and hearts are needed.

I have met great educators from the public schools who care passionately about the children with whom we are entrusted. Providing food, clothing, transportation, and moral support are not parochial or public issues. They are issues of justice—and love.

In my time as principal both at Saint Michael's and at Corpus, I have learned from some of the best. I've learned ways to provide possibility to pupils in poverty. I've learned how much they thrive on being given responsibility. I carry in my heart images of the SWING students proudly at work on their community service projects. Despite our short-lived time at Saint Michael's, Sue Pinero and I created a good model of hope for the future through our cross-age tutoring program.

Pat, a director from Rochester City School District Central Office with soft brown eyes and an open smile, comes to mind.

She and I worked tirelessly to get Bob, the speech therapist provided by Title I funds, to do his job. He hadn't started classes until mid- October. He had excuses and spent hours writing memos about why he couldn't start on time. At the end of one our particularly grueling sessions, listening to him carry on, after he left, we burst out laughing.

"Wouldn't if be great if we could get this guy to put this kind of energy into his job?" I ask.

As she nodded in agreement, she also said, "If you ever need a job, call me, will you?" I remember.

As year-end events begin in earnest, I realize I have to let folks know I am leaving. Or do I? Class picnics and field trips fill the calendar. The annual dinner that includes the school board, faculty, and rectory staff is coming up. I seek counsel.

"Sister Rosalma," I say into the phone, "it's Betty Osta. I'm wondering about the timing of letting folks know I am leaving. I have told only Sister Barbara at the diocesan office so far. Is there a protocol you'd suggest?"

I'm aware that the survival of the school is not dependent on me, but I don't want to do anything that could dampen the enthusiasm of fundraising efforts.

Rosalma pauses for a moment then says, "Let's chat this weekend at the retreat day with Father David, shall we? You're able to attend, aren't you?"

"Yes, Sister, I'll be there. I look forward to our chat."

I realize I'd best keep my plans to myself at the school's annual dinner, which is Thursday night, before the retreat. We are gathered in the church hall, transformed from a bingo space to a dining room: brown metal-rimmed tables now covered with cloth tablecloths, jelly jar glasses full of garden flowers adorning each one. School faculty, church staff, and school board members are all invited, as are all the parishioners, many of whom have children in the school.

I'm seated next to one of the school board members, Ed, a robust Irishman with a wry sense of humor. Across from us is Paul, who has been heroic in leading the efforts to keep the school open. He and Robertina have been in frequent contact. Robertina has sent her regrets for the dinner. No word from Father Cullen. His absence has been noted to me by Clare and Eileen. "Should we be surprised?" Clare had said, shaking her head.

We settle into our seats, and before we eat, Father Delaney introduces the school board and faculty. Then he says, "And now a few words from our school principal, Sister Betty Osta." I am shocked. I'd not been asked to speak or prepare remarks.

Father Delaney, looking older and grayer and particularly frail, turns toward me expectantly. I stand and move to the microphone. I feel almost giddy.

"Thank you, Father, and thank you all for your presence here tonight. I would like to ask you all to help me applaud our fine faculty and school board members who continue to work tirelessly on behalf of our school, helping it remain the best it can be."

I glance around the room at familiar faces open and expectant. Even defiant little Mary's mother is here, smiling. The applause lasts longer than I anticipated. Some new energy of hope fills the air.

I decide against saying anything about the rectory staff. They have not been focused on the school, and none of them are present. "I see here folks who have been a part of this parish and school community for many years. Folks who have worked bingo for many years, whether selling boards or calling numbers. A special thanks to you all."

After the applause, I say, "Speaking of numbers, I'm reminded of a story about the beauty of familiarity and friendship, when folks have been long associated."

I pause and wait to see what kind of reception I might receive. I sense a quieting and anticipation.

"It seems there was a fellow being held in jail overnight for a minor infraction." I'm aware that jail is not foreign to a few in the parish, while others have no experience and might be shocked to know who does.

"As the man is being led to his cell, he hears numbers being called out followed by laughter. A big bass voice says, '72.' It's followed by great chuckles. '47' another voice calls out. Again uproarious laughter. The number '23' is yelled out followed by great guffaws. He asks the warden what is going on with the numbers. 'Oh,' the warden says, his keys jangling as he walks, 'these men have been here so long, they've numbered their jokes. Once they hear the number, they remember the joke.'

"The man is satisfied with the answer until they walk further. He hears another number: '35.' There's not a sound.

"He looks to the warden and says, 'What about that number?'

"'Oh,' says the warden, 'that guy never could tell a joke.'"

The laughter is satisfying.

"My wish for you is that all your numbers, if they aren't followed by 'Bingo!', are followed by laughter. Thank you."

I return to my seat, glad for the applause and laughter. Ed and Phil nod their approval. Then Ed leans over toward me.

"Sister, do you remember when you first came? What you said to me?"

I feel my face flush and wonder what's coming.

"I don't remember, Ed, but I hope it was good."

"Sister, you said you were glad Corpus wasn't a part of CICP, so it could control its own destiny. Do you still believe that?"

"I don't remember saying that Ed, but I sure still believe it. If Corpus is going to go on, and I believe it can, it's the people of this community who will make it happen. I just said to Sister Eileen last night that we have to realize there is no diocesan office. They can't sustain the schools. The answer is in you and the good folks who believe in the school."

I reach for my pop and ask, "Does that make sense?"

"Sister, it makes more sense than anything else I've been hearing. The big meeting is next week. I trust you'll be there."

"I wouldn't miss it, Ed."

The meeting Ed mentions is a much-anticipated one with the school board hosting representatives from the diocese. The few schools that have had a diocesan subsidy want to learn what the future holds. Each of us principals has been asked to outline the potential the school has to exist on its own. Paul and I have drafted a six-page document we think is self-explanatory and thus far confidential. I'm getting good at keeping confidences, especially my own.

The Saturday retreat at the Motherhouse is well attended. The speaker, Father David, has been a favorite of the Sisters for the past year, bringing wisdom and counsel into the tough days that plague the congregation as we move forward after the anniversary of Maureen's tragedy. The healing help of professional counselors for Sisters directly involved has provided needed support. Now those of us still on the front lines are offered additional avenues of healing.

I watch as Sister Jamesine, the petite woman with a large heart whose leadership has been inspirational as she has guided us through the seismic waves of Sister Maureen's trauma, stands to welcome Father Broadbent. She's fair-skinned and, from what I've observed, tough-skinned. She looks out to the assembled group of seventy Sisters, most of us administrators.

"This morning, Father will give us words we can hear and hold, words that will heal and help us continue to care with compassion for this sometimes heavy world of ours."

Applause accompanies Father David as he comes to the podium. He's tall and lean, with not much of his sandy brown hair left.

He begins with a prayer. "Oh God, thy sea is so great and my boat is so small." A peaceful feeling overwhelms me. The secret of my decision makes me feel a bit like I am deserting the ship—yet I feel so light. Ready to go into the sea with my own small boat, trusting in all that is around me.

I listen with half a heart to the words of Father David, my mind going off in a hundred directions. The future survival of Corpus Christi School weighs heavily upon me. I don't want my decision to jeopardize it in any way.

At the break, Rosalma calls me aside.

We step into the small conference room nearby. She smiles and asks how I'm doing.

I feel a strength that amazes me. I feel solid.

"I'm doing better than expected," I say in response to her question of how I'm doing. I smile as I stand behind the chair nearest the window, expecting she will come in and close the door.

Instead she stands by the half-open door, returning the smile. "You look more peaceful," she says.

She comes into the room, leaving the door ajar.

"I talked with the team and with Sister Jamesine. She wants to talk with you directly."

Her pale blue eyes look into mine. I feel a little startled and nod. It's mid-June; graduation will be in two weeks. So much is happening, so much.

I thank Rosalma, and while I wait for Jamesine, I look out the window, the sun painting the grounds with radiance. I breathe the beauty in. Suddenly I am aware what I will say to Jamesine. I haven't seen her since I met with Mary and Rosalma almost a month ago. Now it is time.

When Jamesine comes in, I turn from the window and move to the chair. She takes the chair opposite. She seems troubled, agitated. I sit across from her and can only imagine the burden of her office, especially during these days following Maureen's tragedy. I feel a little guilty adding to her burdens. I greet her with a simple "Good morning" and wait.

Her blues eyes dart about the room, never resting for long on me. She wears the modified veil, her blonde hair and fair complexion bespeaking her Irish background. She has been the Superior General for almost two years, following Mother Agnes Cecilia's retirement.

With no preliminaries she says, "Rosalma told me of your question about the timing for sharing your decision."

"Sister," I say before she goes any further, "I realize what a difficult time this is. I want to offer to stay on another year," I gasp a bit and add, "if it would help."

Jamesine now looks directly at me and replies matter-of-factly, "That won't be necessary."

I wait for her to say more. She doesn't. I feel vulnerable. And a little hurt. No gentle pause or thanks for my offer. Just "That won't be necessary."

I'm not certain whether she intends to be curt, but she is.

I am silent, feeling dismissed.

Jamesine speaks again, as if a checklist on her mind needs to be finished.

"It would be helpful if you wait to share your decision with the faculty and staff until after the upcoming meeting. So it doesn't cloud any issues."

I nod and say, "I can do that Sister. I intended to. " She stands and turns to leave, her focus somewhere else. In that moment it becomes clear: I'm certain something other than my situation is distracting her. Still, I take a deep breath, feeling a bit hurt. I'm reminded of my recent reading of Wayne Dyer's book *Pulling Your Own Strings* where he says that one has to be careful about investing in Institutions. I remember his notion that they don't have arms and can't hug you back.

How right he is.

47

SAVING FAITH

"HELLO, BETTY," Jeanne Malone says, as we pass one another in Midtown Plaza. This personal icon, formerly Sister Helen Daniel, still has regal bearing. I offer a hug that she receives and returns with equal warmth.

"How are you, dear Betty?" she asks, her brows furrowed in concern, her soft gray-brown eyes looking directly at me. I'm with a friend whom I don't take time from these precious moments to introduce.

"I'm very good," I reply, about to ask her the same.

Before I get chance, she asks, her eyes looking sympathetic, "And your work, are you still hard at it as always?"

Here goes, I think.

"I'll be at Corpus until the end of the month, and then," I gulp, "I'm leaving the congregation, a decision long in coming."

Jeanne takes a step back and reaches out for my hand. "Oh Betty, this is good, this is very good."

I smile in agreement.

"You have given your best. Now it's time for you."

I fight back tears, so glad for this affirmation. "I hope to see you one of these days," I say.

"I'd like that very much. Very much indeed," she responds with a characteristic nod of her head. I feel so pleased, my heart pounding with delight.

That's how it is in these days of my leaving. Friendly,

positive responses received from those with whom I share my decision. It is with tenderness that my sister-in-law Nancy receives my news.

"We're with you whatever you need to do," she says with a hug during a weekend visit home.

Mom and Dad are equally open and supportive.

"Dear," Dad says during one of our Friday night dinners at the Westwood, "would you say you're getting out so you don't get burned in the kitchen?" I nod.

He's been with me through the challenging days of Corpus personnel issues. His roles as vice-president of personnel for Niagara Mohawk made my little tasks seem miniscule. I haven't told him everything, but enough that he is more than understanding of my decision.

Mom says little, just as she had said little when I decided to go in. If I did any of it to please her or to get her attention, she is not interested in that. She has never encouraged me to live my life for what anyone else thinks, and that includes her. She keeps her counsel, and my respect. But her sister, Sister Leo Xavier, is ecstatic. She never seemed fond of my joining in the first place.

"Oh yes, my dear, by all means you should be free to leave now. You've done your fair share." She seems eager to hear more, perhaps living vicariously.

I am a little anxious about telling Sadie. I'll miss her fiercely. Living with her has been one of the finest blessings of community living I've experienced. I knock gently on her bedroom door, which is slightly ajar. She's in the midst of her nightly ablutions, nightcap in place, teeth soaking, and bed turned down.

"Can I talk with you for a few minutes?" I ask. It's not

unusual for us to have a little chat at day's end, especially if I haven't been home earlier.

She's seated on her chair, feet up, assessing her bunions. I sit on the edge of the bed.

"I want to tell you that I've made a decision not to make final vows. I'm leaving the congregation at the end of the month."

I'd gotten the hang of keeping the delivery of this message concise.

Sadie looks up, her pink face almost like a baby's. Her sparse gray eyebrows rise up a bit and she says, "You don't say. Well how about that? Are you peaceful?"

"I am," I say, "but there are plenty of people I'm going to miss, you chief among them."

She giggles and says, "You know, if I were your age, I'd do exactly what you're doing."

Tears brim up as I hug her and leave her to finish her evening rituals. I am certain I've just received a gift I'll remember forever. I silently vow to visit and take her out to dinner once in awhile.

Earlier that same night I shared my decision with the other Sisters individually, knocking on doors of those grading papers and finding others at the end of their favorite television show. It's past nine when I finish. Pat, a high school teacher and friend whose room is next to mine and who shares a love of service and laughter, isn't home yet so I leave a note on her bed along with the hand-carved German crucifix I'd received from the priests at Saint Michael's when we closed the school. She'd admired it often over the years that I've had it so what more fitting memento for such an appreciator.

It's after eleven when I hear a tiny tap at my door. She comes in, tears moistening her eyes, but with laughter on her tongue.

"Well," she whispers, her tiny face smiling, "when the going gets tough, the tough get going."

June 30 is fast approaching. This year's graduation goes off without a hitch. Father Delaney is on hand and plays his role as celebrant well. Father Cullen, who has remained relatively removed from the school and has offered no more First Friday Masses, doesn't attend. Clare orchestrates things with precision. The students march in proudly, heads held steady, caps and gowns in place, white for girls and red for boys. Parents stand in the aisles, cameras clicking; joy prevails. The chosen student speaker, Dean, gives a well-rehearsed address that yields enthusiastic applause. As the students march out, "Pomp and Circumstance" never sounded so good, enhanced by trumpet accompaniment from an Eastman School of Music student. In a reversal from last year's anxiety about whether Cynthia could graduate being seven months pregnant, this year, the secretary's daughter, Ann Marie, has invited Cynthia to attend and bring her son. Kindness and compassion: keystones to the future.

The next day, I receive a call from Rosalma. I will meet with her first and then see Jamesine. I have begun giving things away and packing others for home. The question of housing and a car still loom on the horizon. A job, however, has been secured thanks to Pat from the Rochester City School District. I took her at her word, and in confidence, told her of my plans. Within a week she called. She'd given my name to another director, Karen, who hires teachers for classes of students with special educational needs. Right up my alley. The interview rivals my very first one with Ken Harris at BOCES when he put me at ease by asking if I liked his red socks.

This one took place in Karen's office in the executive office building on Main Street, where the district rents extra office space to accommodate the overflow of senior administrators. Pat, whose office is next door, introduced us and left us on our own. Karen indicated the chair I should sit in—an antique oak rocker. My jittery nerves get a workout as I try to steady the chair, make small talk, answer questions about my job goals, and dodge questions about the convent. Karen is sympathetic, the twinkle in her eye so reminiscent of Ken Harris's twinkle, assuring me all is well.

Rosalma is as gracious as ever. Her office is like a sanctuary. Now that I'm not sobbing when I'm in it, I look around and see mementos of a full career: a picture of Father Kevin, an Irish Oblate from her Brazil days, a group photo of the Sisters who were missioned with her in Brazil, times so obviously treasured.

"Do you miss it?" I ask, wondering what I will miss. I'm also cognizant that the vast cultural differences during Rosalma's time in Brazil are mighty and must have played a part in her readjustment upon return.

"I pray for those people, and the religious I worked with, every day, that God's blessings on them continue. Some of the finest people I've been privileged to know."

Her voice breaks a little. I stir in my chair and look toward the desk; a small ship replica sits on the edge next to a note card with my name on it.

"One of my favorites mementos from there," she says, "is this tiny carved sailing ship." She picks it up and hands it to me. "It was crafted in Portugal and carried to Brazil by one of the Oblates. The fine detail and craftsmanship remind me, Betty, of the wonderful work I've witnessed you do. I'd like you to have this as a remembrance from me."

I've cried before in this office and find myself welling up again.

She hands me the card with it that says, "Safe sails to you, dear Betty. May the wind be ever at your back."

Her kindness is magnanimous. I breathe deeply, knowing I am in the presence of greatness. I accept the ship with a little box to carry it in. She also hands me an envelope and waits while I open it. My hands shake as I unfold the letter and discover within a check for fifteen hundred dollars. Rosalma tells me the letter from the congregation is to help me establish credit.

"To help you get started," she says.

I stand and hug her, feeling so blessed and ready.

She tells me Jamesine is waiting for me.

"Godspeed, dear Betty, Godspeed."

Jamesine's door is open when I arrive. She waves me in and indicates I should close the door. She asks if I've seen Rosalma and tells me that the envelope is the result of something the congregation has learned over the years. "Women with no credit rating can have a devil of a time getting started. We're glad to help with that. Let us know if things work out."

I promise I will. I don't bring up anything about offering to stay at Corpus for another year. I realize now, as sincere as I was, how awkward an offer it was. The Congregation has an image to uphold. Whether this institution has arms or not for hugging, it has a long, strong, proud history. *May it continue*, I think.

"Betty, you've come to a crossroads in your life. I need to ask you a few questions as you leave."

I settle into my chair, not sure what to expect but realizing

I'm almost on my way.

I have loved every mission I've been asked to serve on, starting with my month-long stay as a postulant at Saint Ambrose in Northeast Rochester, then on to Saint Thomas More on East Avenue, next Saint Francis Xavier, then Holy Redeemer, Saint Michael's, and of course, Corpus Christi. I've witnessed great and glorious moments of strength of character and leadership. Janice and David Mary come quickly to mind. I've participated in magnificent liturgies that call heaven to Earth, Sister Flora's music transcendent. I've watched teachers touch students with gentleness and firmness, urging the best from them, leading them forward. I've met families of faith whose honest struggles are heroic. And I've watched this congregation go on in faith, love, and hope despite seismic losses and tragedies. I wish them well as I sail into my new challenges, attempting to live everything, even the questions.

Jamesine leans forward and reads from a folder verifying my date of entry, August 30, 1968; my date of reception, September 12, 1970; and my date of promises, July 30, 1972. Then she reads my date of departure, June 30, 1977.

I wince and nod my head. This is it, I think. I'm sitting with the congregational Mother Superior, saying my goodbye.

Any memories of bad times fade as I get closer to the door.

"What you're facing, Betty," Jamesine says, "seems to be a question of faith."

I don't respond. Jamesine continues, words that don't register, words that have no connection to me. There's something missing here. As she keeps talking, I'm stuck on her statement, a question of faith. I can't help but think that she has no idea who I am.

The words to the song, "I Am, I Said," echo back, no one hearing at all, not even the chair.

Jamesine finishes what she had to say and stands. This time she does offer a hug, wishes me well, and sends me on my way. I do know she's right about the question of faith. It is indeed a question of faith. I'm trying to save mine.

I walk down the same black and white tiled hallway where I saw the nuns moving en masse on silent retreat when the fire trucks arrived. I push open the same massive oak door that I opened when I first visited on March 25, 1968. I step out into the clear air, the sky blue above, the sun making silver of the leaves.

"I am, I said."

EPILOGUE

THE DAY IS COOL, a light breeze moving gently as if on a serving platter. Pines and young hardwoods make this private property seemingly more secluded and almost obscure the view over the valley. The blue of the sky on this July morning mirrors that of forty-five years ago, a soft, endless azure decorated by clumps of white clouds. I gaze at the retreat center grounds, pristine and manicured, and I am taken back to a time when I knelt within the chapel, looking out over the valley, sobbing for direction, sobbing to know what would become of me, what I should do.

My postulancy days of polishing stainless steel and buffing floors that already shone had come to an end. It was here in the hills of Massachusetts where I was to determine in a six-day retreat if I would indeed make public vows in the congregation.

The solitude calls to me as I wander along the border of the property, watching birds skitter and chipmunks scamper. How amazing the years have been since I struggled to say "Yes" to religious life and nine years later experienced a different struggle to say a different "Yes."

I stop walking and look across the rolling landscape at the Calvary Retreat Center that contained that first struggle, remembering the priests who listened and, as gently as the breeze, guided.

The location no longer serves Catholic women preparing to make religious vows, now instead serving veterans who have made sacrifices in Iraq and Afghanistan. The high days of the Catholic Church in America have skidded to a halt, many retreat centers such as this one no longer sustainable.

I feel the warmth of the sun, the air swirling around me. I remember praying that prayer would hold me fast for the future, trusting in a God I wasn't sure of, and holding on to a faith that had been inherited at birth.

I turn now toward the circular drive where I once said the outdoor Stations of the Cross, a remembrance of life, death, and resurrection. I see Dave, my husband of twenty years, wander along the front walk. His tall frame, thinner now after diabetes, which he has managed so well, is more like his Navy photograph I keep on our dresser. I think of his journey during his early years, his thirty-four-year-old wife dying of a rare disorder, leaving him with a three-year-old and a one-year-old to raise on his own. All this love, loss, and nurturing helped make him the man who, when he found me seventeen years later, opened my heart to a goodness in life that still brings me to tears.

I'm pleased he has come with me and am glad to see he approves of the new purpose for this property, his Navy years treasured ones.

I signal for just a little more time. I watch as the sun moves toward the afternoon sky and find a bench in the entranceway, the stained glass windows like my memories, muted.

I see myself coming out the door to the waiting car that will take Marnie and me back to Rochester. I feel again the peace and freedom that filled me as I left this place so many years ago, hoping in the future, letting go and trusting.

As I look over at Dave and remember our twenty years together, I smile deeply. How is it that I was so lucky on Easter Sunday so many years ago to go to the First Universalist Church where he is a valued member? I remember the scrolled words atop the sanctuary: Have we not all one Father?

Another image crowds its way in.

Two years to the day that I walked out the massive Motherhouse door, I bent and kissed my father's forehead to say good-bye, his withered body no longer able to fight the cancer that too quickly had eaten at him.

As I placed the tape recorder playing Mario Lanza singing from The *Student Prince* close enough for him to hear the words that last day in the hospital, tears ran down both our faces.

At his funeral Mass, I found myself somehow much more sure of the God I had come to know, the God my father had introduced me to, the God from Sigmund Romberg's *Student Prince*. The God I knew he would walk with now. And the God I have walked with ever since.

I signal to Dave, who joins me at the car as we continue together on our journey home, the words of the song "I'll Walk With God" ringing within me.

I know so fully that I've been given a gift I will never lose.

A saving faith.

ACKNOWLEDGMENTS

DEAR FRIENDS WHO KEPT SAYING, "I can't wait for your convent book," well, here it is. Without your interest, this may never have seen its way to print. Thanks to all of you. You know who you are!

ENDURING GRATITUDE TO WRITERS who gave support, suggestions, and encouragement for so very long. Your words matter. Gregory Gerard, Sonja Livingston, Jenny Lloyd, Lee McAvoy, Pamela Pepper, Jane Shosten, Maxine Simon, and Kathleen VanSchaick.

ARCHIVAL HELP FROM KATHY URBANIC at the Sisters of Saint Joseph Motherhouse and Sister Connie Derby, RSM, at the Diocese of Rochester helped sharpen memories. There's no better gift.

THE EDITING HELP OF WENDY LOW. And the editing, promotion, and production help of Dream Your Book's Nina Alvarez, Carolyn Birrittella, Raquel Pidal, Betsy Alvarez, and Rachael Gootnick.

AND MY PUBLISHER, COSMOGRAPHIA BOOKS, who made it possible for you to hold this book and read this page. (Along with the teacher who taught you to read. They always deserve thanks!)

AND ABIDING THANKS TO FINVOLA DRURY, whose interest in this work inspired me even after her death.

CPSIA information can be obtained
at www.ICGtesting.com
Printed in the USA
LVOW03s1430191117
556905LV00003B/469/P